Withdrawn from
Davidson College Library

Library of
Davidson College

NEW YORK UNIVERSITY STUDIES IN
FRENCH CULTURE AND CIVILIZATION

General Editors: Tom Bishop and Nicholas Wahl

The State and the Market Economy

Industrial Patriotism and
Economic Intervention in France

Jack Hayward

NEW YORK UNIVERSITY PRESS
Washington Square, New York
1986

First published in the U.S.A. in 1986 by
NEW YORK UNIVERSITY PRESS
Washington Square
New York, N.Y. 10003

© Jack Hayward, 1986

Library of Congress Cataloging in Publication Data

Hayward, Jack Ernest Shalom.
  The state and the market economy.

  (New York University studies in French culture
and civilization)
  Includes index.
  1. France—Economic policy—1945–   2. Industry
and state—France.   I. Title.   II. Series
HC276.2.H35   1985   338.944   85–13567
ISBN 0–8147–3435–9

Printed in Great Britain by Oxford University Press

All rights reserved

CONTENTS

List of Figures vii
List of Tables viii
Preface ix
Preliminaries xi

1. States and Markets 1
2. The French Economic Policy Community 19
3. Pressure Groups and Pressured Groups in France 39
4. French Trade Unions as Policy Community Outsiders 56
5. The Nemesis of Industrial Patriotism: the French Response to the Steel Crisis 68
6. Local Economic Decline: Retreating in Good Order? 105
7. Incorporating the Periphery: from Functionalist Regionalization to Contractual Partnership 150
8. Redeploying Resources: Planning the French Economy or Planning the French State? 170
9. Switching to the Strategic Management of Collective Impoverishment 190
10. Changing Direction and Socialist Crisis Management 212

Index 259

LIST OF FIGURES

1.1 The global community of economic policy communities
2.1 The French economic policy community
3.1 Alternative group-government relations in a pluralist context
3.2 The national economic policy community
5.1 French steel: the transition from oligopoly to duopoly
6.1 The local and regional economic policy communities

LIST OF TABLES

6.1 Number of jobs negotiated and actually secured by APEX, 1972–9
8.1 The twelve priority programmes of the Ninth Plan (1984–8)
9.1 The comparative percentage increase in gross domestic product, 1974–8
9.2 Tax and social security charges at a percentage of gross domestic product
9.4 French public expenditure, 1971–8
9.5 Average percentage annual growth rates in French final demand, 1960–79
9.6 Investment and self-financing by non-nationalized firms, 1972–8
9.7 Annual percentage growth of prices, real wages and social security receipts, 1972–8
9.8 Public assessment of Giscard d'Estaing's record in the previous six years
10.1 The performance of the French and UK economies, 1971–83
10.2 Monetary targets and actual percentage growth in France and the United Kingdom, 1977–83
10.3 The two main objectives public enterprises should seek

PREFACE

Although the preparation of this book has occupied much of my time since 1982, I have been preoccupied with its subject matter for the last twenty years. In the mid-1960s, the presuppositions of those who were involved in taking economic policy decisions or in the investigation of these decisions were very different from those that prevail in the mid-1980s. It is instructive to reread the French Planning Commissariat's 1972 forward look to *1985: La France face au choc du futur* and see how remote its intelligent authors were from the realities that were about to erupt within the international economy, quite apart from France's present predicament. By the mid-1970s, it was becoming clear to governments, to their advisers and to their critics that the opulent epoch of sustained post-war economic growth was coming to a close and that a harsh new era of scarcity and austerity was tightening its remorseless grip. This book assesses how France, celebrated for its earlier achievements of ending a prolonged period of backwardness under state leadership and guidance and launching a successful process of modernization and exposure to international competition, has fared in a context which appears less amenable to the mobilization of industrial patriotism.

I would like to thank the editors of a number of collective works in which some parts of this book have previously or will shortly be published for permission to use more or less extensive portions of my contributions. The first and second chapters both draw extensively upon 'Les politiques industrielles et economiques' which will form part of volume IV of *Traité de Science Politique*, edited by Madeleine Grawitz and Jean Leca (Presses Universitaires de France, Paris, 1985). Chapter 3 is a modified version of a 1984 contribution to a collection of essays in honour of S.E. Finer. Chapter 4 is a substantially reworked version of the author's part of a joint paper with Andrew Cox on 'The applicability of the corporatist model in Britain and France: the case of Labour' in *International Political Science Review*, vol. IV, no. 2 (1983). Chapter 5 will be published in 1985 in Yves Mény and Vincent Wright (eds.), *The National Political Management of an International Industrial Crisis: the Case of Steel* (De Gruyter, Berlin). Chapter 6 is a modified version of the author's part of an unpublished comparative study organized by Professors Nathan and Webman of the Woodrow Wilson School of Public and

International Affairs, Princeton University. Chapter 7 incorporates parts of an English version of the article in a special issue on 'Regions' of *Pouvoirs*, no. 19 (November 1981) and of the author's contribution to a joint article with Edward Page in *Politiques et Management Public* (May 1985) on 'Tools, tasks and policy implementation in central–local relations in Britain and France'. Chapter 8 is an updated version of a contribution to Vincent Wright (ed.) *Continuity and Change in France* (George Allen & Unwin, London, 1984), while Chapter 9 appears almost unchanged from Andrew Cox (ed.) *Politics, Policy and the European Recession* (Macmillan, London, 1982).

Some of my intellectual debts are recorded in the notes, but I owe an immense debt of gratitude to Janet Braim who, with equanimity, converted my handwriting into a typescript.

Jack Hayward
Hull, February 1985

PRELIMINARIES

Although each social science has had the imperialist temptation to regard itself as supreme over all others, the study of the coercive, military state on the one hand and of civil society and the economy on the other developed historically along separate disciplinary lines, each providing the focus for an autonomous social science. However, while these disciplines of politics, sociology and economics are distinct, they are not separable because their subject-matter is interdependent. Nevertheless, as they are each considered to be the primary concern of a single discipline, the concerns of the others have been treated as though they were marginal and are in practice neglected for a combination of tactical, methodological and ideological reasons. As it developed in Britain, economics—which disengaged itself from 'political economy' in the century that elapsed between the writings of Adam Smith and Alfred Marshall—came to concentrate its attention upon the market, conceived as self-regulating. The state was there, in the background, ensuring that the various markets would function free from extraneous influences. Such an approach was encouraged by the development of an international market, in which national governments could be by-passed by buyers and sellers of goods and services to whom state boundaries and regulations were increasingly an avoidable nuisance if not an outright irrelevance, a relic of a primitive past.

Sociologists were also inclined to treat the state as secondary to much more deep-seated social forces. While Herbert Spencer in retrospect might be dismissed as an extreme and untypical forerunner, nevertheless the state was generally treated by sociologists (with conspicuous exceptions like Max Weber) as an historically important institution but not as an autonomous factor in the social process. Marx's writings, based upon a conception of political economy but especially influential in sociology, treated the state's activities as a by-product of class conflict derived from the relations and forces of production. If the utopia of most economists is a state-free self-regulated economy, many sociologists' utopia might be said to be a state-free, self-managed society.

While particularly on the legalist European Continent the study of politics traditionally accorded pride of place to the state, its belated emergence as a social science in Britain and America meant that it had to develop its paradigms on ground which its competitor disciplines had already partially occupied. In seeking to clear a space of its own, political science was subjected to powerful cross-pressures. The Anglo-American liberal tradition was suffused with anti-state norms, the principal manifestation of the state—government—being regarded as a sinister and permanent threat to the individual's liberty to speak, worship, produce or dispose of property free from censorship, regulation, legislation and taxation. However, while these liberal values were still in the process of attaining predominance, economic and social developments were creating pressures for governments to intervene increasingly. The causes derived from the activities of the market and social forces, which were creating turbulence and threatening the maintenance of the law and order functions that were regarded as indispensable even to the minimal state, at least until the millennial stateless society was achieved. The tensions and contradictions to which these pressures gave rise are still with us. By contrast, in those countries like France which had long lived within the Roman Law tradition, the state retained a normative and actual dominance, which although contested was relatively immune to the marginalization it faced in the Anglo-American context. While France has certainly not escaped the collisions of social and economic forces with government and has historically even experienced them in particularly persistent and stark forms, still the French state, as the embodiment of public power and as a public service instrument, retained an authority that was largely intact.

The emergence of the 'crown-centred patriotism of the early seventeenth century' in France had as its economic dimension the development of a mercantilist political economy.[1] It was Antoine de Montchrétien, who in his *Traicté de l'oeconomie politique* of 1615 not only first coined the term political economy but explained that natural economic forces had to be subordinated to state authority if private avarice and ambition were to be harnessed to public purposes. Neither he nor his fellow mercantilists envisaged comprehensive state control of the economy, of which the seventeenth-century French state—even that of Richelieu and Louis XIV—was quite incapable. They shared with their eighteenth-century successors—notably the Marquis d'Argenson, advocate of an applied political science, who was the first in 1751 to publish the influential slogan *laissez-faire* and wrote an essay with the programme-title 'To govern better, govern less'—the reliance upon the private pursuit of profit as the motive force of economic action.

Where they parted company in policy terms was that the mercantilists had the state-strengthening purpose of securing the abolition of feudal restrictions on intra-national free trade, while the economic liberals favoured a state-bypassing development of international free trade. The mercantilists advocated a *political* economy because they did not believe that state supervision could be dispensed with, a view that subsequently came under attack but was not superseded in France in the eighteenth and nineteenth centuries. Although political absolutism was destroyed, a democratised sovereign state like the Third Republic was still supposed to play a more active role than that envisaged by the abstentionist doctrine of *laissez-faire*.

Even the turn-of-the-century impact of Durkheim's sociology upon public and constitutional law, notably through the jurist Duguit's substitution of social solidarity for state sovereignty as the basis of legitimate authority, did not dislodge the state from its pivotal position, although it was reduced to the most powerful force in a pluralistic polity. Theorising the normative basis of the interventionist welfare state that was emerging at the start of the twentieth century, Duguit claimed that 'in place of the monarchical, Jacobin and Napoleonic conception of the State as power is substituted a fundamentally economic conception of the State, which becomes the co-operation between public services under the control of the government'.[2] While Duguit's stress upon the economic and social functions of the interventionist state became an increasingly salient feature of twentieth century France, the notion of the state as public power continued to be predominant. Both the state's fearsome aspect as coercive force and its friendly aspect as paternal protector combined to give French public 'servants' the feeling that they were over and above social classes and market forces. While this was in part illusory and self-justificatory wishful thinking, still such attitudes shaped their conduct and frequently imparted to their actions a self-assurance and assertiveness that was foreign to their Anglo-American counterparts. The normative weight of national tradition was tilted in favour of state force rather than market forces and it was taken for granted that governments could decide what they wanted to happen and were able to make it happen provided they had the will.

However, a governmental predilection to act as though it is sovereign is separated from its capacity to do so by the countervailing constraints that social and economic forces exert upon it. So this book will be concerned with how autonomous a set of actors the public 'masters' and 'servants' are, what margin of discretion they enjoy in the context of making and carrying out macro- and micro-economic policies and whether assertiveness of will can be translated into desired outcomes. The specific instances considered, to elicit how state and market interact in practice, are first placed in the context of a 'policy community' approach to an understanding of how the major actors relate to each other on a continuing basis. This seeks to avoid either an Anglo-American inspired pluralist approach presupposing a remoteness of the state from a fragmented society or a neo-corporatist approach which implies such a substantial and institutionalised form of collusion that it becomes difficult to establish whether the socio-economic organizations have colonised the state or the state has incorporated the socio-economic organizations. In place of such dualistic models that often obscure more than they illuminate, preference is given to identifying the major 'insiders' operating within the policy process as a prelude to examining how they relate to each other. Four types of relationship are identified, based upon combinations of crisis or routine decision-making with attempts to arrive at a decision by consensus or imposition. While the cases of domination, endemic conflict and institutional collapse are considered, the type of decision-making dubbed 'concerted politics' is the one with which the 'policy community' approach fits most comfortably in the French context.

The structure of the book takes the form of five pairs of chapters. The first two chapters put the 'policy community' in the historical and territorial context of a series of interconnected sets of economic policy actors. While the emphasis in subsequent chapters is placed upon the national and sub-national actors within the framework of the French state, here the global community of economic policy communities is indicated as constituting the indispensable cast of interlocutors of the state actors. This global community is narrowed down from the international, regional and foreign state levels, with, in each case, representatives of the six clusters of actors: the politicians, the bureaucratic-judicial-military elites, the public and the private economic managers, the leaders of trade unions and professional organizations, the party, parliamentary and media leaders of opinion. Clearly some of these actors are of far greater importance than others, not merely in this or that particular case but generally. They are perceived as such. When a representative sample of the French public was asked in October 1984 to what extent French economic policy was determined by the policy of the

USA, 5 per cent said it was wholly determined and 37 said it was largely determined by the USA. Thus 42 per cent accorded preponderant weight to the policies pursued by a particular foreign country, as against 39 per cent who attributed little or no influence to the USA on French economic policy, while 19 per cent expressed no opinion.[3] Within the global economic policy partnership, there are clearly senior as well as junior partners.

Chapter Two applies the economic policy community approach to France, focusing on the attempt to secure concerted action between industrial firms, banks and governments and the role of firms as national champions of the industrial policies worked out by specific policy communities. Chapters Three and Four look more closely at group-government relations, with trade unions being selected for special, albeit succinct, treatment. This invidious privilege arises from the fact that as 'policy community outsiders' they generally do not figure prominently in the subsequent cast studies and the reasons for this apparent neglect need to be made explicit.

Chapter Five concentrates upon the problems of a particular declining industry, steel, whose leading firms were promoted by the French state as its national champions in the domestic and international market, while Chapter Six focuses upon the local effects of economic decline in the Lille and Valenciennes areas and the attempts by the public and private members of the local economic policy community to organize a retreat in good order. Chapters Seven and Eight examine two ways in which the contractual instrument has been used to link regional economic development with central policy and to redeploy the allocation of public expenditure within the context of national and regional economic planning. Finally, Chapters Nine and Ten consider the response to the impact of the international recession during the Presidencies of Giscard d'Estaing and of Mitterrand, with a view to establishing to what extent those who control the state apparatus are able to modify its economic policies and master the constraints exerted by international and domestic market and non-market forces.

1
STATES AND MARKETS

Constraints and Discretion

It is all too easy to fall into the trap of giving undue emphasis to the proclaimed objectives of official policy makers to the neglect of the obstacles in their path. However, their objectives are themselves curbed by constraints which are often not explicitly recognized. Thereafter, the intentions of decision makers interact with the implementing structures to produce the policy outcomes that are to be evaluated. So, prior to asking how economic policy is formulated, who shares in making it, in whose interest it is made and what are the obstacles to carrying it out, we have to try to ascertain the margin of discretion open to policy makers. If it is accepted that, at its formative stage, 'the central problems of the study of economic policy are to disentangle *discretion* from *constraint*' and that 'Institutions provide both incentives for discretionary action and constraints on it',[1] we should first note that institutional arrangements provide a context making for inertia, for constraint rather than for change. National institutions, operating within a framework of international constraints, partially predetermine the policy agenda, the participants in the policy process and the policy instruments that will be used.

'A satisfactory demonstration of the effects of discretionary interventions on economic outcomes requires what economists describe as a model of *demand* and what political scientists describe as a model of *powers* . . . . The focus on power stresses the restricted process by which preferred outcomes are obtained politically. In contrast, demand assumes a market in which transactions take place'.[2] The market-centred public choice approach to collective decision making, to which we have already alluded, seeks to reduce the matter to individual preferences; but this raises the issue of how these differing individual preferences are to be reconciled. It is assumed that rather than a power struggle, such reconciliation is achieved by mutual adjustment and compromise. However, the transition from self-interest to public interest remains impossible without a normative leap, and Buchanan has conceded that in *The Calculus of Consent*: 'Explicitly and deliberately' he and Tullock 'defended constitutional limits on majority voting . . . We defended the existence of constitutional constraints *per se*; we justified bounds on the exercise of majoritarian democracy.'[3] These ethnocentric constraints upon the use of public power have a global importance because of the fact that the United States has been able to impose some of its values on the rest of the non-communist world through its domination of the international market.

An approach that also comes from economics but with a different normative inspiration is that of economic policy optimization developed by the Dutch economists Tinbergen and Theil. Here it is not the individualistic preferences of consumers—deemed to be sovereign—but the preferences of a political authority, deemed to have precise policy priorities that are to be optimized: 'The optimizing model contains two sorts of relationships, an *economic constraint* and an *objective function*. The constraint is a set of equations linking the economic variables to each other. Many values of the economic viables will be consistent with the constraints imposed by the structure of the economy. These values form a set of *feasible* outcomes.'[4] The objective function measures the costs and benefits associated with each variable, so that it 'provides a means of evaluating every *feasible* outcome. The central assumption of the optimizing model is that the chosen outcome will have the highest utility value of those that are feasible, subject to the constraints. For this reason the problem is described as one of *constrained optimization*. . . . The authorities usually have goals for many of the uncontrolled variables such as inflation and unemployment, which are spoken of as *target* variables.'[5] The task of the public authorities is to use policy instruments which they control to guide the target variables in such a way as to approximate the outcomes they are seeking to achieve.

It is flattering to politicians and bureaucrats to believe that decisional *volontarisme*—such a feature of French public policy rhetoric—is relatively free from constraint and that outcomes can be expected accurately to reflect intentions, with blame and praise allocated accordingly. The notion that the government has sovereign command over the complex domestic and international forces that will decide the fate of its economic policy initiatives flies in the face of reality. Yet, while it is seldom openly proclaimed, it frequently is the inarticulate major premise underlying the judgements made of public policy. Such unrealistic expectations are based upon an excessive emphasis on the preferences of policy makers and insufficient concern with the economic, political and bureaucratic constraints. A formal model, capable of separating the specifically structural economic constraints from the government's policy intentions, needs to supplement knowledge about the relationship between policy instruments like public expenditure and economic targets like reducing inflation with a more sophisticated institutional conception of the context. For example, one could hypothesize that a fragmented political structure will increase the 'response lag' of economic policy to any problem. Thus unitary countries like France and the United Kingdom, with a strong bureaucracy and a weak parliament, with a traditionally high—but decreasing—level of party discipline (United Kingdom) and traditionally low—but increasing—level of party discipline (France), might be better able than a fragmented country like the United States to define objectives and rapidly react to policy issues. Rule following curbs the public authorities' capacity to act in an unpredictable way, constraining the discretionary power of the *volontariste* decision maker. If assistance is given to firms according to established rules rather than *au coup par coup* and *à la tête du client*, then the government's power to discriminate has effectively been abandoned.

The capacity to measure outcomes and to calculate how far they are due to the discretionary choice of the public authorities—or of any other actors for that matter—is vital but frequently absent. Alt and Chrystal point out that: 'Many large changes in the targets and instruments of policy arise "automatically" rather than through choice. An example is the decline of revenue in a period in which national income declines. Economists refer to such changes as *automatic stabilizers*.'[6] Another example is the rise in tax revenue as inflation results in more people becoming liable to pay income tax because the tax bands remain the same. It is not always clear whether 'fiscal drag' is the consequence of a deliberate political decision or whether inaction is to be attributed to inertia. The use of particular policy instruments varies in part because of the institutional structure in particular countries. Thus, the contrasting character of the money market in France and the United Kingdom results in the central bank in the United Kingdom exerting monetary control through the buying and selling of government securities in the open market, whereas in France selective credit allocation is the preferred instrument. Although such attempts at policy optimization have made only limited and partial progress, they remain the principal hope for a behavioural analysis of economic policy. Such an ambitious analysis is not attempted here.

Economic Policy and Industrial Policy

The term 'economic policy' is used to mean a process by which a variety of identifiable actors belonging to the economic policy community contributes to a government decision on how, within the framework of its general policy aims, its economic objectives should be implemented by existing or reorganized institutions and policy instruments. Let us unpack this definition. It refers, firstly, to a process, involving a complicated sequence of overlapping stages, by which economic policy issues are recognized and acknowledged, appear on the agenda and may proceed through the stages of formulation, elaboration and decision, before being implemented and evaluated. Whereas policy-making models borrowed from economic theory tend to focus upon the formulation, elaboration and evaluation stages of the process and organization theory stresses the elaboration and implementation stages, a political science approach will adopt a more systemic and comprehensive treatment of the process rather than concentrating upon the preferred policy outputs or the internal dynamics of the interacting policy-making and delivering organizations, important as these are.

The bulk of this book is concerned with how a specific nation state, France, has sought to resolve its economic problems by reference to a plurality of domestic actors, arranged into six clusters (see below p. 49) which constitute the economic policy community: the domestic heads of the partisan national executive; the senior civil servants in charge of the major economic ministries and, where relevant, the judiciary; the heads of the major public and semi-public financial and industrial corporations; the leaders of the main financial, industrial, commercial and agricultural enterprises and their representative organizations (peak confederations, trade associations, local and regional chambers of commerce); the heads of the major trade unions and professional organizations; lastly, the leaders of the political parties, in parliament and in the elite and mass media, concerned with the democratic mobilization, communication and legitimation of economic policy. However, like any other state—even economic super-powers like the United States, although with a different power relationship with foreign extra-state actors—the French actors have to contend with a plurality of others who constitute a global community of economic policy communities (see Figure 1.1). Thus, each of the actors within the specific nation state that may be the focus of one's interest will have a variety of other potential interlocutors. While it might be most natural for the

States and markets

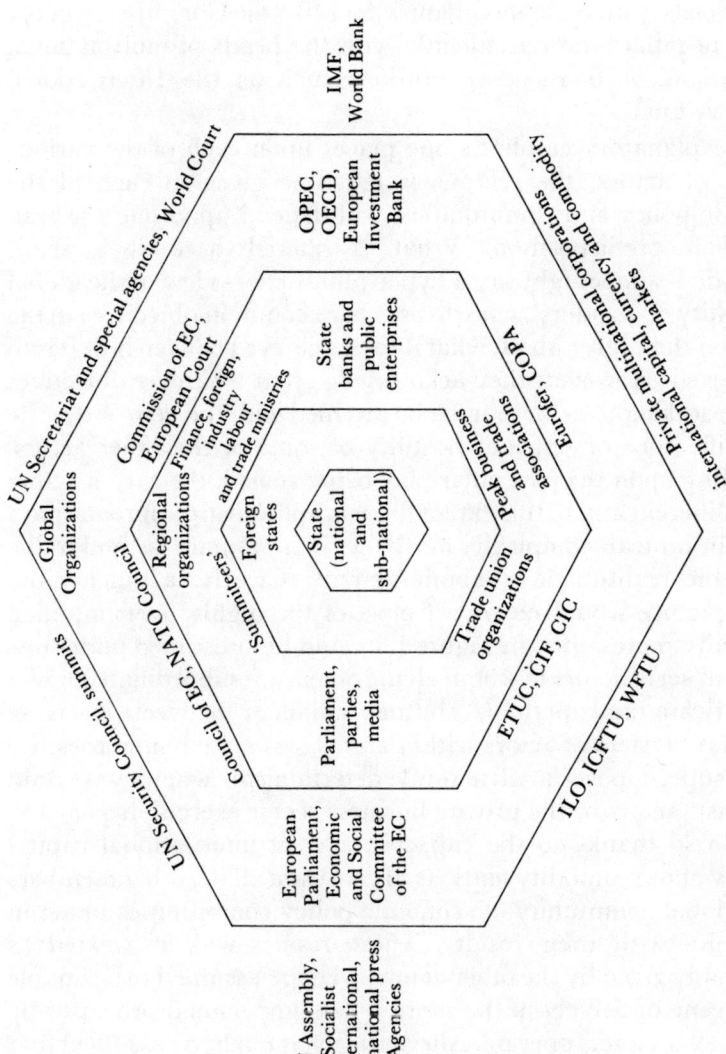

Figure 1.1 The global community of economic policy communities

senior officials of the French finance, external affairs, labour and trade ministries to think of their 'colleagues' in similar ministries in the foreign states with which they have frequent dealings as their most immediate 'partners' in the wider economic policy community, this need not necessarily be the case. They may have stronger ties with officials from regional organizations like the Commission of the EC, or negotiate more frequently with the heads of multinational corporations or financial institutions such as the International Monetary Fund.

The explanatory emphasis one places upon each of the various clusters of actors, the relative weight one gives to each of the economic policy sub-communities, will depend upon one's overall theoretical predisposition. What is offered here is a semi-pluralistic—some might say a hyper-pluralistic—view of the global community of 'insiders', who do not share common objectives in the sense that they agree about what is to be achieved or even how it is to be achieved. However, they acknowledge that whatever objectives they are seeking to achieve must be attained with the help or despite the indifference or outright hostility of some of the other actors. Depending upon the particular play being staged, the cast of actors will be different and to this extent the semi-pluralistic approach pays a price in protean complexity for the desire to remain faithful to the observable realities of economic activity. Clearly, a much more simple picture would emerge if most of the highly oversimplified complexity represented in Figure 1.1 could be subsumed under one dominant set of actors to whom all the others are subordinated. Over the intricate and perhaps shifting alliances between parts of particular clusters of actors within and across state boundaries, we might superimpose a structural determinism whereby certain 'capitalist' actors in the private business sector exercise hegemony. They do so thanks to the capacity, say, of international capital currency and commodity markets to constrain all the other members of the global community of economic policy communities to act in conformity with their results. These results will be treated as insuperably given by the other actors, who are assumed to be unable to intervene decisively in the more or less impersonal processes by which such markets operate. Alternatively, it might be assumed that the crucial actors are located in the state sector. The master puppeteers are alleged to be either the political leaders, the central bankers or the techno-bureaucrats of one or more states who manipulate the other actors. Yet again, it might be the top officials of the International Monetary Fund who pull the strings to which the others dance. The particular view one takes will, *inter alia*, be influenced by whether one is sitting in New York, Tokyo, Paris, Moscow, Rio or Singapore. A virtue of the semi-pluralist approach adopted here is that it does not preclude any of the above hypotheses as *partial* explanations of how economic policy emerges at various levels and particular locations within the global community of communities.

Just as we have used the concept of an 'economic policy community' to suggest a network of identifiable actors engaged in an interactive process by which aims are implemented, so the narrower notion of industrial policy needs to be located within a particular cultural and institutional context. As Hogwood has suggested (but note the characteristically one-sided emphasis on government intervention in industry rather than the reciprocal reality): 'the overall pattern of governmental involvement in industry is not so much the sum of the effect of all the policy instruments as a product of the way they and the agencies administering them interact'.[7] Industrial policy should not be considered in isolation from either the rest of economic policy, with which it interacts or from the network of institutions and actors, located in a particular spatial and temporal milieu. What imparts some semblance of unity to a collection of piecemeal expedients, dignified with the spuriously singular appellation of 'industrial policy', is the underlying industrial culture characteristic of a particular country and subsidiarily of the industrial sub-structure and sub-culture of a particular local or regional territory. It frequently takes the explicit form of economic nationalism. Dyson has applied the notion of 'different industrial cultures, contrasting concepts of the firm and its relationship to the wider capitalist society' to 'state-oriented' France and Federal Germany compared with 'society-oriented' United States and United Kingdom.[8] Precisely because of its dedication to a liberal 'institutional isolation', epitomized in the firm's self-sufficiency, the world of industry is damagingly separated from the other actors in the pluralist industrial policy community, with the result that when they need to collaborate, 'their crisis interventions (are) reactive, defensive and ill-prepared'.[9] By contrast, as we shall see, Japan has been able to achieve a rather more effective 'political–bureaucratic–industrial complex' than France, thanks in part to *amakudari*, the charmingly dubbed Japanese version of *pantouflage*, which means 'descent from heaven', the Japanese heaven being service in the top echelons of the bureaucracy.[10]

The economic nationalism that is a particularly marked feature among advanced industrial societies in general, as well as both Japanese and French industrial policy in particular, is partly attributable to reliance upon governmental leadership to overcome a strong sense of economic backwardness. Although it is therefore frequently to be found in developing countries, most of these countries lack the cohesive industrial policy community capable of mobilizing their society for the developmental goal of economic growth. The 'situational nationalism of the late industrializers' combined with 'strong inter-organizational linkages increase the level of operational preparation of policy makers by provision of an institutional structure of communications and control that facilitate agreed, rapid and unified action'.[11] However, this ephemeral and exceptional combination of a formidable driving force and a smooth mechanism to harness that force cannot be expected to be a usually successful strategy of national industrial policy. Consequently, industrial policy is normally not a unitary, closely coordinated or planned programme of state intervention in association with a network of actors and cohesive industrial policy community. Rather it consists of an improvised amalgam of *ad hoc* instruments and inconsistent objectives intended to influence firms to behave in ways that would not have spontaneously occurred in a market context. The instruments may be, in varying degrees, specific or comprehensive in their coverage, temporary or permanent in their duration, direct or indirect in their impact, coercive or persuasive in their methods, defensive or offensive in intent. The more fragmented the industrial policy community, the more its members are attached to the market pluralism of the classic homes of liberal capitalism such as the United Kingdom and the United States, the less likely will industrial policy be an acceptable type of activity. At the limit, to acknowledge the existence of an industrial policy community would be regarded as tantamount to a conspiracy against the public interest, rather than a way of giving practical expression to such a public interest. We shall return later to the subject of industrial policy. Meanwhile, such cultural contrasts suggest that, before we proceed further, some attention should be devoted to the ideological and normative dimension of economic and industrial policy.

The Normative Context: Mercantilism and Market Pluralism

Whereas much of the ideological argument about economic policy has been conducted in terms of individualism versus collectivism or capitalism versus socialism, in practice nationalism in the service of industrial development and state power is a much more enduring and potent undercurrent. Max Weber remarked that mercantilism (which under the stimulus of the 'new mercantilism' may recover from its neglect) was the earliest example of 'the economic policy of the national state' and that: 'The first trace of a national economic policy on the part of the prince appears in the fourteenth century in England'.[12] It began hesitantly with piecemeal pragmatic expedients to deal with particular emergencies. It was used by monarchs in their state-building activities, being popularized by the champions of sovereign state power, such as Bodin in sixteenth century France. However, Weber set the scene for the contemporary debate when he described mercantilism as 'a league between the state and the capitalistic interest'. In Britain, once 'the industrial interests, which were now in a position to dispense with mercantilistic support' preferred 'market opportunities' to monopolies, 'irrational and rational capitalism faced each other in conflict' and Adam Smith's *Wealth of Nations* (1776) was the intellectual landmark of the new anti-mercantilist conception that was to conquer the public mind in the nineteenth century.[13]

Macpherson explains that the possessive market society which emerged in seventeenth-century England 'does not require a state policy of *laissez faire*; a mercantilist policy is perfectly consistent with the model and may indeed be required at some stages in the development of a possessive market society'.[14] Just as the weaknesses of declining market pluralism—the cases of 'market failure' that most economists seek to treat as exceptions to the general rule—have in the twentieth century led to extensive state intervention and regulation, so in the period when market pluralism was emerging, the state acted to assist some types of trade and industry and to restrain others. While the older restraints on competitive acquisitiveness continued to provide a framework of social order and prevented some of the more extreme consequences of market society's treatment of labour as a commodity and employment as dependent upon market circumstances from being fulfilled, profit calculations were modified rather than superseded. However, the classical economic foundation for market pluralism having been laid, the oppressive and inefficient visible hand of the state was presumed to be unfit to manage the market forces of supply and demand.

Adam Smith's economic liberalism, which led to the conception of a self-correcting economic system that spontaneously tended towards market clearing of all commodities, including labour, acquired disciples on the continent, notably Jean-Baptiste Say. Although some non-conformists like Sismondi argued that endemic under-consumption could lead to a disequilibrium between supply and demand, Say's assertion that supply created its own demand prevailed. As the latter-day non-conformist John Kenneth Galbraith has argued: 'By the 1930s, the notion that production created its own sufficient demand had been economic scripture for more than a century. It was given formal expression as Say's Law of Markets. Whether or not a person accepted Say's Law was, until the thirties, the prime test by which economists were distinguished from crackpots.'[15] It required Keynes's *The General Theory of Employment, Interest and Money* of 1936 to destroy the neo-classical equilibrium that was supposed to guarantee full employment even when it was clear that mass unemployment persisted. Liberal economics also dominated official teaching in France in the nineteenth and early twentieth centuries. The *Ecole Libre des Sciences Politiques* had as one of its founders and teachers Léon Say (grandson of Jean-Baptiste Say) several times finance minister in the early decades of the Third Republic. So, there was bound to be strong resistance to the 'intellectual repeal' (Galbraith's formulation) of Say's Law and the introduction of Keynesian macro-economics, even though Keynes was not challenging the market management of the economy but merely ensuring public support for deficient market demand. An appeal to an older, indigenous statist tradition—in combination with the Saint-Simonist anticipation of a technocratic managerialism—was in important respects to equip France to adopt a more assertive conception of economic policy than the Anglo-American Keynesians.

Henri de Saint-Simon was a friend of Jean-Baptiste Say, but his main claim to our attention is that—in association with Auguste Comte and thanks to a group of brilliant disciples—he pioneered the view that economic activity should be collectivistically organized, society being reduced to a rational system of economic functions and its members to economic functionaries. Although it was Engels who in *Anti-Dühring* popularized the view that 'The government of persons would be replaced by the administration of things and by the conduct of the processes of production', it was probably Comte rather than Saint-Simon himself who in *L'Organisateur* (1819) first argued that a scientific and engineering elite, such as was produced by the *Ecole Polytechnique,* could be entrusted with the economic management of society.[16] It was to the technocratic products of this *grande école*, rather than to the *Ecole Libre*, which trained so many of France's senior bureaucrats from the inception of the Third Republic, that the 'administration of things' should be confided.

While Saint-Simon had sought to reduce politics to the science of production and to transfer power from a parasitic, aristocratic leisure class to the productive industrialists, it was the Saint-Simonians who systematized his intuitions into an exposition of socialist doctrine. Thus the primacy of society's industrial constitution, based upon the institution of property, required the abolition of inheritance so that only those who earned their remuneration by their contribution to the productive process would share in the national income. Exploitation of man by man would be abolished along with the class distinction between proletarians and proprietors. The nationalization of the banks and industry was clearly advocated in the 1829 *Exposition* of Saint-Simonian doctrine. Hayek, the ultra-liberal opponent of socialist planning, credits the *Exposition* with being the 'Old Testament' of both socialism and 'the religion of the engineers'[17] that from the 1930s acquired a renewed influence among the French economic elite. Their role in promoting the development of French railways and inspiring the construction of the Suez Canal has often been recalled. However, it was their 'bancocratic' (Proudhon's epithet) advocacy of a centralized public banking system to organize production and the mid-nineteenth-century practice of the *Crédit Mobilier* type of industrial banking—which was more successful in Germany than in France—that best reflect their anticipation of both twentieth-century entrepreneurial state capitalism and planned socialism.

The Normative Context: Planned Capitalism and Planned Socialism

Less dominated by implicit generalization from partial US experience, Andrew Shonfield's *Modern Capitalism*, rather than Galbraith's *The New Industrial State*, provides the best analysis of the pre-1970s trend towards state control of market forces. His comparative consideration of a wide range of (predominantly European) national experiences led him to a more circumspect formulation of the institutional tendencies identified by Galbraith. Firstly, the role of public authorities in macro-economic management has been massively expanded, even when the instruments might be mainly entrepreneurial public corporations in one case or the banking system in another. Secondly, market competition was subject increasingly to selective as well as general regulation, and governments frequently encouraged collaboration between firms or became directly involved in the pursuit of public industrial policy objectives in crucial decisions such as investment, research and development, prices and incomes, or industrial training and retraining. Thirdly, the increasing macro and microeconomic policy roles of government, in the context of medium and long-term forward looks, required political skills and resolution of a higher order than had hitherto been necessary. 'The central question is how far an active government wielding great and varied economic power, intervening in the detailed conduct of private business affairs, discriminating between one citizen and another on the basis of subtle and complex judgements of the community's needs ten or twenty years ahead, driving bargains with particular interest groups as administrative convenience dictates, can be subjected to democratic control.'[18]

How to achieve such democratic control is where Shonfield's analysis is at its weakest. As an economist, he was particularly concerned with the efficient attainment of objectives, and the efficacy of the instrument of discretionary power represented by the French meritocratic elite of senior economic bureaucrats impressed him. 'The essential French view, which goes back well before the Revolution of 1789, is that the effective conduct of a nation's economic life must depend on the concentration of power in the hands of a small number of exceptionally able people, exercising foresight and judgement of a kind not possessed by the average successful man of business. The long view and the wide experience, systematically analysed by persons of authority, are the intellectual foundations of the system. The design and efficiency of the machine of government then determine the degree of practical success achieved.'[19] Whereas many nations had used particular interventionist instruments piecemeal and packaged them into a policy, Shonfield claimed that 'no other nation has so self-consciously fought to make a coherent system out of the devices which have been adopted more or less haphazardly elsewhere . . . Postwar French planning can be regarded as a device that mobilized a number of instruments of public enterprise and pressure which had been lying around for some time, and pointed them all in the same direction.'[20] While one must make allowances for the fact that Shonfield was writing before the 'ardent obligation'—de Gaulle's 1962 rhetorical flourish—had cooled, he can nevertheless be taken to task for presuming there to be a much greater integration of state policy than in fact was or is the case in France. While it is true that, despite Galbraith's claims about the existence of a 'technostructure', from across the Atlantic or the Channel France seems to have interlocking business–bureaucratic economic and industrial directorates. These lead to enviably cohesive economic and industrial policy communities, but France has not attained the planning capacity of its Japanese equivalent. This is not merely due to cultural and structural differences but to the enduringly fragmented nature of the very state machine that aspires to impart unity to a pluralistic whole.

Charles Lindblom, whose study of *Politics and Markets* distills the results of decades of reflection, not only goes deeper than either Galbraith or Shonfield, but also ranges more widely, a fundamental part of his analysis being a contrast between synoptic policy making in the Soviet manner with strategic policy making, characterized by market interaction, negotiation and voting. This book was foreshadowed by his work, nearly a quarter of a century earlier, written in collaboration with Robert Dahl, *Politics, Economics and Welfare: Planning and Politico-Economic Systems Resolved into Basic Social Procedures* (1953) and a seminal 1959 article on 'The science of "muddling through"'. However, by the mid-1970s, when he compared communist and non-communist economic planning, it was not to argue that whereas the latter was incremental the former was not. Rather, communist economic policy making was described as 'the planned adaptation of secondary decisions to unplanned primary decisions'.[21] He went on two years later to argue that like market pluralism, communism was 'driven by ignorance and uncertainty to endless improvization rather than synoptic plans'. Communist policy making was capable of 'extremely rapid sequences of incremental change' to overcome specific problems accorded political priority rather than comprehensively and simultaneously solving a range of related problems.[22]

In his *magnum opus*, he shifted the focus onto the pivotal role of productive enterprise, which became the centre of his analysis of the interaction between markets and politics. Whereas communist systems manipulated markets to distribute most consumer goods and services and to attract labour, apart from agriculture they were seldom used to settle how inputs were allocated and what was to be produced. Lindblom argues that communism was an 'organizational revolution rather than a social one' and so 'the principal innovation in communism has been administrative: a new form of business enterprise, together with a new method of setting its assignments, coordinating it with other business enterprises, and putting resources at its disposal . . . . Communism applies those authoritative, hierarchical and bureaucratic controls that operate *within* large enterprises in all industrialized systems to relations *between* enterprises.'[23] However, despite the slowdown in the Soviet growth rate since the 1960s, there is a stubborn reluctance to move to market socialism. This is partly because it seems to be an ideological retreat towards capitalism, partly because of fear of loss of control over its COMECON 'partners', and partly because of reluctance to let consumers retrieve some power over prices from the party leadership. Most of all, however, there is an anxiety that the resulting increase in the autonomy of enterprises might encourage trade union autonomy and more especially that it would lead to 'the duality of leadership characteristic of market-oriented systems and to the privileged position of enterprise managers in them'.[24]

Whereas in market pluralist societies macro-economic coordination occurs without the need for a coordinator, large firms have come to play a dominant part. Lindblom seeks to explain why this is so because it is difficult to reconcile with democratic principle and is 'largely ignored in conventional political science. To understand the peculiar character of politics in market-oriented systems requires, however, no conspiracy theory of politics, no theory of common social origins uniting government and business officials, no crude allegation of power elite established by clandestine forces. Business simply needs inducements, hence a privileged position in government and politics, if it is to do its job.'[25] In words that would be fully understood by French socialists after 1983, although not necessarily before that date, Lindblom explains why businessmen are not just one sectional interest like any other, why they enjoy virtual economic veto power. Businessmen 'appear as functionaries performing functions that government officials regard as indispensable. When a government official asks himself whether business needs a tax reduction, he knows he is asking a question about the welfare of the whole society . . . . Any government official who understands the requirements of his position and the responsibilities that market-oriented systems throw on businessmen will therefore grant them a privileged position. He does not have to be bribed, duped, or pressured to do so. Nor does he have to be an uncritical admirer of businessmen to do so. He simply understands, as is plain to see, that public affairs in market-oriented systems are in the hands of two groups of leaders, government and business, who must collaborate and that, to make the system work government leadership must often defer to business leadership. Collaboration and deference between the two are at the heart of politics in such systems. Businessmen cannot be left knocking at the doors of the political systems, they must be invited in.'[26]

In his 1979 revision of his highly influential paper on 'muddling through' of twenty years earlier, which presented incrementalism as the antithesis of planning, Lindblom returned to the situational and structural hegemony of business firms within the political economy of market pluralism. 'Having assigned many or most of the great organizing and coordinating tasks of society to business enterprises, then subjecting the managers of these enterprises to market inducements rather than commands . . . the only way to get the assigned jobs done is to give businessmen whatever inducements will in fact motivate them to perform.'[27] He goes on to suggest that the result is 'a structure of veto powers that makes even incremental moves difficult', with firms having the privileged position of exercising a veto within the market pluralist system. So, far from seeing big business and government enjoying a corporatist-style interdependence, Lindblom remains committed to a business-biased pluralism. Nor does he subscribe to Galbraith's conception of a technostructure linking the mature corporations of the planning industrial system and government, recognizing that although there is convergence between Soviet and 'western' style policy making, it is muddling through more than planning that unites them.

Having reviewed various theoretical approaches to the subject of whether it is the imperfections of the market or of government that are the greater threat to formulating and implementing a satisfactory economic policy, it remains to examine more closely the major public and private members of the economic policy community and to investigate the problems of converting preferences into outcomes in matters of public economic intervention. Without necessarily subscribing to Lindblom's general proposition that 'business' is the brightest star in the market pluralist firmament, it is perhaps appropriate to start with the major firms, although not confining our remarks to industrial at the expense of financial firms as both Lindblom and Galbraith do.

The Economic Policy Community

As a link with the discussion of the evaluative context and emphasis upon the role of big business on which we ended the preceding section, we should bear in mind Galbraith's remark: 'There is nothing in the American tradition of dissent so strong as the suspicion of private business power.'[28] Lindblom characteristically puts the point in a more universal form. 'The large private corporation fits oddly into democratic theory and vision. Indeed, it does not fit.'[29] True, Lindblom argued earlier that: 'However poorly the market is harnessed to democratic purposes, only within market-oriented systems does political democracy arise. Not all market-oriented systems are democratic, but every democratic system is also a market-oriented system.'[30] Lindblom confesses that he does not fully grasp the connection between market economy and political democracy but when what Wright Mills called the pluralist 'semi-organized stalemate'[31] masquerading as a power paralysis results in practice in big business vetoes rather than pluralist compromise, this failure suggests that political democracy is the main casualty.

What clearly disturbs people committed to liberal democracy and market pluralism, whose progenitors sought to eliminate the problem of power, is that public policy cannot simply be assumed to be made according to the dictates of the unconstrained popular will. What we have to do is to understand the validity of this preoccupation with the power of business and whether its US exponents are presenting experience that is in significant particulars culturally specific to the United States. What are the consequences of what Karl Polanyi called 'the running of society as an adjunct to the market? Instead of economy being imbedded in social relations, social relations are imbedded in the economic system.'[32] How do societies like France, which have resisted subordinating their traditional economic practices to market pressures, adapt to the retreat from paternalist state protectionism? Who matters most within the economic policy community and how do they relate to the other members with whom they cooperate and conflict? How closed and cohesive a community is it and does any single participant enjoy general and permanent dominance? In what follows, we shall confine ourselves to how the economic policy process operates in market pluralist and planned capitalist societies.

In their striking study of *Community and Policy inside British Politics*, the subtitle of *The Private Government of Public Money*, Hugh Heclo and Aaron Wildavsky suggested the existence of an 'expenditure community' in which the policy that emerges depends upon the interpersonal sense of community of those who share in making it. The members of this policy community are 'sometimes in conflict, often in agreement, but always in touch and operating within a shared framework. Community is the cohesive and orienting bond underlying any particular issue.'[33] There is a tension between the goals of efficient policy making and a harmonious sense of community: 'between adapting actions and maintaining relationships, between decision and cohesion, between governing now and preserving the possibility of governing later.'[34] To pursue each of the constituent elements of the policy community too exclusively at the price of the other leads to failure. An overemphasis upon community leads to the evils of 'delay, ambiguity, contradiction, self-absorption. Delay arises because of the time-consuming efforts to bring along other officials and departments. Ambiguity helps paper over the cracks of disagreement so that officials can cooperate a while longer. Contradiction emerges out of efforts to appease contending forces, often giving each a little and neither enough. Self-absorption comes from the close proximity of small groups of powerful men who depend on each other's good opinion.'[35] When one is impatient with a government because its policy is slow to emerge, equivocal and pointing simultaneously in opposite directions, a measure of understanding, if not of tolerance, may be induced by appreciating that these propensities to sluggishness, evasiveness and inconsistency are the price of communal continuity and cohesion. To all the constraints upon policy makers imposed by external forces and realities must be added the self-restraint necessary for the preservation of the policy community itself. That this involves sacrifices in relation to some abstract optimal policy is not to be denied. Although community must sometimes be sacrificed for policy results, the capital asset of the policy partnership itself should not be squandered in the pursuit of ephemeral increases in income.

In chapter 3 we shall see that six clusters of national actors play a predominant part in the 'hexagon of limited pluralist power', but we must now specify which of these form the economic policy community 'insiders' and which of them are 'outsiders', whose activities impinge only in a peripheral way upon the policy process. Where it can be identified in any precise fashion, the economic policy community is based upon the convergent assumptions and purposes of two types of partners: the select leaders of the major financial and industrial enterprises (public or private, national or multinational) together with the heads of their representative organizations and the elected or selected state officials who run the ministries, public enterprises and banks responsible for economic management on behalf of society. It is their reciprocal relationship of enduring partnership—sometimes strengthened by a unilateral or bilateral exchange of members—that leads to the constitution of a macro-economic policy community, superimposed upon a series of policy sub-communities. These more specialized policy communities, dealing with industry, energy, incomes, employment and so forth have their own more or less institutionalized memberships. We shall try to identify whether there are a few strategically placed people who play an active part in many of these sub-communities as well as in the macro-economic policy community. To the extent that we do so, we shall be able to give some precision to the term 'limited pluralism'. Let us make it clear immediately what this means. *Most of those who are essential to liberal, social and economic democracy are excluded from the economic policy community, whereas most of those included—notably the elite economic bureaucrats and the select business leaders—have no democratic legitimacy.* Among those excluded for most purposes are: the voters, political parties and parliament; the local authorities; the trade unions; the press; the mass of consumers. This does not mean that some of these outsiders do not occasionally play an important part in the making of economic policy. (Even if legislation only plays a limited role in matters of economic policy, law is still a significant if formal instrument in the hands of decision makers.) However, they intervene episodically and can usually be ignored by the public policy partners who are inclined to see themselves as the true guardians of an enduring public interest.

2
THE FRENCH ECONOMIC POLICY COMMUNITY

Attempts to describe and evaluate the specific relationship of the state and the market in France are bedevilled by the presuppositions with which the subject is approached. Two aspects of this difficulty need to be explicitly faced at the outset. Given that socio-cultural factors usually play an important part in explaining political and economic action, the 'prescriptive' values that are intended to shape and authenticate the conduct, of all those who make and expound public policy, those who carry it out and those who have to live with its consequences must be distinguished from the actual conduct of the actors.[1] A country's peculiar policy style, the institutional and cultural legacies that constitute the normative framework by reference to which policy is defined and that changes relatively slowly, must not be equated with the day-to-day behaviour of members of the policy community, from which it may diverge sharply under the pressure of circumstances. It has been argued elsewhere that mobilizing private interests in the service of public ambitions constitutes the salient element in the French policy style, but the will to act initially by way of assertive and innovative imposition does not preclude recourse to responsive and conciliatory consultation and negotiation where a *fait accompli* proves difficult to achieve without a costly conflict. However, it is maintained that in France, while an 'active policy style does not in practice mean integrated or decisive government action, it implies a *capacity* for policy initiative, a *potential* for far-sighted planning and a *propensity* to impose its will when it is necessary to attain public objectives.'[2]

This leads to another preliminary issue: To what extent is the French state autonomous from the market? While the Marxists initially focussed attention on the extent to which in a capitalist society the state had any autonomy from the productive forces of economic determinism, the ensuing debate was almost exclusively 'theoretical' in the worse sense, that is divorced from an examination of the 'facts'. Some American scholars have been fascinated by the contrast between their fragmented, federal political structure operating in a market-dominated, pluralistic political and economic system and France's centralized, unitary political structure, superordinate to a society in general and market forces in particular. However, whereas John Zysman has somewhat circumspectly argued that the French state can be treated 'as a powerful, independent force in political life . . . and thus at least partially autonomous', Harvey Feigenbaum categorically asserts that, because it has been captured by the economically powerful, 'the French state is strong but it is not autonomous.'[3] The latter statement is based upon an examination of the relationship between the 'state', represented by the President and Prime Minister, other ministers, senior officials in the ministries, and the legislative and judicial bodies on the one hand, and the partially or wholly nationalized oil companies on the other, that are held to dominate the relationship. 'Essentially autonomous public and private petroleum companies are responsible for the framework which shapes the options available to government. Both by omission and design, French and foreign-based companies enjoy considerable freedom of action.' Feigenbaum concedes that: 'Certainly there is in France, as in most Western countries, a remarkable coincidence between the policy objectives of public officials and the broad interests of the petroleum industry', but he argues that: 'Companies are both . . . the main repositories of expertise and active promoters of policies that administrators are all too inclined to accept.'[4]

We shall return at the end of this chapter to a closer examination of the oil industry case, but here and now it is necessary to point to the dubious presupposition that *either* the 'state' *or* the 'market' represented by the oil companies is 'autonomous'. If one envisages the relationship not as one of unilateral domination of either firms over government, or the reverse, but rather as one of collusive interdependence in which the oil companies may in some key respects be the senior partners in the joint enterprise, one is closer to behavioural reality. The tendency to separate state from society and to regard one or other as dominant in a general way is both implausible and simplistic. It neglects the capacity of the various members of the economic policy community—none of whom is genuinely and generally autonomous—to exert influence on policy outcomes in the course of the continuing process of interaction and in the context of a shifting balance of power, as circumstances and issues change. We shall return in the final chapter to the specific issue of public enterprises, which has become even more important in the 1980s. However, we must first look retrospectively at the traditional French state–market relationship.

In the illuminating comparisons he drew between the market-oriented United Kingdom and *étatiste* and *dirigiste* France, Andrew Shonfield explained that whereas in the United Kingdom 'there is an established principle of strong unitary central power, there are other potent traditions ingrained in the political system which impede the development of active, interventionist government. There is an abiding prejudice which sees it as the natural business of government to react—not to act.' In France, thanks to a combination of active techno-bureaucratic leadership and passive democratic support, 'a set of institutions which were largely pre-capitalist in design could be adapted more readily than others to serve the purposes of the new capitalism, with its large built-in segment of public power, in the second half of the twentieth century'.[5] John Zysman has elaborated on the same point, but he shows that the state had a stabilizing as well as a developmental role. 'The anti-market tradition in France has its origins in the very process of industrialization, which was initiated by a strong and centralized state and tended to leave in place and even reinforce many of the institutions and social groups of the traditional economy. . . . In France the market-place was never really allowed to impose its will on the community; a full-blown market system was slow in evolving, and the structure of social relationships preserved in the political arena set the channels through which industrialization would flow. Closed borders, active entrepreneurial intervention by the state, and negotiation rather than competition between business within France have all served to insulate the economy from the market.'[6]

In the new context of exposure to an EC and international market, the old intransigent and assertive *volontarisme* has become much more difficult to sustain and the pressure to adopt a more accommodating attitude has proved hard to resist. Yet in November 1968 the president of the peak business organization CNPF (Conseil National du Patronat Français) asserted that far from the growth in foreign competition requiring a withdrawal of the national government's protective and supporting intervention, it was a further justification of such assistance.[7] French governments were only too ready to respond to this call but 'the French state, accustomed to imposing its will on the marketplace, has been unable either to isolate the French firms or to alter the structure of the international industry. In this setting, forcing the firms to conform to the goals of the state slowly weakened them in the marketplace. . . .

However, allowing the firms to conform to the constraints of the market would have required the government to abandon or to redefine many of its policies.'[8] In the 1970s and 1980s, the managers of the proud French state have been humiliated into just such a painful, fundamental reassessment.

If the term 'economic policy community' is to have any operational meaning, its members have to be able to communicate with each other in more or less institutionalized and regular ways. Insofar as it ever is achieved, overall coordination of the official parts of economic policy making is carried out through an elaborate network of formal and informal committees of ministers and senior officials of the main economic ministries. While some decisions are taken personally by the President, the Prime Minister or Finance Minister with the advice of their personal staffs, the weekly economic interministerial committee meeting represents the regular domestic economic summit, of which only its chairman—the Prime Minister—and the Finance Minister are permanent members. Others who are frequently invited to attend are the President's economic adviser, the Governor of the Bank of France, the Planning Commissioner and the head of the Regional and Spatial Planning Delegacy (DATAR), with spending ministers coming as appropriate to the matters under discussion. Attempts to concentrate responsibility for economic policy in one ministry (currently called the 'Economic, Finance and Budget Ministry' but we shall use the traditional name Finance Ministry for short) have always been resisted because of the concentration of power this would imply. In any case, it is too complex a ministry to be cohesive, its two great bastions being the Treasury and Budget Divisions, which are most directly involved in what has been called the role of 'the state as economic player', by contrast to its customary roles as economic regulator and economic administrator.

Zysman argues that France and Japan are among the rare countries whose governments organize state-led development. 'As a *player*, it pursues specific outcomes on a case-by-case basis, assembling packages of incentives which can be used to persuade or coerce. It discriminates among firms and applies administrative rules and regulations to accomplish particular objectives.'[9] Zysman gives pride of place as the instrument of state action to the Treasury Division: 'The *Trésor* is the point at which the pinnacle of the French state bureaucracy joins the administered character of the financial marketplace.'[10] This is because he regards the key economic instruments to be financial, with credit allocation being the most important of them. However, he admits that the tiny Treasury Division has to operate through intermediaries, although he is less ready to admit that they do not passively implement its wishes. The Bank of France, the Economic and Social Development Fund, the *Crédit National* and the *Caisse des Dépôts* may act in conjunction with the Treasury Division, but they have their own priorities and are not subordinate members of the public economic policy community. In the key decisions concerning national and international monetary policy, public borrowing and the loan of public funds for private and public investment, they are powers in their own right. Besides, the Budget Division is unduly neglected by an analysis that claims that the Treasury Division 'cannot be overemphasized',[11] while even in its diminished place within the economic policy community, the Planning Commissariat helps to avoid economic policy disintegrating *merely* into a series of improvised, piecemeal expedients. Finally, the nationalization of most of the French banking system in 1982 has, as we shall see in the final chapter, not appreciably increased the Treasury Division's control over credit. The earlier experience with banking nationalization after the Second World War provides extended and eloquent testimony to the difficulty of exerting the type of central Treasury control presupposed by Zysman. It has been pointed out that the pre-1982 nationalized banks 'pursued inflationary interest and money creation policies, diverted investment out of France and then speculated against the franc. Moreover, the nationalized banks were the most recalcitrant in applying the government's credit directives in 1973–5.'[12] If the Treasury Division is the pinnacle of state financial power, it meets in the shape of the state banks veritable 'states within the state'. In other words, the French economic policy community is more pluralistic than is often claimed (see Figure 2.1).

Despite the apparently 'pyramidal' nature of French state authority, this highly simplified picture of the exposed tenth of the iceberg has already conveyed something of the plurality and fragmented character of the French public economic policy community. When it comes to dealing with the private sector, the Treasury Division of the Finance Ministry—the nerve centre of the state's banking power—is looked upon as the decision maker, but in fact power is dispersed among semi-autonomous sub-systems, each pursuing its own policy objectives, with its own industrial clientele.[13] Each economic policy—trade, industrial, energy, monetary, prices and incomes, employment, regional and so forth—has its own particular state–society sub-system so that the attempts to

24   *The State and the Market Economy*

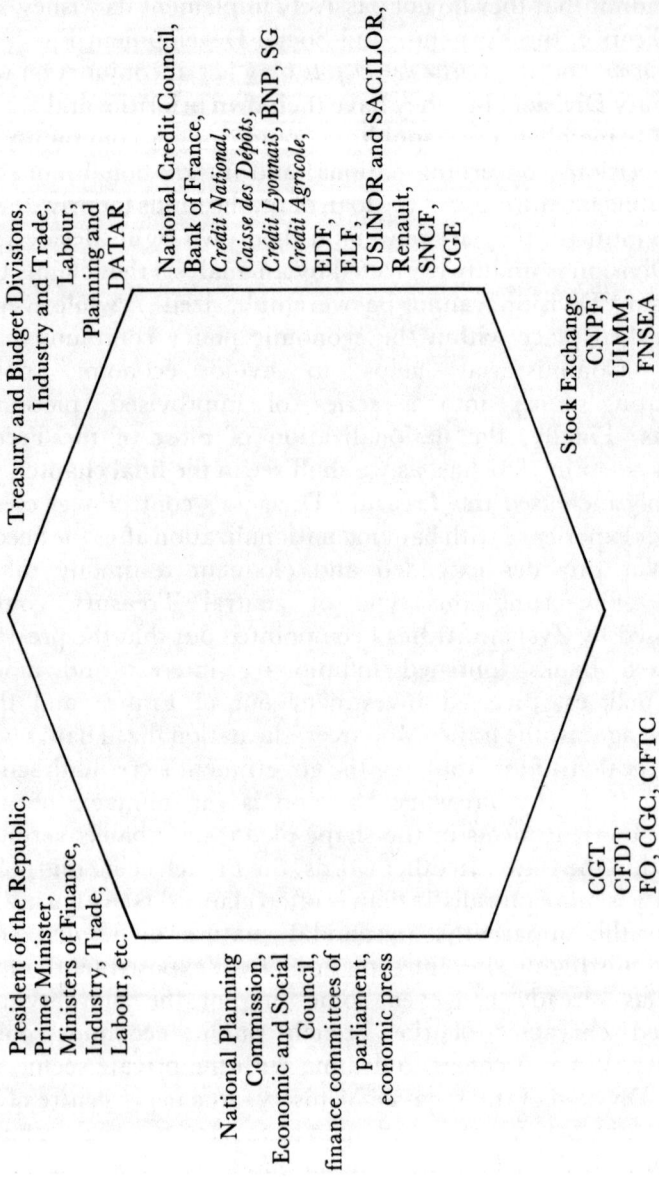

Figure 2.1   *The French economic policy community*

coordinate them, by the Finance Ministry or either its Budgetary or Treasury Division, by the Planning Commissariat, by the Interministerial Economic Committee or by the Prime Minister or President of the Republic, are illusory. We see here why attempts to define terms like 'industrial policy' rigorously are bound to disintegrate. This is because the reality they attempt to describe is highly heterogeneous, with decisions being taken piecemeal, case by case, with non-economic criteria—whether political or bureaucratic—predominating and a consistent set of actions being the exception rather than the rule. We shall examine an example of this—industrial policy—more closely later. Let us meanwhile consider two types of interventionist relationship between the French state and its economic environment and how the emphasis has shifted from a traditionalist, 'paternalist', regulatory and protective role to a modernist, entrepreneurial, selectively interventionist and promotional one. Both are opposed simply to leaving decisions to emerge in the market.

Towards Concerted Action by Firms and Government

In the traditional system, the state sought to reduce social conflict and preserve the status quo by regulations restricting both foreign and domestic competition, slowing down the pace of change because this helped both to preserve social harmony and France's capacity to go its own way within the world economy. Business performance was only a secondary matter. The prime concern of firms was access to the supervisory sub-division of their sponsor ministry, usually through their representative trade associations, so that the government's use of its regulatory powers, over matters like tariffs and quotas, prices, credit or taxation, could be negotiated to their satisfaction. Although the state's regulations were general, indirect and impersonal in form, they were the subject of piecemeal negotiations not merely with nationally representative bodies forming the economic policy community but more specific industry and even product policy communities. The distant, legalistic and circumspect attitude adopted by public officials was reciprocal to the suspicious and potentially rebellious attitude of predominantly family-owned businesses. The ministry officials knew little directly about the firms and relied upon the trade associations for their industrial statistics.[14]

Suleiman has acutely perceived the significance of the French distinction between 'pressure groups' and 'lobbies' on the one hand, the 'professional organizations' on the other. What is the criterion by which the former are dismissed as sinister sectional interests, unrepresentative, retrograde and demagogic, which threaten the public interest, whereas the latter are respectable, representative and dynamic? It is simple. Those groups that collaborate with the embodiments of *raison d'état* and act as their (junior) social partners have attributed to them the seal of legitimacy. The leaders of such acquiescent, pressurized groups become state-sanctified notables. They can at best persuade their spending–sponsor ministry to identify to some extent with the group's goals and absorb some of its values, in return for giving the division or ministry support in intra-administrative conflicts or vis à vis the politicians. At worst, the group may become a semi-autonomous extension of the state apparatus, providing assistance in the implementation of public policies over which it has little or no influence. A survey of *directeurs* of Paris ministries in 1968–70 indicated that they considered the main advantages of contacts with *organisations professionnels* were that they facilitated the implementation and—to a lesser extent—the formulation of policy, as well as enabling the government to anticipate opposition. Lesser advantages were the opportunity to acquire information from the interest groups and the ability to explain to the groups decisions that had already been taken. If the virtue of contact with the interest groups consisted essentially in disarming opposition to *faits accomplis*, the principal disadvantages were: the leakage of information led to the mobilization of opposition to the action contemplated by the government; constant pressure prevented the 'correct decision' being taken; lastly, officials resented the 'time wasted' by such meetings.[15]

However, rapid post-war industrialization, combined with the exposure of the French economy to the effects of European and international competition, led successive governments to adopt a much more active, entrepreneurial role than they had hitherto attempted. Their most perceptive public servants had anticipated this development soon after the Second World War, notably the group of economic planners that gravitated toward Jean Monnet and the Finance Ministry and other officials that looked to François Bloch-Lainé for intellectual and administrative leadership. It was around the ambiguous notion of 'concerted economy' fathered by Etienne Hirsch, Monnet's close collaborator from 1946 before succeeding him as *Commissaire Général du Plan* (1952–9), that the modernizing forces rallied. Monnet saw his crucial problem as being: 'How to lead an immense collective effort without being in control of decision making in the state or in industry', which meant deploying persuasive powers of a high order.[16] The catalyst was planning legitimized by a process of socializing the key decision makers into accepting a common set of norms and thanks to Bloch-Laîné and de Gaulle, Monnet's view that 'It was as much by hammering home a few simple ideas as by virtue of its weighty reports that the Plan became a household word' prevailed.[17]

The person who popularized the notion of 'concerted economy' was Bloch-Laîné, who as head of the Treasury Division from 1947–52 had helped the First Plan to become a financial reality and who as director general of the *Caisse des Dépôts et Consignations* from 1952–67 made it one of the Plan's banking instruments.[18] In a 1960 comment for the review *Jeune Patron* upon the 1959 lecture that launched the term on its way to being the key French official economic cliché of the 1960s, Bloch-Laîné declared: 'The term concerted economy was mentioned as early as the First Monnet Plan. . . . It is currently fashionable because it embraces ideas and activities calculated silently to revolutionize our organization and practices in economic and social affairs; attempts to break down the futile doctrinal opposition between liberalism and *dirigisme*, reconciling in a realistic way the freedom of firms and the new role of the state.'[19] While he admitted the need to beware of the formula that implies an illusory and facile reconciliation of opposites, he made it clear that he wanted businessmen, unions and government to abandon outdated ideological disputes for the calm of partisan discussion of economic realities.

However, his definition of 'concerted economy' makes clear that the 'partners' in this consensus building were essentially the key public and private actors: government officials and businessmen. Although he later rejected the term 'regime' as inadequately pluralist, Bloch-Laîné's initial formulation was: 'it is a regime in which the representatives of the state or its subordinate bodies and those of business (whether public or private) meet to exchange information, compare their forecasts and together either take decisions or present advice to the government. It is a regime in which the major investment, production and exchange decisions do not wholly depend either on the heads of firms or of government bodies alone but are based upon continuous collaboration so that the public and private sectors do not correspond to two sets of separate, autonomous, unconnected acts.'[20] He assumed as self-evident that the economic segregation between business and government stipulated by a strict adherence to liberalism was 'nonsense'. The public authorities needed to be informed of the decisions and plans of the businessmen, while the latter had to be aware not only of what the former did but of what 'the state knows, forecasts and plans'. With rapidly evolving markets and technologies, businessmen had less to fear from the relatively well informed and neutral state than from their competitors. Furthermore, 'the state's own activities and those of its satellites in economic matters are now so varied and so extensive that there are few private industries that, as suppliers or as clients, can remain indifferent to them.' He was well placed to know that 'since the last war, few investments have really been private.... Every firm of any size must nowadays deal with the banker state.' In trying to persuade businessmen to play the game of a 'depoliticized' exchange of information with the government about their forecasts and plans, Bloch-Laîné warned that an ill-informed state was more inclined to be inquisitorial and *dirigiste*. 'Those that think that the less the state knows the less will it intervene are wrong. The reverse is true, since it is no longer conceivable that it will not intervene.'[21]

Bloch-Laîné advocated joint investment programming based upon production planning between the government and major firms to attain precise objectives with the financial means provided in part by the state and its banking agencies. The Planning Commissariat— 'the discreet promoter, in practice, of the concerted economy'[22]— was not the only place where the public and private sectors learned to work together. The movement of managerial staffs between the senior civil service, the public enterprises and large private firms had broken down the ideological prejudice against nationalization. As part of his early 1960s tendency to play down the significance of ideology, Bloch-Laîné correctly anticipated Federal Germany's subsequent attempt to develop its own version of *concertation*, despite its liberal rhetoric, declaring in his 1959 lecture: 'The German miracle owes as much, if not more to government organization and action as it does to the spontaneous inspiration and unimpeded activity of its businessmen.'[23] Retrospectively, in the mid-1970s, Bloch-Laîné adopted a less sanguine view of the development of the 'concerted economy', asking whether 'the Right has killed the concerted economy by taking it over.'[24] He regretted that the Left-wing version of *concertation*, represented by the notion of democratic planning publicly championed by the CFDT and by Pierre Mendès France in his *La République Moderne* in the early 1960s, with planners Jacques Delors and Jean Ripert providing much of the inspiration, had failed to make headway.[25] However, it is clear that the trade unions were not given a major role in Bloch-Laîné's initial formulation of the idea, his main concern being the key members of the economic policy community, not the peripheral workers' representatives, who decisively rejected the attempt to apply wage restraint to them under the guise of an incomes policy in 1963–4.

By 1968 Bloch-Lainé and his associates like Jacques Delors and Simon Nora, reflected in *Pour Nationaliser l'Etat*,[26] had become reconciled to the idea that the bridging of the previously sacrosanct separation between public and private sectors had principally allowed the state officials from the *grands corps*—especially the *corps des Mines*—to move into the technologically advanced industries. Suleiman has shown that this exodus has led to the substitution of capitalist values for those of public service and the *Ecole des Mines* has become the most successful business school in France. Industrial management education has become the foundation of this corps' training, and Suleiman quotes the objectives set in 1969 by two former directors of the *Ecole des Mines* as the pattern for future *grandes écoles* activities.

1. *Industrial policy of the state*. Initiate and above all stimulate governmental strategy within a certain number of important technical and economic ministerial divisions: for example, initiate and stimulate (which means 'defend and illustrate') French energy policy, policy of acquisition of raw materials, etc. This role which has always existed in countries where public authorities do not practise pure and simple *laissez faire* is tending to take on greater importance in all industrialized societies.

2. *Strategy of large enterprises*. Industrial policy can under no circumstances be limited exclusively to the planning stage. To defend and illustrate a policy in an economic sector is also to implement it at the level of the productive sector—that is, in the public enterprises and in the large private enterprises (the differences between these two sectors, as far as management is concerned, being less important than the points in common)'.[27]

Suleiman has shown that the corps of mining engineers and of finance inspectors hold many of the key industrial and banking posts. What has proved attractive to the private firms in these former public servants is that they combine the legitimacy and politico-administrative skills that French businessmen otherwise conspicuously lack. Apart from profit seeking, 'the businessman exhibits a remarkable incompetence. He is unable to defend himself in the political arena and his social vision is practically nonexistent.

The need to compensate for this lack is what accounts to a large extent for the business community's desire to have as its leaders former state officials.' Suleiman argues that: 'It would be difficult to pinpoint a coherent set of policies that the *Inspection des Finances* or the *Corps des Mines* are committed to within the areas of the economy or of energy' because 'it is not the policies *per se* that matter, for policies are judged according to their impact on the power and position of the elite.' Such policy pragmatism has meant that the elite corps have been able to adapt to the need for change both in government and in business. Suleiman concludes his discussion of the elite and the new economy: 'The lack of commitment on the part of the corps to a set of definable policies, as well as their overriding need to find outlets and "colonize" sectors, ultimately coincide with the private sector's need for officials who can defend industry's interests through their access to decision-making centres.'[28] This development has important implications for the economic and industrial policy process in the first instance, and subsequently for the policies themselves. The entrepreneurial state and the statized enterprise concentrate their joint energies and resources upon industrial development, focused upon the firm. Under the remorseless stimulus of foreign competition, the mobile members of the *grands corps* became the heads of the 'national champion' enterprises, dedicated not so much to compete inside France as with foreign firms, particularly the US multinational corporations.

Qui Gouverne les Groupes Industriels?, based upon empirical studies of major French firms, offers an overlapping but less administration-centred view of business leadership. Bauer and Cohen argue that in a context in which collusion—with other businesses and with government—plays an increasing role at the expense of domestic competition (without stressing the enduring importance of international competition), industrial groups are recruited and run by a 'coopted oligarchy'. They alone decide the group's industrial strategy, because whereas the rest of the management is confined to specialized and limited tasks, the self-recruiting, self-perpetuating and (where possible) self-financing oligarchy maintains a general oversight, decides the firm's organizational structure, its planning and budgeting, the formulation, elaboration and implementation of its policy, where necessary in negotiation with other private or public actors. In France, they rise from the top, coming principally from the public *grandes écoles*, rather than from private business and law schools as is the practice in the United States. In France, as in Japan, it is experience in the higher echelons of the civil service that lead to senior positions in industry and in the banking system, adding, as their preparation for business competition, merit tested in competitive examinations to their success in the school of administrative life. However, whereas in Japan the transition is made on completion of their official career at 55, in France it often occurs much earlier, when they have more time and energy to devote to their business careers.

Bauer and Cohen explain the need to coopt from outside to the leadership group by its internal system of divide and rule between subordinate specialists and directing generalists. 'The qualities sought are those that cannot develop within the industrial group because specialization and the fragmentation of responsibilities are carried to extremes. The skills sought outside are those that the ruling system monopolizes: control over the state resource, and especially the knowledge-power of negotiation, the preparation of strategic plans and their imposition.'[29] The resulting preference for generalists doubtless explains the tendency for the *Ecole Nationale d'Administration* (ENA) to play an increasingly important role compared to *Polytechnique*; the former are better equipped both to offer general leadership within the big business firm and to deal with their counterparts at the head of major ministries, whereas the latter mainly provides the recruiting ground for lower-level, specialist managers who often go directly into industry without *pantouflage* after experience in the public service. Whereas senior civil servants, especially from the *Inspection des Finances*, frequently move into public and—until 1982—private banks, it is not established that these banks have been particularly willing to risk funds in industrial ventures.[30]

The Ministry of Industry in France and Japan

By comparison with the highly fragmented public power of the federal United States, France seems to have an assertive, purposive and close government–business relationship even outside the 'military–industrial complex' but it has not achieved the level of sustained and generalized mobilization for industrial development attained by Japan's 'GNP machine'. While they share the 'situational nationalism of the late industrializers' and more recently the resilient pride of the defeated nation, Japan has perfected 'the most successful strategy and intentional development' based upon highly consensual economic and industrial policy communities.[31] In contrast with the communist command economies and the capitalist market economies, the Japanese have developed a large number of *ad hoc* financial, industrial, political and social institutions appropriate to a 'plan-oriented market economy' based upon the interdependence of the key actors in the state and business sectors working in developmental cooperation.

Chalmers Johnson suggests that 'the broad pattern of development since the late 1920s has been from self-coordination (the state licensing private firms to achieve economic goals) to its opposite, state control, and then to a synthesis of the two, cooperation.' This Japanese version of 'concerted action', which worked best in the 1950s and 1960s, combines competitive private ownership and management with public target setting, accompanied by an acceptance of administrative guidance. Japan's elite economic bureaucracy 'makes most major decisions, drafts virtually all legislation, controls the national budget and is the source of all major policy innovation in the system.... This power, which amounts to an allocation of discretionary and unsupervised authority to the bureaucracy, is obviously open to abuse.... But it is an essential power of the capitalist developmental state for one critical reason: it is necessary to avoid overly detailed laws that, by their very nature, are never detailed enough to cover all contingencies and yet, because of that detail, put a strait-jacket on creative administration.'[32] What the Japanese policy style shows, thanks in part to the 'descent from heaven' process of mobility from the senior civil service into private management and Right-wing politics which we compared to French *pantouflage*, plus cultural and situational circumstances, is a perfected market-conforming, interlocking business–state intervention. The price in terms of subordinating those who are excluded from this elite policy-making community is high.

In France, as elsewhere, Japanese industrial policy has become a model of successful public intervention in the market system, with the added virtue of its relative organizational simplicity. In Japan, industrial policy is an umbrella term covering 'a complex of those policies concerning protection of domestic industries, development of strategic industries, and adjustment of the economic structure in response to or in anticipation of internal and external changes which are formulated and pursued by MITI in the cause of the national interest, as the term "national interest" is understood by MITI officials.'[33] The capacity to develop a high-growth, state-guided industrial system was facilitated, even more than in France, by an earlier 'closed economy in which all . . . contacts with the rest of the world were mediated and brokered in government offices.' Over time MITI developed a balance between business market-mindedness to secure competitiveness and public control to enforce state priorities. While it lasted—MITI's key control over imports declining from the 1970s—MITI's industrial policy effectiveness was due in large measure to the comprehensive economic control that it wielded, linking industrial intervention with general economic management. As Chalmers Johnson puts it: 'MITI's experience suggests that the agency that controls industrial policy needs to combine at least planning, energy, domestic production, international trade, and a share of finance (particularly capital supply and tax policy).'[34]

The contrast with the fragmented and feeble French Ministry of Industry could not be more striking. Erhard Friedberg's study of the French Ministry of Industry at the end of the 1960s stressed its lack of integration between appropriately named divisions controlled by different *corps*, pursuing separate policies. In the absence of a comprehensive and consistent industrial policy, the ministry's capacity to intervene was concentrated in its few strong divisions, there being little correlation between bureaucratic strength and industrial importance. For example, the weak divisions include not only textiles but DIMEE, concerned with the mechanical and electrical industries. Administrative rather than industrial criteria are decisive in determining how sectors and firms are treated. The strong divisions are those with a well-established regulatory tradition, the clearest example being the Fuels Division, the *Direction des Carburants* (usually known as DICA), to which we shall return in connection with energy policy. They tend to supervise sectors with a few large firms, but Friedberg argues that their capacity to exert influence within the industrial policy community is due to the fact that they can use the *corps des Mines* network both within the bureaucratic–financial public sector and with the heads of the firms concerned, making it *possible* to formulate and carry out a dynamic industrial strategy. These direct links mean that they do not have to bother with the trade associations, which the weak divisions have to rely upon in impersonal dealings with a multitude of small and medium firms. While the Ministry of Finance is beyond their reach, the members of the *corps des Mines* alone among senior civil servants have a significant industrial training, so they acquire an expertise which the *Service des Interventions* officials of the Treasury Division lack, with the result that the recommended firms receive the lion's share of public funds. (The advice of the *Crédit National* and of

DATAR also play a part in grant decisions.) Repeated attempts at policy coordination have failed to overcome the juxtaposition of compartmentalized sponsor divisions, with the result that piecemeal, *coup par coup* intervention has predominated over the pursuit of general policy objectives.[36]

From the early 1970s a number of analysts detected a change to a new model 'entrepreneurial state' in France, despite the liberal rhetoric with which Giscard and Barre enveloped it. It was generally agreed that new doctrine was expounded in the official 1968 Montjoie report on industrial development and the Nora report on public enterprise, as well as in the Sixth Plan industry commission report, although the most forceful assertion of the new approach came in a book *L'Impératif Industriel*[37] by a member of the *corps des Mines*, planner and future minister under Giscard, Lionel Stoléru. The state became directly involved in industrial restructuring and its micro-industrial approach was increasingly focused on direct dealings with a selected few national champion firms. The key issue is how the power to make industrial policy has been shared between the two major 'partners'. This has often been put in general terms: 'the basic institutions of industrial policy have been centralized by the state ... but often they have no centre, all too often focused solely on the firms. All this has encouraged the piecemeal negotiation of the sensitive major programmes directly between a few senior civil servants and a few managing directors, at the expense of overall coordination .... Ultimately, industrial policy would sometimes seem to be confined to a few people, knowing each other and mastering the problems.'[38] So, far from the Industry Ministry being able effectively to control industrial policy, the latter tends to disintegrate into a plurality of policies of each of the major firms in the industrial policy community, promoted to the status of national industrial champions.

Bauer and Cohen seek to explain the paradox of a state with immense potential power that usually ends up underwriting what the major industrial groups decide among themselves and consolidating their power. They stress a large firm's monopoly of legitimate expertise, the stability of its management compared with the frequency with which the state's representatives change and the conflicts between the various public sector actors. From the national champion's capacity to take advantage of the fragmentation of the state administration and its inability to formulate a consistent and comprehensive industrial policy, Cohen and Bauer conclude that the state's financial resources are used to further the firm's autonomous strategies, rather than the supposed state industrial policy. They also discount the view that either the state deposit or merchant banks have a consistent industrial policy, with the result that within the industrial policy community pride of place is accorded to the major industrial groups.[39]

National Champions or Sectoral States within the State?

To illustrate the danger of assuming that a national champions policy—even when the firms in question are nationalized—means that they are docile instruments of a deliberate, consistent and sustained public policy, let us consider two French public sector examples, EDF and ELF, drawn from the administered and from the market economy energy sector respectively. Even if the polemical epithet '*Etat-EDF*' is set aside as extravagant, in matters of energy policy EDF has been a state within the state, the prime author and moving force behind the 'all-electric' energy policy and the inordinately ambitious French electro-nuclear policy. Naturally, all large firms seek autonomy through control of their environment, extending their hold over supplies and market, over technological innovation and over finance. While energy policy was dominated by cheap and then by expensive oil from the 1960s, and although it has been largely determined within France by three clusters of actors—political (President, Prime Minister, Industry Minister), financial (Treasury and Budget Divisions of the Finance Ministry) and operational (the electrical and petroleum public corporations)—one thing emerges strongly: even before the onset of the 1973 crisis, there was a switch from imported oil to domestically produced nuclear energy. 'There can be no reasonable doubt that the initiative for almost all aspects of the nuclear programme comes from the EDF.... There is a remarkable similarity between the propositions of EDF in the late 1960s and early 1970s and the basis of the present national energy policy.'[40] EDF's dominant influence must be credited in part to the tandem of its managing director Marcel Boiteux and chairman Paul Delouvrier, but more especially to its control of the advisory body that shaped public policy decisions: the consultative committee for the production of nuclear-based electricity, commonly known as the PEON committee. However, to achieve its dominant position, it had first to assert its primacy over the Atomic Energy Commissariat (CEA) and protect itself from the constraints that the Finance Ministry sought to impose upon its expensive ambitions.

By 1970 EDF appeared to have achieved both these goals. As long as de Gaulle was President, his prime commitment to nuclear power for an independent deterrent and his insistence on relying upon French rather than US technology meant that the CEA was in the driving seat. However, his replacement by Pompidou meant that a political obstacle was removed; the cabinet in November 1969 took the crucial decisions about the use of US reactors that substituted the primarily commercial preoccupations of EDF for the military and industrial patriotism of the CEA. Thereafter EDF and CEA worked closely together to overcome the Finance Ministry objections to the demands for massive provision of capital to fund the enormous electro-nuclear investment programme. Following on the 1967 Nora report recommendation that public enterprise autonomy should be promoted by signing medium-term contracts with the government, EDF saw its opportunity to free itself from financial constraint. However, the programme contract was short-lived because of the rapid rise in EDF indebtedness. This allowed the Finance Ministry to restore a measure of financial control over EDF, although without preventing it from proceeding with its massive investment programme, its electro-nuclear investments amounting to 47 per cent of its turnover in 1979. The fact that the Mitterrand presidency has led, despite lower demand, to a modest cutback in the electro-nuclear programme was predictable, given that three-quarters of the Socialist Party's energy committee before 1981 consisted of EDF and CEA staff.[41]

The severance of control from ownership has reached the point in certain profitable multinational nationalized champions that former President Giscard d'Estaing could complain: 'The power of appointment is virtually the only influence that one can exercise over the policy of these enterprises.'[42] This lack of control applied particularly to petroleum policy, and to ELF–Aquitaine and its managing director for its first eleven years (1966–77) Pierre Guillaumat, under whose aegis the ludicrous *avions-renifleurs* project to prospect for oil was initiated. Guillaumat was appointed by de Gaulle as head of the Industry Ministry's DICA (1944–51) and became head of CEA (1951–8). On de Gaulle's return to power, Guillaumat was made Minister for War but informally Minister of Oil in the early years of the Fifth Republic, before taking over as first head of ELF–Aquitaine. A DICA official is reported as asserting: 'No one could say Guillaumat was controllable.'[43] His influence was perpetuated by his protégé André Giraud, who like Guillaumat was director of the DICA before heading the CEA and becoming industry minister under Giscard.

The pivotal place of the DICA in the energy policy community must be stressed. 'This department serves both as the conduit of policy imperatives to the industry and as the repository of technical advice to the government. It is here that responsibility for licences is decided, based on predictions of French market needs as well as other related licensing, e.g. new refineries, distribution points, etc. Contact with the industry is . . . continuous, both because DICA officials sit on national company boards and because of their continuous consultation on government subsidized projects (technical research), approximately weekly pricing meetings and of their general technical role in the determination of long range policy.'[44]

Lucas has documented how, prior to the 1973 oil shock, the energy policy community in 'France cheerfully embraced the penetration of oil. It did so because a policy of cheap oil suited three powerful groups for three quite different reasons. It suited the Ministry of Finance because it brought low prices and demanded no investment from the state. It suited the Ministry of Industry because it engendered an international competitive manufacturing industry. It benefitted a coalition of Gaullist politicians and oil company executives (not always distinguishable) who perceived an opportunity of creating an extensive and secure structure of oil supplies based upon French crude.'[45] Whereas the policy enshrined in the 1928 'charter' of French petroleum regulation was the creation of a national champion—Compagnie Française des Pétroles (CFP) in the first instance—to act as an instrument of *dirigiste* state directives, the cheap oil and need to adapt to the international market in the 1960s led to a loosening of the link between the state and its chosen instruments. Not merely was the *tutelle* of the Industry Ministry and the planning process circumvented in practice. Giraud, as the head of the DICA, explained in 1966 that the 1928 Act itself recognized the prime importance of the oil companies and delegated to them the flexible implementation of a minimally specified policy based on the common interest of companies and state.[46] Giraud was Guillaumat's choice as his successor at the head of ELF, but Giscard—exercising what we have earlier seen to be the only power he had over the public corporations as President—instead chose a fellow finance inspector and market liberal Albin Chalandon.

Giraud as Minister of Industry was in the late 1970s to be less sanguine about the autonomy of ELF when he came into conflict with its head Albin Chalandon, the President-imposed intruder into what had been a preserve of the *corps des Mines*. ELF had enthusiastically embraced the Nora Report invitation to act commercially and took its cues from the multinational oil oligopoly.[47] A 1974 parliamentary report revealed that CFP and ELF resorted to tax evasion, withheld and falsified information about prices paid for crude oil, as well as conspired with French affiliates of the multinationals to raise jet fuel prices to the nationalized Air France. The Schvartz Report pertinently wondered: 'One may well ask where is the state? Is it in the DICA, in the Energy Agency or is it at the head of ELF–ERAP?' The government had allowed too much freedom to its national champion with the result that it was forced to negotiate with a rival power, 'the general interest being supposed somehow to emerge from these conflicts'.[48] More generally, it is not clear that French national champions acted differently from other oil companies because 'the profit-maximizing orientation of French public enterprise leads to behaviour that is inconsistent with the purported goals of French petroleum policy.'[49] Paradoxically, the proud national champions policy seems in practice to dwindle into ensuring that French firms are partners in the international oil cartel, even if the price is that they put their loyalty to this international oil company community above that to their national policy community.

We can no more generalize from the spectacular example of French energy policy than we can from other French industrial policies: the rearguard action on behalf of declining industries—the 'Red Cross State'—or those to be protected from foreign competition or those high-technology industries that are to be given priority promotion. What we have sought to do with these concluding cases is to exemplify some of the general propositions we advanced earlier. The policy-making process is conceived as operating within semi-pluralistic, elitist decision-making communities, which in the case of economic and industrial policy give pride of place to the discretion of actors in the major business firms, to the public and private bankers, and to the politico-administrative leaders, exercised within a framework of domestic and international constraints. The varying roles of these actors will emerge more fully in later discussions on economic policy making and implementation at the national, regional and local levels.

3
PRESSURE GROUPS AND PRESSURED GROUPS IN FRANCE

The term 'pressure group'—when abstracted from the working of the politico-administrative system generally—is not merely too narrow but too one-sided and too all-embracing as well. For a start, the word 'group' is misleading because many of the major actors in the policy process—notably large public and private enterprises—are sufficiently powerful to act in their own right, without seeking collective strength through combination. However, the companion word 'pressure' presents more complex difficulties. Pressure groups work within a multilateral and reciprocal system of influence in which groups are pressured as well as exercising pressure. The study of pressure groups was pioneered by scholars in the United States and the United Kingdom, and unconsciously incorporated a value-laden liberal and unilaterally pluralist emphasis upon societal influences upon the state rather than vice versa, characteristic features of their own 'Anglo-Saxon' political systems. This bias was uncritically adopted by the pioneer in the field of French pressure group studies, Jean Meynaud, in his initial overall description of the subject. His later work was more speculative and divorced from detailed empirical verification, the necessary work having simply not been done. For the most part it still remains to be done.[1]

Sensing perhaps that there was a missing dimension to his work, notably in the field of economic policy, this former economist went on to become a pioneer investigator of the phenomenon of technocracy, but he did not live to bring the two sides of his work together.[2] The techno-bureaucratic preoccupation came naturally to a fellow countryman of Saint-Simon, but it was Henry Ehrmann, whose superb pioneering study of the French peak business organization, the CNPF, had brought him into direct contact with the interface between the most conspicuously capitalist pressure group in French society and the major techno-bureaucratic agencies of the French state, who focused on group–government links.[3] In a remarkable article in 1961 on 'French bureaucracy and organized interests' (which has never been followed up by the large-scale systematic investigation for which it cries out), he suggested that the relationship between big business and government was not just reciprocal rather than unilateral, but it was frequently collusive.[4] This insight was exploited by others, notably by Andrew Shonfield in the contrast he made between France and Britain in his magisterial investigation of *Modern Capitalism*.[5] So, the term 'pressure' is misleading in yet another way. Through the notion of institutionalized 'concertation' between selected 'insider' groups and government agencies, leading perhaps to a consensus that avoided zero-sum confrontations and conflicts, the way was open for a re-emergence of the notion of corporatism, the linkage in the French case being indicated by Ehrmann in his 1957 study of French big business.[6] However, in the 1960s, the analysis remained essentially a pluralist one, with clear indications that it should be slanted in a neo-corporatist direction, characterized by concerted capitalism-cum-statism.

The pluralist character of Ehrmann's analysis was emphasized by the way in which he argued that, despite the monolithic structure attributed to the French state by legalistic studies, both sides of the state–society equation were highly fragmented. It was not just French society that was the prey of endemic and profound cleavages; the French state was itself fractured by numerous fissures. While 'horizontal' ministries, notably the Finance Ministry, sought to assert an overall public or general interest, the bulk of the state machine consisted of 'vertical' ministries which worked primarily with a single interest, exercising powerful, joint, fissiparous, distintegrative pressures in the making of public policy. While Ehrmann's analysis was understandably oversimplified (for example, playing down the splits within the Finance Ministry), nevertheless the broad picture is accurate. Detailed studies of French administration have subsequently shown that such fragmentation is a feature not merely of relations between ministries but between *directions* (divisions) in the same ministry and between *bureaux* in the same *direction*.[7] While in Britain the permanent secretary at the head of each ministry, much more than the passing ministers, provides the capacity for effective unitary bureaucratic coordination, the more collective and transitory French style of coordination by a *directeur de cabinet* and the minister's personal staff, not only offers greater scope for pressure group penetration, but also leads to more intra-ministerial conflict between line and staff and accentuates the inherent tendencies towards administrative pluralism. However, counterbalancing this propensity to dissensus is the historically and culturally dominant status of the French state and its agents, with their claim to represent the general interest in a way few political leaders have surpassed. The salient twentieth-century example was General de Gaulle, for whom the general interest simply equated the General's interest.

However, as Ehrmann had already indicated, whereas the interpenetration of certain groups with particular parts of the government apparatus might, and sometimes did, lead to the group leaders absorbing something of the senior officials' general interest values, the senior officials might, and sometimes did, identify the public interest with one or more specific private interests. Although officials in the Budget and Treasury Divisions of the Finance Ministry or in the Planning Commissariat, 'who have to assign priorities to what are frequently contradictory demands, believe themselves to be free of the corporatist[8] leanings for which they criticize their colleagues in the vertical branches', in practice this is far from the truth. 'What is obviously intended is to eliminate the top political organs from the determination of important community purposes and to place the full responsibility for the manipulation of interests in the hands of the administrator and his like-minded counterparts representing those very interests . . . . They are also frankly selective about the interests to be admitted to the process of common decision making, inasmuch as they share the preferences of many of their colleagues for large-scale interests deemed to be less rapacious and less narrow-minded than organizations of "little men".'[9] Ehrmann circumspectly concluded, on the basis of early post-war experience (the Fourth Republic and the start of the Fifth Republic) and in the light of the notions of 'concerted economy' developed by Bloch-Lainé from the planning practice of Jean Monnet,[10] that the main impetus for *economic* policy had come from a bureaucratic–big business alliance. 'The best-organized forces in the nation, the bureaucracy and the large economic interests, leaned on each other and drew increasing strength from mutual support until, *at least in some cases*, authoritative decision making became the result of a near-amalgamation between them.'[11] In his turn, Shonfield and others analysed and explained the failure of the United Kingdom to achieve a comparably rapid and sustained rate of economic growth after the Second World War to the failure to establish such a beneficent alliance between selected big businessmen (normally former senior civil servants who had moved to the semi-public or private sector) and senior state officials.[12]

Before leaving the subject of terminology, one could certainly substitute the term 'interest group' for pressure group, given the latter's misleading implications. However, interest group is a term not without its own problems. Finer—while conceding that it is more neutral—reduced it to a sub-category, contrasted with disinterested groups promoting a cause. Whereas this type of distinction had its vogue, it has a major weakness, reflecting an introspective pluralism, *almost exclusively preoccupied with the groups themselves*, their motivations and capacity to attract members, *rather than their extrovert relationships with government and other groups*. If we were to focus upon this latter distinction, which reflects current concerns more closely, one would instead contrast the 'insider' groups, which have acquired a more or less formally institutionalized relationship with one or (usually) more agencies of the state and 'outsider' groups. The latter are denied official recognition—and the legitimacy that goes with it, especially in countries like France, with a long statist tradition—as well as the routine, regular access to public decision makers which the 'insider groups' enjoy as a matter of course. The clientele-conferred 'legitimacy from below', which is particularly characteristic of the United States or the United Kingdom is not wholly absent from countries such as France and Federal Germany, which normatively rely to a greater extent upon a state-sponsored 'legitimacy from above'. The crucial notion of 'social partnership'—which attains its full development in neo-corporatist systems such as Austria—is confined to the representative, responsible, respectable, cooperative, useful and trustworthy 'insider' groups. Regular contact with them would not taint the official paragons of the public interest with the pitch of particularist demagoguery.

In France, the distinction made by senior civil servants is between the reliable *organisations professionnels* and the unrepresentative, irresponsible, disreputable, potentially disruptive pressure groups or lobbies, the use of the foreign term being intended to suggest that they are outlandish, untrustworthy and undesirable imports that disturb domestic state–society harmony.[13] In the United Kingdom and the United States, the absence of a dominant public law tradition on the hierarchial superimposition of state authority over society, and the strength of liberal and pluralist norms, inclines group–government relations to be conducted—in principle—between equals. The opposite is true in France. Those groups that are accepted by government bodies as 'social partners'—a more select category than those formally recognized as 'representative'—

acquire this status on the understanding that they are junior partners. Public recognition constitutes a privilege, selectively according a measure of public legitimacy to private organizations. In return, the government's social partners strengthen the position of their official patrons by lending them support from outside the public decision-making system. In France, the juridical chasm between public and private actors is bridged in part thanks to the collaborative activities of these intermediaries or mediators. So, a preliminary step in studying any public policy sector must be to identify which, if any, groups have acquired the privileged status of social partner, when they attained it, who the actors on both sides are, what form their transactions assume and with what frequency they occur. This is necessary before investigating their role within the policy process from problem identification through to the implementation of practical solutions, whose defects prompt the re-emergence of problems.

Why some groups are selected for privileged 'insider' status depends, as we have seen, in part upon their willingness to act as (junior) partners. However, the transigent or intransigent behaviour of any group is usually derived from other, more fundamental factors—in particular the structural and functional indispensability of some groups, which confers upon them what Finer has called 'socio-economic leverage', defined as the 'power to disrupt society'.[14] A similar notion was adumbrated earlier (without Finer's gift for garbing a concept in an arresting formula) by Grant McConnell: 'Through the private associations, it has time and again been possible to discover authoritative spokesmen for segments of the population which have the capacity to disrupt common life. Through these leaders, it has been possible to strike bargains permitting a reasonable degree of social peace.'[15] Thus, whereas Finer—preoccupied with the disruptive capacity of British trade unions which was such a feature of the 1970s—dwelt upon the negative, dissentient aspect of socio-economic leverage, it may also take the positive, acquiescent form of a capacity to help society work more smoothly. More generally, thanks to their strategic location in the socio-economic system, some groups acquire a major capacity materially to help or hinder decisions by offering or withholding their cooperation or engaging in various forms of covert or overt opposition to defend old privileges enshrined in the status quo or to extract new ones.

In discussing this indispensability—traditionally attributed to business and more recently to trade unions—Finer argued that: 'It is the power to withhold a function that constitutes their strength; not their power to coerce'.[16] Ultimately, when it becomes a trial of strength, the coercive power at a group's disposal is decisive, particularly in the case of outsider groups such as trade unions to some extent still in the United Kingdom and France.[17] The strike has been historically and still is in these countries at least as important an instrument of popular participation in the political process as the vote. This may not fit comfortably into the traditional constitutional rules of liberal democracy but as against would-be totalitarian political systems, pluralist democracies or polyarchies are conspicuous for the existence of groups that operate independently from government. While the coming of universal suffrage has reduced somewhat recourse to more or less violent direct action in the United Kingdom and France, public demonstrations which may degenerate into riots continue to provide a medium for mass pressure when public opinion fails to influence the governing elites. Extra-parliamentary and extra-partnership action continue to be available for use by exasperated dissentient groups that are outside the organized and authorized channels of communication between the mass of the powerless and the powerful elites provided by the major political parties and insider groups. Any theory of the relationship of groups and governments needs to take account of the groups that remain, as it were, outside the normal political processes, particularly because almost all groups are willing, on occasion, to cross the legitimacy boundary. However, the insider groups are conscious that they will pay a high price if they become outlaws for more than the briefest crisis episodes.

A number of alternative models of interest group–government relations have been proposed to account for the complexities of the French case. Vincent Wright suggested a fourfold classification: 'domination–crisis', 'concerted politics', 'endemic conflict' and 'pluralist'. These models are based on attempts by others to offer an overall explanation that only partially accounts for some of the phenomena observed.[18] I have attempted to reformulate this characterization—with a major amendment—into two pairs, each having a heroic or crisis style decision-making variant and a humdrum or routine style variant along one dimension and a consensus/imposition variant along the other[19] However, as I regard all four situations as types of general pluralist relationship, I replace pluralism with 'institutional collapse' as the fourth variant in the matrix (see Figure 3.1). Thus 'concerted politics' combines the day-to-day, normal, routine relationship of social partnership between insider groups and government capable of habitually achieving and jointly enforcing comprehensive consensus. 'Domination' corresponds to crisis situations, when a breakdown of the customary capacity to secure consensus leads to either the government or one or more groups seeking to coerce the other, without threatening the survival of the political regime. Shifting to the imposition dimension, 'endemic conflict' describes a stable, routine situation in which group activists see their function as that of wresting piecemeal concessions from an unresponsive, arbitrary or oppressive government. For its part, the government's officials and ministers regard the groups as prone, at worst, to indulge in violent confrontation and to have recourse to illegal direct action tactics or at best to mass demonstrations and rabble-rousing campaigns calculated to discredit public policies. Finally and catastrophically, there is the situation of 'institutional collapse' in which one or more groups push conflict—intentionally or unintentionally—beyond the attainment of piecemeal concessions to the extent of bringing about a comprehensive paralysis or collapse of the regime. This situation, while more common in the military coups-prone countries of Africa, Latin America and Asia, is not unknown in France (for example, 1940, 1958) when war has put the political system under intolerable pressure. The fantasy that trade unions in the United Kingdom might paralyse the economy and polity does not survive more than a moment's reflection but the Polish free trade union movement Solidarity did threaten to bring about institutional collapse, leading to the Jaruzelski coup of 1981.

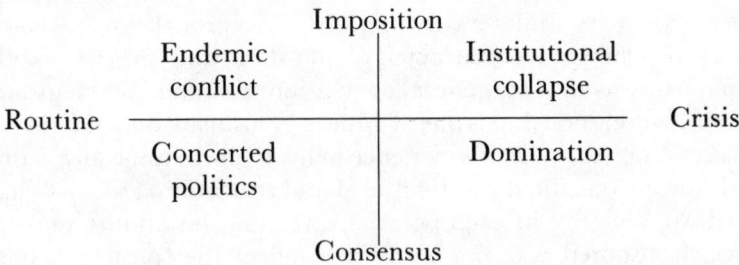

Figure 3.1. *Alternative group–government relations in a pluralist context*

In France, group–government relations are best analysed—depending upon the type of actor and policy issue involved—in the context of the typology of endemic conflict, concerted politics and domination, with the possibility that any particular predicament can be tackled at different phases by methods appropriate to more than one of these models. General characterizations of group–government relations in France should be treated circumspectly. While the cultural norms and historical tradition may make domination more 'normal' in France than in the United Kingdom, where endemic conflict is tolerated with greater equanimity, there are numerous examples in both countries of state domination and non-insurrectionary group exertion of socio-economic leverage. What is less common is the attainment of the stable state of social partnership, which in its most advanced form is characterized as neo-corporatism.

A different typology has been used by Frank Wilson, involving either three or four theoretical models specifically to explain French interest group–government relations. In a 1982 study, he proposed four alternatives: the pluralist, marxist, neo-corporatist and protest models, while in 1983 he dropped the marxist model and confined his analysis to the other three.[20] Having distinguished eight characteristic features of interest group activity concerning the boundary between state and groups, consensus on procedures and goals of government, group autonomy, group access to decision making, perceived equality of access, expectations about involvement in decision making, attitudes towards participation and motives for participation, Wilson specified how interest groups (his preferred term) could be assumed to behave. Despite the interesting nature of his findings, based upon an opinion survey of ninety-nine interest group leaders, one should stress that it is conceived in an Anglo-American perspective, with the focus on the groups themselves. This unilateral rather than reciprocal emphasis—as well as the subjective character of the data and the size of the sample—means that his general conclusion: that the French group–government relationship is one of 'limited pluralism' does not take us very far. Whereas Wilson's evidence helps to undermine any claims that France—outside the agricultural and educational sectors—has moved appreciably in a corporatist direction, he admits that the approach adopted was not likely to confirm the 'protest' model. Finally, the neglect of the state side of group–government relations in the survey means that it has to be introduced *in extremis*. He sums up: 'The absence of political consensus in the ruling elite decisively explains the absence of corporatism in France . . . . Our final conclusion is that the French government is above the interest groups. The executive is so powerful that it is better to talk of a situation of limited pluralism rather than just pluralism.'[21]

Having on occasion myself engaged in such sweeping generalizations, it ill becomes me to do more than state that unless the analysis is broadened to subject the government side of the equation to equally rigorous scrutiny and unless the actual behaviour of group and government actors in policy contexts is investigated, we will have done little more than scratch the surface of part of the problem. This ambitious task will require the work of many scholars, who may be stimulated by Wilson's courageous return to a fascinating, yet neglected area of the subject. Meanwhile, it may be useful to indicate who the major 'insider' actors are in the public policy area and at what stage they tend to intervene in the policy process, preparing the way for the formulation of hypotheses that will be qualified or refuted after detailed empirical inquiry.

The Domestic Hexagon of Pluralist Power

How can we give concepts like 'limited pluralism' a less elusive and more operational embodiment for purposes of cross-national comparison, while going beyond concepts like 'tripartism'? This notion had a 1960s and 1970s vogue in the United Kingdom, at and after the time when the National Economic Development Council and economic planning looked as though they might occupy the central place in public economic policy that the Planning Commissariat and the national plans were already beginning to lose in France. Some observers have suggested that this 'toothless tripartism' was a staging post or even the actual embodiment of neo-corporatism, based upon the peak collaboration of government, business and the trade unions, whereas others more presciently perceived that neither trade unions nor business were able or willing to accept incorporation.[22] In any case, the model referred primarily to economic policy making and important though this is, it is neither all-embracing or even all-determining. It would be most convenient for political analysts if all matters of major significance could be traced to one set of decision makers. Intractable complexity precludes such simple solutions and depending upon the type of policy decision and policy area one is investigating, the policy actors either will be different or will exercise different degrees of political influence on the eventual outcome.

However, the political system is not an ultra-pluralist free market in which no pattern of control can be discerned, with decisions emerging in wholly unpredictable fashion from the confused mêlée of a mass of individual or group wills. Between these extremes, it may be helpful to offer a less drastically over-simplified middle-range model of a hexagon of pluralist power, provisionally and artificially excluding here both the influences external to the particular state investigated and the local levels of power. Furthermore, this model focuses its attention upon the 'insider' actors, who engage simultaneously, successively or alternatively in tactics that conform with the typology of endemic conflict, domination or concerted politics. Finally, the model gives pride of place to those actors that impinge most directly upon the economic policy process, which we have already conceded is only part of reality. For example, the role of the church or cultural institutions other than the media of elite and mass communication does not find a place in this hexagon of pluralist power. It should also be made explicit that this is a static model, focusing upon intra-systemic change and that it would be necessary to add a temporal dimension at a later stage. With all these limitations, let us see how far we can proceed.

In Figure 3.2 (and proceeding in a clockwise direction) the heads of the partisan national executive in France—which together with the heads of the 'permanent' senior civil service, judiciary, police, military, public financial and industrial corporations constitute the public sector—are formally assumed to be at the summit of a pyramid of state power, with which 'private' groups have to deal, either directly or through the mediation of political parties, parliament, and the elite and mass media of communication. Familiar conceptions such as 'presidential government', 'prime ministerial government' or even 'cabinet government' personalize the partisan executive. In France, the President of the Republic contrives to be both the partisan head of the efficient executive and the non-partisan head of state, and this is not only significant at the meta-political level. Given the need to transcend or compromise conflict within and between each of the clusters of decision makers who participate in the hexagonal process of persuasion, 'bribery', cajolery, and outright coercion, this capacity to utilize the headship of state more directly than is possible in the United Kingdom, where the two functions are separated, strengthens the hand of the French president. However, the existence of a prime minister in France leads to another kind of duality which presents its own advantages and difficulties. The extent to which the partisan executive is drawn into the policy process—either collectively, through its head or through particular ministers acting individually or through cabinet committees—varies a great deal with the type of issue. Sometimes,

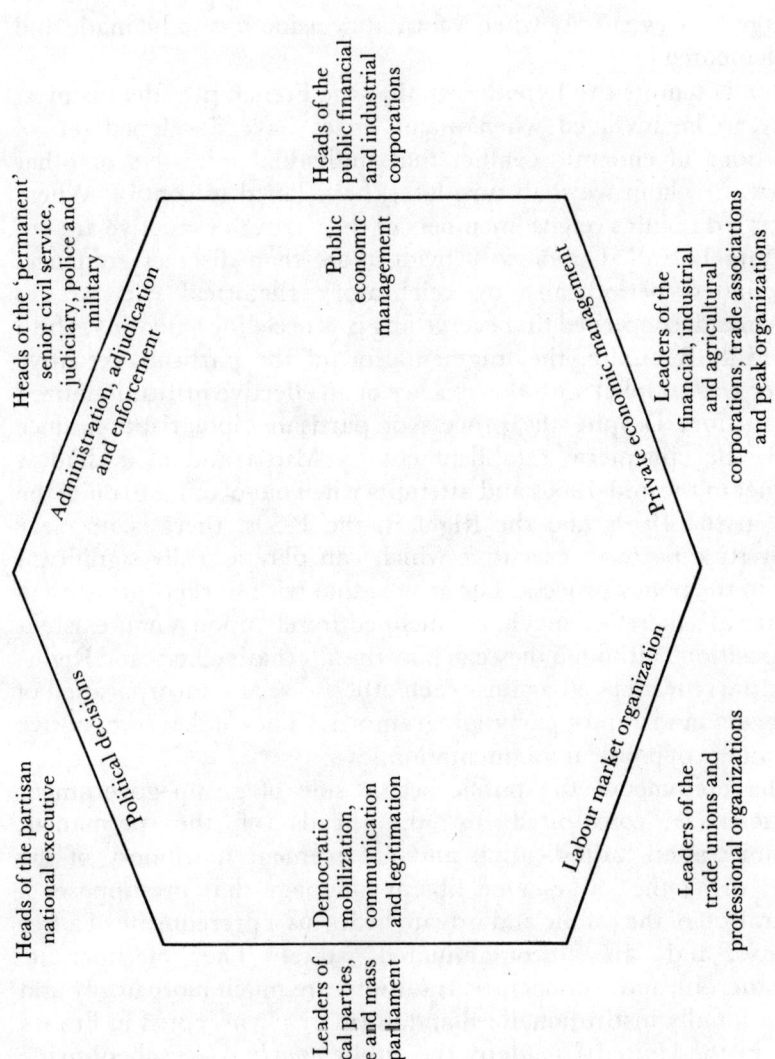

Figure 3.2 The national economic policy community

they may initiate consideration of the matter, placing it upon the policy agenda without being prompted. Much more often, they will be responding to external 'pressures' and will only become involved when a practical solution has to be devised for the problem that has emerged, or even only when a formal decision has to be made and implemented.

One is tempted to hypothesize that the French president is most likely to be involved when major crises have developed out of situations of endemic conflict that individual ministers or other actors, to whom we shall turn later, have failed to control. Where concerted politics reigns, members of the partisan executive are not likely to be called upon to provide more than discreet guidance, punctuated periodically by celebratory rhetorical exercises to reassure all concerned that everything is proceeding smoothly. Until the Fifth Republic, the fragmentation of the partisan executive power was coupled with the absence of an effective institutionalized Opposition. Despite the process of partisan bipolarization since 1958, the ephemeral establishment by Mitterrand of a shadow cabinet in the mid-1960s and attempts when out of office to unite the Left in the 1970s and the Right in the 1980s, there is no clear alternative partisan executive which can play a really significant part in the policy process. The groups that wish to exert pressure in France are therefore much less inclined to rely upon a non-existent 'Opposition', although they can play the alternative Left- and Right-wing party leaders off against each other to secure incorporation of their demands into party programmes. They take competitive advantage of political fragmentation.

The epitome of the public sector side of group–government relations is constituted by the heads of the permanent administration, adjudication and enforcement machinery of the state, using the value-laden liberal language that presupposes a separation of the public and private 'sides' as a prerequisite of a free society and an uncontaminated state. The meritocratic, bureaucratic and technocratic traditions are much more firmly and operationally institutionalized and normatively accepted in France than in the United Kingdom, the public *grandes écoles* school-made men being regarded as entitled to influence public policy decisions because they embody a disinterested and elevated conception of the public interest. When pushed to extremes, this statism can amount to a desire to dominate all private group manifestations of a potentially disorderly society, prone to the seductions of sinister sectional interests.

Despite the French tradition of judges working in conjunction with the police to enforce the law, emphasis upon their collaboration should not be overdone, notably because the French administrative courts have restrained the abuse of power by developing a remarkable measure of state self-restraint.[23] However, most groups are either reluctant or unable to use the courts to further their cause vis à vis government or each other, cost and delay being decisive factors for those who cannot afford to pay or to wait. Unlike third world countries, or even those advanced societies that have come under the influence of a 'military–industrial complex', outside the specific sphere of defence policy the irruption of the military into the centre of the French political stage, coupled with claims that it is the guardian of the national interest, only occurs on the rare occasions when crises need to be dominated by recourse to armed force.

Normally, the spending ministries, which have close clientelistic ties with 'their' groups, seek to develop 'concerted politics' practices, although the relationship usually stops well short at the consultative level, when not actually embroiled in 'endemic conflict'. While the senior civil servants sometimes play an important role in identifying problems, they come into their own in the preparation of detailed projects and in the final stage of implementation, although cost may play a major role in preventing proposals proceeding to the legislative or regulatory stage. The sponsor ministries' freedom to strike bargains is constrained in numerous ways, especially by the general financial constraints enforced by the Budget and Treasury Divisions of the French Economy and Finance Ministry and the Bank of France. This leads us to the next cluster of actors, those responsible for public economic management.

While the policy role of the permanent civil service is not devoid of ideological controversy in France, it has not taken on the harsh and acrimonious tone of the United Kingdom under Mrs Thatcher's leadership. Since 1981, the massive extension of the public sector in French banking and industry, with the consequent change in heads of the enterprises concerned, has represented a dramatic shift in the balance within the mixed economy (accounting since 1982 for a one-sixth of gross domestic product and over one-third of investment); even though it is different members of the same school-made elite that continue to run large business in France, whether public or private. Whereas public utilities do not belong to the *Conseil National du Patronat Français*, the industrial enterprises in the competitive sector belong to their relevant trade associations as well as to the CNPF.

In contrast to the traditional, autonomous, world-wide financial power of the City of London's merchant banks, French state agencies have usually managed to keep a fairly firm control over credit. Banking has remained primarily national in the scope of its activity as well as its management. The contrast between the two countries was accentuated by the extension in 1982 of public ownership in France from the three major deposit banks to cover over 90 per cent of bank deposits. In some areas of public policy, notably nuclear energy, French public enterprise has played a crucial role in the closed politics initiation of an exceptionally ambitious policy that was driven through to implementation, albeit at the cost of an astronomic level of indebtedness. State financial control has been minimized because *Electricité de France* (EDF) had political and techno-bureaucratic backing at the highest levels.[24] While avoiding the journalistic extravagance of the polemical epithet 'EDF-State', it is significant that in a much more pluralistic type of policy context, that concerning the Rhine–Rhône canal, a key factor in the recurring cycle of indecision has been the opposition of EDF.[25] Without generalizing from the case of EDF (which is far from isolated, if one considers the ELF petroleum corporation or Renault) French public corporations are much more uninhibited actors in the policy process than doctrinaire political and cultural constraints usually allow them to be in the United Kingdom.

The agricultural organizations (with the conspicuous exception of MODEF) have been the most inclined of all organized interests to accept cooption as the acquiescent clientele of the government, in their case the Ministry of Agriculture. Being little concerned to influence public policy outside the farm sector, although in many respects they have developed corporatist-style structures, attitudes and behaviour, the farm leaders are parochially pluralist in their lack of concern with non-agricultural matters.[26] In France, I have argued, 'the farm organizations, usually controlled by the farmers who would prosperously survive the transmutation to a market-oriented agriculture, have made a show of resistance to public policy. They have usually been resigned to slowing the process down and extracting the maximum financial concessions in return for controlling the more desperate of their condemned members.'[27] In industry the major firms are seldom allowed to collapse completely because of the politically and socially intolerable consequences, governments being concerned primarily to organize a retreat with a semblance of good order.

Business groups exercise a substantial measure of *indirect* influence through friendly political leaders and parties, with financial contributions moving from firms and actual or former politicians moving into firms as directors. French governments' periodic resort to price freezes and restraint agreements reflects a complex combination of state domination and concerted politics, mainly in the industrial sectors with endemic conflict, mainly in the service and distribution sectors. The most interesting development since the 1960s in France has been the proliferation of contractual agreements between firms and government, reflecting a partial move to a stronger kind of concerted politics, contractual politics.

Peak business organizations have a complex about their public role, partly because of their poor image and their apparent lack of influence. The employers' associations have resisted attempts to increase worker participation through their trade union representatives in decision making within the firm. The unions have themselves been ambivalent about direct involvement in decision making, either within government or within the firm. The trade unions have not wholly abandoned the 'outlaw' mentality they acquired during the nineteenth century, when they were regarded as illegal conspiracies. The two largest trade union confederations are committed not so much to the improvement of the material conditions of union members as to the displacement of the existing elites and even the abolition of the capitalist system. However, in reality these unions have had to confine their inordinate ambitions to acting rather negatively, resisting policies that they disliked rather than promoting policies which they desire. They have been ineffective in this 'veto group' role, partly because their political friends were out of office for most of the Fifth Republic.

The Mitterand presidency has presented them with similar problems to those faced by the Trades Union Congress during periods of Labour government in the United Kingdom, notably the acceptance of sacrifices in their members' standard of living in return for policies of which they approve, without anything like a formal 'social contract' being proposed. The Socialist-led unions (the CFDT, Force Ouvrière and the teachers union, FEN) remain jealous of their autonomy, while the Communist-led CGT is capable of greater control over its rank and file, but is less inclined to use it. This is because the policies pursued owe little to the views of the French Communist Party, which from 1981–4 was a dispensable minority in a Socialist-dominated coalition. So, whereas state domination over the unions is less appropriate than it was in the de Gaulle, Pompidou and Giscard presidencies, and neo-corporatist social partnership is unacceptable, the government–trade union relationship in France has settled down to a more or less amicable form of endemic conflict. The unions—and more especially their members—find it difficult to accept that the international economic constraints mean that, far from 'everything being possible', what they regard as essentials—job security and rising incomes—have become luxuries.[28] In the case of middle-class liberal professions, the conflict has taken a much more acrimonious form, with the use of weapons like strikes and direct action by French doctors in 1983 against the policies of a Left-wing government. In an economic context in which the government has to improvise solutions to immediate domestic and foreign pressures, hopes that a decentralized and democratic planning process would give the major organized interests an important place within the priority-setting and decision-making process, generally and not merely in relation to their own sectional concerns, have had to be played down. So, full employment—a major trade union gain in the post-1945 period—important for its indirect leverage effects as well as for itself, is no longer an agreed objective of public policy to whose attainment all are committed.

The sixth cluster of decision makers within the hexagon of pluralist power is made up of the liberal democratic agencies of partisan mobilization, the media of elite and mass communication, and the institutions of legitimation. The leaders of the major political parties, inside and outside parliament, are supposed to play an important part in processing, selecting, modifying and transmitting the pressures from society—whether or not they have originated from the major organized groups like trade unions or trade associations—to the executive authorities. Because the heads of the partisan national executives acquire office thanks to electoral victory, they have to ensure that they act in such a way as to win the necessary popular support, if not at all times at least in the medium term. So, while the political party does not play the monopoly role that it enjoys in the one-party state and parties pursue less divergent policies when in power than would be expected from their ideologies or programmes in opposition, it continues to have an important place among the plurality of political actors in France.

The complex, confusing and constantly shifting party system has in recent years stabilized into a bipolarised double duality, so that although coalition government continues to be the order of the day, both the Left- and Right-wing coalitions at least end up with a leader when in office. In France, where party government has never been fully accepted, it is the successful presidential candidate's programme, not a party programme as such, that sets the formal policy agenda. However, all the other hexagonal actors come into play to reinforce the partisan commitments they welcome and may have contributed to formulating in the first place or to block or amend those to which they are opposed. In this process, the role of the media of communication, the daily and weekly press, the radio and television, often plays a crucial role, particularly when they are independent actors in their own right (that is not propagandists for one of the other actors: government, public or private corporation, trade union, political party).[29] Because of the secrecy that these other actors seek to preserve while they consult, negotiate and exchange concessions, the power of publicity that the communication media exercise can play an especially decisive part in the most delicate, 'closed', confidential stages of the policy process.

4
FRENCH TRADE UNIONS AS POLICY COMMUNITY OUTSIDERS

Although at the turn of the century an activist minority of French trade unionists—the revolutionary syndicalists—argued that the workers could paralyse the economic system by a general strike and thereby bring about a total transformation of the economic and political system, this was more a matter of sustaining a weak movement with extravagant hopes rather than a realistic assessment of the trade unions' revolutionary capacity. Having for nearly a century—from the Le Chapelier law of 1791 to the Waldeck–Rousseau law of 1884 legalizing trade unions—been treated as outlaws, the trade union activists either looked to their own strike power or to winning political power through working class parties as their chosen instrument of collective emancipation from subordination to their economic and political masters, the employers and the government. They refused to collaborate with their exploiters and oppressors, and chose to continue to behave like outlaws even though they were no longer officially regarded as conspirators in restraint of trade in labour. In France, various Right-wing attempts to tempt the worker organizations into a rejection of class conflict—from late nineteenth-century Social Catholicism to mid-twentieth-century Gaullism—fell on deaf ears. They were, it is true, only being offered junior partner status within a system of social partnership in which their potential for disruption would be bought off. With the emergence of strong Socialist and Communist Parties, having the capacity to participate in coalition governments, the opportunity to secure legislative reforms increased. Thanks in part to a combination of electoral and industrial pressure, the conditions of the working people improved, although the bulk of the workers never joined either industrial or political organizations, and the major amelioration came after the Second World War, owing principally to the thirty years of sustained economic growth France enjoyed.

Although the French trade unions' hostility to the modest attempts at incorporating them into the economic policy community have a rather different explanation from that of their British counterparts, it is instructive to contrast the reasons for their common revulsion. The emergence of the proletariat historically preceded both democracy and socialism in the United Kingdom, while in France the opposite was the case. Consequently, at the start of the twentieth century, in the United Kingdom 'labourism' operated through an industrial labour movement that was a relatively powerful, united force within civil society, which sought representation in the political system through the Labour Party but was able to *defend* itself through collective bargaining in the industrial system; whereas in France 'socialism' found its main expression through a number of political movements, divorced from the weak and fragmented, mainly anarcho-syndicalist, unions whose prime function was that of ideological mobilization outside and against the liberal democratic system. Despite the claims of those who argue that modern technological determinism has produced a convergence that overlaps this disparate historical experience, we would agree with Gallie that it has led in France and the United Kingdom to neither of the rival over-simplifications in the assessment of industrial societies: incorporation of the workers or the exacerbation of class conflict. On the basis of empirical studies of British and French industrial workers, supported by secondary sources, he came to the conclusion that 'the differences between the attitudes of the French and British workers could best be understood as the result of the interaction of the workers' specific patterns of aspiration and normative expectation with fundamentally different institutional systems of power. . . . There was no sign of the two systems becoming increasingly similar over time; rather, during the 1960s they moved further apart.'[1]

So, prior to seeing how the French trade union movements have proved refractory to political incorporation, it is necessary to compare how the workplace style of managerial authority and the level of popular aspirations interact, as well as how the legal framework (or lack of one) impinges upon this interaction. Gallie suggests that: 'A critical difference . . . was that the French workers, with higher substantive and procedural expectations encountered an institutional system that allowed a very much lower degree of participation in the decision-making process. This made it far more likely that they would reject the basic procedures of decision making as illegitimate, that they would be dissatisfied with the substantive rules of the organization, and that they would have an image of management as essentially exploitative.'² So, French workers were and are dissatisfied with their (higher) earnings and living standards, whereas British workers have—at least until recently— been satisfied. French workers are far more militant over work process issues like manning and shift work; are more critical of the remoteness of French management and regard the firm's power structure as illegitimate, in contrast to British worker perceptions. These contrasts are related to the much greater coercive power of British as compared with French trade unions. 'In Britain the costs of bargaining were outweighed by the costs of conflict. In France, in contrast, management quite correctly believed that the unions were unable to impose major economic losses on the firm, and the cost of conflict was considered negligible compared to the probable cost of bargaining.'³ When this is taken in conjunction with the legal provision that virtually prevents any one French trade union from monopolizing representation of any group of workers (much less permits the institution of a closed shop) which is regularly reinforced by elections that pit the unions against each other, the fragmentation of French unionism has increased rather than diminished.

There are five trade union confederations that are officially recognized as 'representative' and together account for about 15 per cent of the French workforce. The largest, with about one million members, is the CGT, which has a Leninist-style relationship and an interlocking directorate with the Communist Party, that it unconvincingly attempts to explain away. The refusal to admit this link openly is significant because in many other western European countries (notably the United Kingdom), there are close and overt ties between trades unions and Social Democratic or Labour Parties. Clandestine Communist Party control over the largest trade union is to a limited extent matched by the fact that the second and third largest unions, the CFDT and FO (the latter may have overtaken the former in the early 1980s as well as partly closing the gap with the CGT) both have Socialist general secretaries. However, unlike Henri Krasucki and his predecessor CGT general secretaries, Edmond Maire and André Bergeron deliberately do not play an active and leading part in Socialist Party politics. While the CGT's support is declining in trade union elections to well under half the total vote, it continues—especially in the bigger industrial firms and in the nationalized sector—to set the pace and determine the atmosphere of industrial relations. It has, ever since it adopted this aggressive position after the Second World War, used it—in 'objective alliance' with the CNPF (the French peak business organization)—to prevent the emergence of corporatist-style relations by pursuing a rhetorically aggressive maximalist strategy of mobilizing for a political revolution that did not come and a defensive industrial resistance that slowed down, but seldom prevented governments and business from getting their way.[4] The CFDT adopted a more ambiguous stance, which sought to sustain a heterogeneous union whose ideology included residues of Social Catholic corporatism, as well as self-management syndicalism, via contractual collective bargaining and 'democratic planning', all in the service of creating a wholly new society.[5] Two smaller unions—the CGC and the Catholic rump of the CFTC—followed a line that was broadly similar to that of *Force Ouvrière*, which collaborated with business in the labour market but refused corporatist links with government, either institutional or in relation to restricting free collective bargaining as part of an incomes policy.

The attempt at institutional incorporation of trade unions attained its most ostentatious manifestation in the 1960s' attempt by de Gaulle at reform of the Economic and Social Council, which has been fully discussed elsewhere.[6] Suffice to say here that although the CGT was the originator in 1919 of the idea of a functionally representative National Economic Council, all the trade unions united resolutely to oppose the amalgamation of its Fifth Republic incarnation with the Senate fifty years later in 1969. This failure of summit incorporation should not have been unexpected as at plant level there is only a very weak system of collective bargaining, much less the kind of social partnership presupposed by corporatism. Whereas one can argue about whether the peculiar French legal and industrial structures are the cause or the concomitant of an industrial relations system characterized by habitually unilateral decisions by employers and recurrent state intervention, it is the case that the state has—apart notably from minimum wage regulation—usually delegated management of industrial relations to business. Whereas the state usually sets the norms in other areas of public life, it has—since the 1936 Popular Front—in an attempt to encourage employers to bargain collectively, legally provided that agreements signed by only one of the nationally 'representative' unions can be extended to all employees within a bargaining unit, even if the union concerned in fact represents very few workers in the firm.[7] It will come as no surprise to those familiar with the 'free rider' paradigm that such unilateral extension discourages French workers from joining trades unions, while exacerbating the hostility of the CGT and CFDT to 'the system', whose members nevertheless secure such benefits as ensue without feeling any commitment to the industrial system in general or their firm in particular. The weakness of French trade unions and the lack of a general system of institutionalized collective bargaining results in recourse to more or less violent direct action aimed at achieving relatively modest results or the resort to demonstrative strikes intended to politicize industrial issues, to bring the employers to the negotiating table by involving the government.[8] The feeble French Ministry of Labour has never played the kind of influential interventionist role developed by the British Department of Employment in the 1960s as an adjunct of incomes policy.[9] Although in both countries prime ministerial crisis supercession and outright dispossession by the creation of *ad hoc* agencies to deal with functions like industrial training, relegated the trade union interlocutor in central government to a subsidiary or peripheral role, it was only the advent in 1981 of the Socialist-dominated Mauroy Government that created a political context in which the Ministry of Labour might occupy a more significant role in the industrial relations system.

As was the case in the United Kingdom, the attempt to secure an incomes policy—or what in France was sometimes more indelicately but accurately described as a 'wages police'—revealed the unwillingness of the French trade union leaders to adopt the stance of industrial statesmen. Prior to the tentative attempts under the Left-wing Mauroy Government to resume the search for an incomes policy, the French experience was largely confined to the 1963–4 attempt by Planning Commissioner Massé to secure a consensus following the coal miners' strike of 1963. As Raymond Aron put it at that time: 'The state intervenes too much in the working of the economy to rely solely on market mechanisms. If it wishes to reduce constraint to a minimum, it must find among the representatives of socio-economic groups the appropriate interlocutors, who are concerned about the stability of the whole as well as their special demands. Perhaps the immediate purpose of an incomes policy is to find the partners to a dialogue who agree to speak the same language as those who are responsible for achieving economic equilibrium.'[10] French trade union leaders were prepared to collaborate with government and business in discussing national economic policy in consultative bodies, but were not able to do more than take limited advantage of the status and information they secured as a result because of the bitter conflict that continued at factory level, where the reality of wages and working conditions were determined by employers who exploited to the full the tactics of 'divide and rule'. Sedate summit collusion could not go far along the corporatist road when industrial disputes involved sequestration of the management and fighting at the factory gates, with police sent to retrieve the employer's property or protect the right of some workers to break strikes while accepting the benefits that would accrue if the strike succeeded. As another perspicacious French sociologist expressed it: 'Workers distrust the militants; the militants distrust the leaders and refuse to give them (the) means to build responsible organizations. Weak unions try desperately to maintain the facade that enables them to speak in the name of an active, aggressive and unruly working class.'[11] So, the trade union leaders remain outsiders committed by ideology, political conviction and concern to retain the support of their membership in the conflicts that bring them into more or less brutal collision with employers and agents of the state, to resist integration.

Whereas the trade unions could be ignored with impunity in most areas of public policy, the attempt to control either the volume of income—to deal with inflation—or the distribution of income—to secure greater social justice—necessarily involved the trade unions. They were naturally rather more interested in increasing social justice than in reducing inflation, whereas government and the employers reversed the order of priority. Furthermore, the consequent interference in the private settlement of wages was obnoxious to the employers and, to a variable extent, the trade unions, partly because of the sensitive issue of differentials. Although substantial numbers of workers still do not receive the legal minimum wage, this does influence the overall wage scale. In the era of economic growth and especially since the 'events of May 1968', it has been accepted that the minimum wage should increase faster than the rate of inflation, to allow workers paid the *salaire minimum interprofessionnelle de croissance* (SMIC) to share in rising living standards. However, such general governmental pressure has either been counteracted by some unions (for example, the CGC) seeking to maintain differentials; others, notably the CFDT, have sought systematically to promote the narrowing of differentials; whereas the CGT regards arguments that split wage earners as undesirable and concentrates on more for all. As for the employers, they have sought to *individualize* wages to the point that, by virtue of discretionary, *ad hominem* payments and bonuses, each employee is paid a different amount, thereby reducing worker solidarity.

De Gaulle's failure to coerce and defeat the coalminers in the spring of 1963 (a lesson Heath failed to learn a decade later, to his cost) was the immediate cause of the Incomes Policy Conference in autumn 1963, which continued with nine meetings until January 1964, as well as of a July 1963 law restricting the right to strike in the public sector. 'The CGT and FO were most suspicious of the motivation of the proposed incomes policy. They both feared the "integration" of the trade unions into the Gaullist regime and stressed that free collective bargaining was the instrument *par excellence* of trade union action. They feared that an incomes policy would be merely a disguised form of centralized wage restraint.' By contrast, 'the CFDT favoured a *dirigisme contractuel* in which, in return for restraining wage increases, the trade unions received certain guarantees. In the firm, works committees must have the recognized power to require essential information about all aspects of the firm's operations and in particular its investment, employment and wage policies', which was opposed by the employer organizations 'because it undermined the authority of the employer. At the industrial level, the CFDT insisted that real earnings and differentials should be fixed, rather than minimum rates which left the employer uncommitted in practice and allowed "wage drift" to distort relative earnings. At the national level ... the CFDT stressed the need for structural reform to deal with the basic causes of inflation', while 'to deal with regional disparities, public enterprises should be established in economically backward regions and a National Investment Fund set up to provide the credit to stimulate private investment.'[12] The Auroux laws were to satisfy in part some of these CFDT demands—nearly twenty years later.

Faced by trade unions that either opposed an incomes policy in principle or demanded such substantial concessions as to make the price too high, as well as by large and especially small business opposition, the hope of an interest group consensus evaporated. Instead, the Pompidou government directly imposed a wages policy in the public sector and relied upon price control to secure indirect wage restraint in the private sector, firms not being allowed to pass on higher wage concessions in higher prices. Although there was public encouragement of profit sharing from the mid 1960s, the attempt to move the unions in a corporatist direction was effectively blocked. On the principle '*tomorrow* we shave free of charge', a long forward look working party in 1964 predicted that 'In 1985, the necessity for incomes discipline will have been recognised by the various social groups, and incomes policy as defined by public authority will have become the instrument of a new social contract.'[13] This notion of a social contract was to play an important role in the mid-1970s collaboration between the TUC and the Labour government in the United Kingdom but it has never caught on in France, although tentative attempts were made to revive it by Jacques Delors, Finance Minister in the Mauroy government as it came under greater international pressure to restrain wage increases.

After the 1968 wage explosion, consequent to the 'events' that were a direct challenge to such neo-corporatist tendencies as existed, as well as to the more prominent statist and technocratic forces in France, and following the fiasco of de Gaulle's attempt to create an 'Economic Senate' in 1969, Pompidou's prime minister Chaban-Delmas launched a 'New Society' programme which sought to promote incomes policy simultaneously with collective bargaining. The person behind this programme was Jacques Delors, former CFTC/CFDT representative in the Economic and Social Council, who had been appointed by Massé as his 'social adviser' at the Planning Commissariat in 1962 and *rapporteur* in 1963 of the solution to the miners' strike, before playing a part in the 1963–4 incomes policy conference.[14] As he was to become Economic and Finance Minister in the Mauroy government of 1981–4, Delors' wish to shift France decisively in a 'social democratic' direction, in which a strong, institutionalized trade union movement would have close contractual relations with both government and the employers, was widely regarded as aimed at developing a Left-wing form of corporatism. In the meantime, the leadership of his old trade union, the CFDT, had evolved a long way to the Left, embracing the fact of class struggle and seeking through worker self-management a way of avoiding capitalism, communism and a bureaucratic social democracy. The CFDT continues to remain riven between those—a minority—who wish to achieve a radical and comprehensive change in French society and those—identified with the strategy known as *recentrage* or *resyndicalisation*—who wish to strengthen the trade union's role in a genuine collective bargaining and look to social rather than political change as their prime instrument.

Industrial policies—whether one is considering the promotion of technologically advanced industries by officially designated national champion firms or rearguard action in support of declining lame duck firms by the 'Red Cross State'—have been the subject of a bipartite, not tripartite, corporatist relationship between government and large firms, with the trade unions conspicuous by their absence, except as far as dealing with the redundancies *consequent* upon industrial decisions. Concerted action in the matter of the volume and location of industrial investment, backed by an armoury of interventionist controls that were partly dismantled in the late 1970s (notably price control, since restored by the Mauroy Government) facilitated by a *grand corps* trained interlocking directorate between the banks, large public and private firms, senior civil service and political class, gave French industrial planning much of its continuity and boldness. Though in some cases, such as computers and steel, there have been resounding fiascos, in many other cases, notably the electro-nuclear programme, telematics and aerospace, there have been striking successes. The Mauroy Government's ambitious desire to plan simultaneously from above and below, regionally and industrially, involving trade unions as well as business, in a context of recession rather than expansion, has encountered much comprehensible scepticism. It looked to a generalization of the ultra liberal–pluralist device of contract—with public and private corporations, with trades unions and with regional councils—to achieve what it called, borrowing one of the CFDT's conceptions of 1959, 'democratic planning', but what some would regard as in practice reflecting neo-corporatist aspirations.

The same problem recurs in the current experiments in democratizing the management of public enterprise, part of the problem being to what extent it is to be the *trade unions* or the *workers* that will have an increased role. The crucial question is how the avoidance of statism by recourse to socialization—in which the organizations representing workers and consumers can be given decision-making functions alongside the nominees of the government—can receive an institutional consecration. The traditional CGT solution of a tripartite board representing the government, workers and consumers, developed just after the First World War, could be regarded as extending anarcho-syndicalism in a neo-corporatist direction by eclectically juxtaposing it with a dose of statism and consumer representation. However, post-Second World War nationalization resulted in practice in techno-bureaucratic management, with the tripartite boards having hardly more influence than the shareholders' representatives in private industry. Because the workers have not had a sufficiently large share in decision making in the public enterprises, they have remained outsiders who seek to extract maximum benefits rather than share in sometimes painful managerial responsibilities. The increased role for workers representatives enacted by the Mauroy Government, not merely at board level but also in the workplace, is not likely to overcome trade union reticence towards what might be construed as an attempt at incorporation. Although there will be some shift in the balance of power towards the trade unions, the government-selected management continues to remain in charge of the old and new public enterprises.[15]

During the 1970s, the CFDT, like the CGT, appeared to be looking to the advent of a Left-wing government to create the conditions for the attainment of their objectives. The collapse of the PS–PCF *Common Programme* in 1977, prelude to defeat at the 1978 general election, strengthened the hand of those that distrusted reliance upon political salvation. The Mitterrand presidential election victory in 1981, quickly followed by an absolute parliamentary majority for the Socialist Party, took the unions by surprise. Neither the CGT—whose Communist masters 'entered the government on their knees'—nor the CFDT—whose favoured Socialist leader Rocard had been out-manoeuvred by Mitterrand—were particularly in sympathy with the new regime. The leading unions welcomed the programme of decentralization, nationalization and planning, as well as improved rights for workers—notably a legal requirement to negotiate annually—and a shorter workweek, enacted by the Mauroy Government, to whose ministerial staffs several CFDT officials had been appointed. However, both the CGT and the CFDT—for different reasons—were reluctant to sacrifice their independence and accept integration from a Left-wing government which they had resolutely refused to successive Right-wing governments. Delors-style 'social compromise' experiments in neo-corporatism made little progress because the trade unions prefer to retain their autonomy from a government that, like the Labour Government of 1974–9 in the United Kingdom, offered attractive legislative and policy concessions but wanted support for unpopular wage restraint in return that could not be delivered except in the short term. The early 1980s have not falsified the assertion that: 'French experience of the last two decades proves that no necessary correlation exists between advancing capitalism and the development of "corporatist" patterns of collaboration between organized labour, the state and private sector employees',[16] not even when the state is in the hands of the Socialist Party.

Two major circumstantial factors that inhibited the trade unions from becoming economic policy community 'insiders' after 1981 were the rising unemployment which the Mauroy Government managed to stem until 1983, but which thereafter increased rapidly, and falling trade union membership as from the later 1970s. Increasing unemployment prompted the CGT—compelled to tone down its opposition to the Socialist policies pursued by the presence of four Communist ministers in the Mauroy Government until July 1984—to unleash its criticism and stimulate the unenthusiastic workers into active opposition. The fact that the CGT general secretary, Henri Krasucki, was one of the leading 'hardliners' in the Communist Party leadership exacerbated this reversion to maximalist demagoguery. Rising unemployment forced the CFDT to argue—embarrassing for a trade union—that solidarity with the jobless meant that work sharing through reduced working hours would have to be accompanied by some reduction in wages. Although it was the major inspiration behind the Auroux laws increasing the workplace rights of workers and trade unions to information, free expression and negotiation,[17] the CFDT was conscious that only limited progress had been made towards its objective of a self-managed socialism. So, although the CFDT was the union most willing to play an active part within the economic policy community at national, regional and factory levels, it found that it was being consulted rather than taking an effective share in decision making.

National unemployment climbed from 615,000 to nearly 1.7 million between 1974–81 and duly reached some 2.5 million by the end of 1984. The recession-induced unemployment, especially in the older coal, steel and shipbuilding industries, reduced trade union membership, especially in the case of the CGT and in the old union bastions of the Nord and Lorraine. The unions could not countenance the closure of mines, furnaces and yards, competing with each other in their defence of existing jobs but lacking the capacity to do more than slow down the inexorable process and negotiate favourable terms for those displaced. This unenviable role simply confirmed the marginal place of disgruntled trade union leaders within the French economic policy community as the weak, but increasingly acceptable partners of employers and government. While the author does not subscribe to a single-answer solution to the French relative success with concerted economic policy making and implementation, it is true that a contributory factor has been the *de facto* exclusion of labour from influence over the direction, if not the pace, of change. 'The French system of organized industrial growth succeeded not because of agreement on the necessary strategy between labour and capital, but on the ability of those at the centre of the process to subordinate the interests of labour and other groups in their plans. It was predicated on and required the traditional political weakness of wage-earning groups in French politics. It would otherwise never have succeeded.'[18] For the insiders to make their compromises, uncompromising outsiders are kept at arm's length.

5
THE NEMESIS OF INDUSTRIAL PATRIOTISM: The French Response to the Steel Crisis

The singularity of steel

The deserted industrial cathedrals of France, represented by the abandoned blast furnaces and rolling mills of Lorraine and the Nord, bear forlorn visual testimony to the failure of a faith whose erstwhile worshippers have been compelled to seek other shrines. At least until the financial collapse of USINOR and Wendel, the two French basic steel firms in 1978 and—although less confidently—even since then, there has been an explicit assumption, shared by all the public and private members of the policy community of steel decision makers in France: the survival of the national industry was a categorical imperative. Isolated sceptics like Jean-Jacques Servan-Schreiber who proclaimed in 1969: 'L'Oréal oui, de Wendel, non. Il faut changer de patriotisme industriel' were not treated seriously. The president of the Steel Trade Association replied peremptorally: 'the French steel industry will not be content with a policy of whipped cream and cosmetics.'[1]

The view that a basic steel industry was an indispensable attribute of a self-respecting advanced industrial society is shared by all sectors of political opinion, with the RPR and the Communist Party being especially eloquent proponents of these paleo-industrial national champions. No less a person than Alain Boublil, the former economic planner, who in 1981 became the industrial advisor on the Socialist President of the Republic's staff, wrote in 1977, well after the onset of the crisis and on the eve of its culmination: 'Because the steel industry commands, in terms of industrial location, metallurgical manufacturing, which itself feeds the heavy mechanical engineering and automobile industries, it should be regarded as a priority industry, whatever the external constraints.

Withdrawal from the steel industry would have such "downstream" consequences that the impact on the whole of industry would be disastrous. There is no major industrial country without a powerful steel industry.'[2] Clearly, giving up basic steel had ceased to be unthinkable, but there is still no disposition to regard it as less of a national industrial imperative.

Industrial nationalism, exemplified by the traditional association of steel with military strength and political power, came under increasing international pressure in the post-war period. The Coal and Steel Community was desperately resisted by the French steel firms,[3] and only in the 1960s did the realization dawn that Europe-wide and even world-wide competition was threatening their prosperity and then their very survival. This development was not peculiar to the French steel industry because the acceptance of the consequences of dependence upon international trade in a country traditionally wedded to protectionism involved painful adjustments. However, in the case of an industry, which pretentiously described itself as '*the* profession' just as the Communist Party was widely referred to as '*the* party', this meant descending from the pedestal from which it had advantageously surveyed the antics of lesser beings. A distinguished economic journalist and historian of the *Comité des Forges*, notorious predecessor of both the *Chambre Syndicale de la Sidérurgie Française* (CSSF) and *Conseil National du Patronat Français* (CNPF), has placed the traumatic effects of the changed circumstances facing famous family firms like de Wendel in historical context. 'From the time when artillery had a decisive influence in war and until it ceased to have this influence, that is up to the Second World War, there was a necessary interaction between the men in office and the steel masters. Each needed the other. It is not always possible to say which of the two had the greater share in making the major decisions. And other industrialists will always envy this very special industry, linked by its origins with the aristocracy, privileged and protected in its activities, never fully subjected to the stern law of competition.'[4] The ability to identify its sectional interest with the general interest and to have this symbiosis accepted by the political and administrative authorities, ensured that these hereditary economic rulers were able to conduct their affairs within a mercantilist and 'divine right' capitalist context.

The establishment of the European Coal and Steel Community (ECSC) quickly led in 1953 to an *Entente à l'Exportation des Producteurs de l'Acier* or *Entente de Bruxelles*, to fix minimum export prices. The ECSC High Authority was set to dissolve the *Entente* on the ground that its activities also restricted competition within the ECSC. However, opposition from national governments in the Council of Ministers led to the High Authority's retreat, being an early demonstration of the intergovernmental character of the EC's forerunner and the repudiation in practice of the official Community commitment to the liberal dogma of unrestricted price competition. 'By declaring steel prices to be free, the High Authority in fact opened the way to a continuation of control by the member governments, which refused to accept the doctrine that the steel industry should be permitted to escape the orbit of national policy.'[5] Given this failure to create a functional economic federalism, governments remained free to protect and promote their national firms. France was not backward in taking full advantage of this tolerance.

However, the stable pattern of routine state–steel industry relations, which we shall explore later, was disrupted by forces beyond the mediating control of the French government. It has been persuasively argued that 'the state can stand as intermediary between a national industry and the international market—cut off the national economy from the world economy, as it were—when by its own actions it can ensure a stable supply of the product and control the market in which the product is sold. Such an intermediary role depends, it would seem, on an autonomous capacity for leadership in domestic industry, and on the ability to coordinate and direct diverse state powers in support of politically defined economic outcomes. This is easiest for stable products sold to a handful of consumers who are open to influence from the state, and it is more difficult for rapidly evolving products sold to a diverse and diffuse consuming public.'[6] Basic steel certainly conformed to this pattern. Additionally, high transport costs, product specialization and international steel cartels, based upon mutual respect of domestic markets which were themselves cartellized, created classic oligopolistic relations to deal with a particularly unstable, cyclical-prone product. The steel industry has been a case where, prior to the crisis that necessitated first covert and then overt nationalization, the French state was able 'to manipulate the ownership patterns of an industry in order to obtain specific changes in its production capacity and technology.' What is much more questionable is the claim—made at the time when the crisis was in full swing—that 'the capacity of the state to initiate and force investments and reorganizations that will permit growth is an invaluable asset.'[7] There is little evidence that state intervention successfully corrected the mistakes of the major industrial firms and plenty of evidence to suggest that it encouraged the sluggishness with which they adapted to rapidly changing conditions. We must first consider the steel industry and government arrangements and actors who were together responsible for what, in 1979, was described as 'the greatest mess we have seen in France for thirty-five years'.[8]

Public Control without Public Ownership

A leading French public servant set the scene thus in 1961: 'Because it might have been nationalized in 1946–7; because it wasn't; because it might be; because it has profited more than any other private industry from public financial aid; the steel industry occupies a special place in the national economy and its behaviour has been clearly influenced by these factors.'[9] Even in *dirigiste* France, steel was singled out for especially stringent, albeit primarily negative, control. As client and supplier of services (transport) or raw materials (coal), through credit, fiscal and tariff policy, through control over steel prices (which represented a 'systematic violation' of the ECSC treaty) the government directly and, via the nationalized industries, potentially had a firm grip on the industry. One commentator maintained that the distinction between an unprofitable nationalized industry like coal and (because of price control) a low-profit private industry with a low rate of self-financing like steel, was 'more a matter of degree than of kind', control in both cases being primarily a matter of control over investment funds.[10] However, the difference in ownership meant that what could be obtained in the coal industry by an exercise of authority had, in the steel industry, to be obtained by a difficult process of negotiation, owing, until 1981, to the government's unwillingness (for ideological and political reasons) to contemplate outright nationalization as a means of exercising a comparable measure of direct control. The distinction between a private and a public corporation therefore was a crucial one.

Combination in the French steel industry was by horizontal rather than vertical integration, accentuating its 'closed' and introvert character, whereas a shortage of labour discouraged diversification of industry through the localization of engineering firms. Because of the traditionalistic and familistic character of the steel firms, this process of concentration took a financial rather than an industrial form, leading to the creation of larger holding companies rather than bigger production units. This process was facilitated by the fact that all the major and even some of the smaller steel companies were linked with investment banks, guaranteeing their autonomy by controlling their own source of credit. 'There is perhaps no branch of French industry which is dominated to the same extent by financial capital resulting from the fusion of industrial and banking capital' observed a Communist commentator.[11] The prime motivation for the intricate financial interconnections that have existed in the French steel industry was the preservation of family control. Hierarchies of holding companies and of joint subsidiaries were the staging posts (together with a multiplicity of bilateral agreements sharing out markets and sources of supply) in the process of eliminating the appearance of free competition after having covertly suppressed the reality.[12] In conjunction with the activities of the *Chambre Syndicale de la Sidérurgie Française* (CSSF), this habit of working closely in concert was seen, as early as 1961, as 'leading either to "professional" (trade association) planning or at least to a co-ordination of plans at the level of the profession.'[13]

While the major steel firms shared with the government the desire to dominate rather than submit to market forces and in fact had long pursued such a policy with a view to promoting their financial interests, under the leadership of the CSSF they became accustomed to fitting their medium-term investment projects into the framework of national planning, although they preferred to work through private bilateral dealings with the government. However, it was simpler not to have to conduct a number of bilateral bargains, even if this involved an opportunity to play off one firm against another. Because of the complexity of its task, the Ministry of Finance (in France as elsewhere) placed great store by having one spokesman for the industry and was therefore an important contributor to the increasing importance of the trade association, which returned the compliment by acting as a rationalizing and modernizing agent, explaining and securing support for government policy. As M Jacques Ferry, then Vice President of the CSSF declared in 1959: 'To secure the continuity that is indispensable to our factories, our production and investment programmes must be planned jointly by the industry, in contact with and after obtaining certain guarantees from government departments.'[14] This government help was often an essential bait to secure the collaboration of the firms and in this delicate exercise the CCSF played an indispensable intermediary role.

Although it is generally true to say that a trade association's functional importance is inverse to the concentration of the industry, a dispersed industry with a large number of small firms being more dependent upon the association to coordinate, aggregate and articulate its group interests, the CSSF was—ever since the days of the *Comité des Forges*—a prototype of the powerful trade association. This was because the mutual suspicion and reluctance to collaborate of exclusive, dynastic family firms necessitated a powerful intermediary to reconcile internecine conflicts and act as spokesman for the industry. As a senior civil servant at the Ministry of Industry has written: 'Steel is an industry where the trade association structure is strong and the leaders' authority unquestionable. It provides the state with an ideal group interlocutor, capable of effectively committing its members when it enters into commitments' and avoiding the necessity of conducting negotiations piecemeal.[15]

The gravity of the industry's financial crisis—in particular its growing indebtedness—forced the family firms to concede power to the President of the CSSF as their negotiator with the government, who for its part, did its best to strengthen his position as a force for modernization in the steel industry. Although born in Lorraine, Ferry had no family ties with the steel industry, representing the managerial elite drawn by *pantouflage* after a brief period in the public service.[16] He was prepared to accept an unprecedented degree of responsibility for the human consequences of industrial change in return for government help in surmounting its financial consequences. Tough and articulate—the latter not being a conspicuous characteristic of the patrimonial employers—Ferry fortified his power base, the CSSF, by making it the indispensable intermediary for planning change in the steel industry and securing favourable financial terms from the government. As long as the steel firms were solvent yet financially dependent upon the government, his position appeared secure, thanks in particular to the CSSF's financial arm, the *Groupement de l'Industrie Sidérurgique* (GIS) of which, significantly, M Ferry was also president.

Established in 1946, GIS did not get into its stride until 1953, after which it annually issued a collective steel industry debenture loan on the capital market. It had a council of twelve members from the industry and a four-man committee—with representatives from the Ministries of Finance (Treasury Division) and Industrial Development (Metallurgical Industries Division) as well as the Planning Commissariat—whose vital task was to allocate the funds obtained. This public control, through the agency of the GIS, over access to the capital market and over the investment projects to which these loans were assigned, gave the *Crédit National* and the Ministries of Finance and Industrial Development the ability to ensure conformity between the steel firms' investments and public policy.[17] The GIS was an essential instrument of the authority of the president of the CSSF in his role as intermediary between the steel companies and the government, the bait to induce collaboration being specially favourable borrowing terms.

Given the reluctance of the government, until the advent of Mitterrand, to assume direct responsibility for the steel industry, there was great scope for the CSSF to influence the government agencies which were apparently in such a strong position to control the activities of its member firms. Quite apart from the sympathies and ties that might have existed between the politicians who were temporarily in charge of the state apparatus and specific business interests, there were additional sources of comfort for the 'administered'. The various government agencies with which it dealt were by no means united, and there was abundant opportunity for playing them off against each other. In particular, the Ministry of Industry's Metallurgical Industries Division, the Ministry of Finance's Treasury Division and the Planning Commissariat, acting under the aegis of the Prime Minister, were its regular interlocutors. Bargaining with them on a confidential, bilateral basis, it was often possible for the CSSF to secure the support of its sponsor ministry and—in return for concessions—of the 'expansionist' Planning Commissariat against the economy-minded Ministry of Finance, custodian of the public purse against the depredations of private interests. The Ministry of Industry's senior ranks saw their function as that of the indulgent father whose role was to guide his frequently feckless or spendthrift (when they were not timid and tightwad) sons, in the ways of righteousness (that is conformity with the government's desires) but generally willing to support their claims on the family funds.

The creation of the USINOR Dunkirk plant, which was the French prototype of a seaside steel mill using foreign coal and ore, resulted from the collaboration between new-style managers and the Ministry of Industry. It reflected the more dynamic approach of this type of steel businessman, more willing to face increased indebtedness as the price of innovation compared with the more cautious family firms of Lorraine, which furthermore were reluctant to establish a coastal steel mill away from their traditional fiefs and national iron mines. The low cost of transport and advantage in the export trade were decisive factors in the choice of a coastal location, the latter factor being particularly attractive to the government. The Ministry of Industry's Steel Division, rather than either the Planning Commissariat—whose regional vocation was only embryonic in the 1950s—still less the DATAR (the Regional and Spatial Development Planning Delegacy), which did not come into existence until 1963, played an important part in the decision to choose the Dunkirk location and in securing public financial support for the project which it regarded as an invaluable step towards the modernization of the steel industry. In the process, it was a welcome ally for USINOR when Antoine Pinay, as Minister of Finance in 1959, sympathetic to the interests of small-scale family firms rather than the big corporations, opposed the project until he was convinced of its desirability by his Director of the Treasury.[18] The shadow of mass unemployment had not yet fallen over the industrialized Nord when this showpiece industrial installation was conceived and built, so regional considerations did not play a major part in the decision.

The Fos Folly

A more spectacular example of a state-sponsored, regionally oriented exercise was the case of Fos.[19] In contrast with the 1954 Marseille project of an isolated steel plant, the local promoters in 1962 who began acquiring land at Fos and especially the Regional and Spatial Development Planning Delegacy (DATAR), who became involved in 1964 and took command of the project, conceived matters on a much broader and more ambitious scale. As well as being the launching pad for the industrial development of the rapidly expanding population of the south-east, Marseille–Fos was to become the Mediterranean answer to Rotterdam on the North Sea, the southern 'europort'. Given that Fos had already been considered as a candidate for France's second integrated shore-based steelworks, it is not surprising that when in 1965 DATAR's consultants reported on the industrial development prospects of the area, a 6 million-tonne steel plant (subsequently expanded to 7.5 million tonnes) headed the list. The problem was that only the Lorraine firms could create a new coastal steel mill and they were reluctant to do so, particularly in a steel market that appeared to be contracting, because this would mean closing down some of their older plant in areas which they had traditionally dominated.

(Lorraine's mono-industrialism—one-seventh of the region's active population worked in the iron and steel industry—had prompted the regional saying: '*La Lorraine compte quatre départments, plus un cinquième qui s'appelle la sidérurgie*', which was more important that the other four put together.) They were worried by attempts to determine the location by reference to regional development policies. Through the Fourth Plan Steel Commission's report, they made clear that a capital-intensive industry like steel would yield few jobs and that its indirect regional expansionist 'multiplier' effects were unlikely to be commensurate with the vast input of funds. They also secured acceptance for the view that the idea of establishing a new coastal plant should be postponed until the latter half of the Fifth Plan (that is the late 1960s).

Ferry accepting that the location should be determined on political grounds, Marseille–Fos was adopted by the Prime Minister in December 1968. The post-1968 boom, especially in the steel industry, made Wendel–Sidélor much more enthusiastic about putting its future into Fos. It tried to obtain foreign partners—first Italian and Spanish, then German—on its terms (that is majority French control) but IRI decided to double the size of its own Taranto works, while the Spanish government preferred to go into partnership with US Steel in its own country. Wendel–Sidélor decided at the end of 1969 to proceed on its own, with the help of a substantial state loan obtained after protracted negotiations with a reluctant Finance Ministry. In November 1970, the *Société Lorraine et Méridionale de Laminage Continu* (Solmer) was established as a subsidiary of Sollac, itself a subsidiary of Wendel–Sidélor, half the Sixth Plan steel investment programme being allocated to Solmer. Taking enough space—half the total—to expand if necessary to a 20 million-tonne plant, Solmer was expected to account for only a third of the 37,000 jobs created, even if one includes the Ugine–Kuhlmann special steels plant. However, it was believed that a total of some 170,000 jobs would be generated, increasing the population by nearly half a million. These perspectives encouraged a flood of officially sponsored hyperbole about Fos becoming the spearhead of a 'French California'.

The drying up of Wendel–Sidélor's cash flow in 1971 dispelled the hope that it could finance most of Solmer by self-financing. The government seemed to be trapped by its own propaganda, because it could not face a withdrawal by Wendel–Sidélor from Fos, the largest investment project ever launched in France. Too many commitments had been entered into with firms and local authorities.

With its shares at rock bottom and under pressure from the banks that had loaned money for Solmer to Wendel–Sidélor (the American Eximbank, guaranteed by four French banks, including the three nationalized deposit banks) it speeded up redundancies in Lorraine in November 1971, which threatened to have unfavourable political consequences for the government parties in the March 1973 elections. In May 1972, the government secured the services of Jacques Ferry of the CSSF to persuade the head of USINOR —who was on very bad terms with the head of Wendel–Sidélor—to come to the rescue. The 'competition for the non-financing of Fos' seemed to be settled in October 1972 when USINOR and Wendel–Sidélor agreed to joint control of Solmer under the chairmanship of Ferry, but the increased burden of indebtedness on the two basic steel giants played a notable part in their subsequent collapse when they faced the full brunt of prolonged recession.

The Showpiece of Contractual Industrial Planning

The French steel industry was included in the national planning process from the start, when it was the only manufacturing industry covered. The question, however, arises of the extent to which conformity between what the Plan stipulated and what the steel firms did should be attributed to the influence of the Plan in shaping the behaviour of the firms or rather to the influence of the firms in shaping the content of the Plan. If there was any industrial planning commission that corresponded to the Communist stereotype criticism of the planning process as 'limited to registering the intentions of the monopolies, introducing a measure of consistency between them and adapting the public sector programmes to suit them', it was the Steel Commission.

According to the idyllic ideology of 'concerted economy' planning, the industrial or 'vertical' planning commissions were supposed to be the place *par excellence* in which the various interests involved came together to reconcile their views of the industry's prospects from the perspective of the national forecasts and objectives propounded by the government and its experts and accepted their responsibility to contribute towards the implementation of these objectives. Even though their meetings are not public, their work was, however, still far too 'open' to be more than solemn and official occasions for the formal ratification of investigations, discussions and decisions taken or undertaken elsewhere. The superficiality of trade union participation in the planning process, which had many causes, was due most directly to the fact that the workers' representatives were in general absent from the regular contacts between members of the government and administration (from the Prime Minister downward) and the spokesmen of business. This resulted in the trade unions being presented with *faits accomplis*. This pre-arranging of the planning commission business by prior unofficial contact was interspersed with *ad hoc* meetings of an interministerial committee on the government side to coordinate the views of the various government agencies. On the business side, in the case of the steel industry, the work of the Steel Commission was prepared in advance at the monthly meetings of the CSSF's *Commission Consultative des Questions Techniques* and when necessary by *ad hoc* meetings to deal with specific questions.

The business attitude towards industrial planning was that it was primarily an exercise in medium-term market research of a not too accurate kind. The participants expressed wishes but could not take decisions. The Plan registered decisions taken elsewhere in the governmental or industrial system. Forecasting the size of the market for steel products over the five-year planning span was a salient feature of the Commission's work and its starting point, being dealt with in the first chapter of the Commission's report. It was natural that the market should be the dominant concern of the producer; government, for its part, being particularly concerned with the export prospects. However, the implications of achieving a particular level of productive capacity and the concern to maintain competitive capacity through cost reductions led to discussion, in the second chapter, of the industry's investment programme. Government saw its role as that of restraining the industry's investment enthusiasm in periods of boom and overcoming its excessive pessimism in periods of market recession and low prices. It was also concerned to avoid duplication by coordinating the investment programmes of the oligopolies. Further, the Commission was concerned with the financial implications of the more or less ambitious investment programme which had been adopted and looked to the government to provide direct and indirect assistance. 'Voluntary over-estimation' of demand by the steel firms, leading to an ambitions investment programme 'results in financing problems which give weight to their demands in the spheres of prices, taxation and loans.'[20] Finally, the Commission was concerned with the raw materials, research and employment implications of its production and investment programme and here, once again, the government was involved.

Because it was the CSSF that had most of the data required by the planners to undertake any serious forecasting, the Commission leaned heavily on it. As the planning official principally responsible for liaison with the Steel Commission in the Fourth and Fifth Plans declared: 'The number of firms and plants being few, it is possible to have real planning, to question each firm and each plant and work out a consistent general programme which is then broken down into particular programmes . . . . Steel is a small world, the competitors broadly know each other's position and as a result we can achieve a coherent set of (investment) projects.'[21] However, the firms were undoubtedly more willing to communicate information to the Commission through the CSSF which created a dependence of the former on the latter. The acquiescence in this by the Planning Commissariat was a reflection of relative bargaining power as well as a matter of convenience.

The inability of substantial sections of French industry to attract long-term investment capital from the market had, ever since the Second World War, necessitated dependence upon public sources of finance at lower than market rates of interest. The price was a willingness to accept a measure of public influence over investment policy. Government control over prices had reduced profit margins and thereby the steel industry's capacity to self-finance its investment projects. In the 1960s private capital avoided the key capital goods industries (such as steel, electronics and chemicals) which were risky because they were exposed to increasing foreign competition and was turning to the safer consumer goods industries and especially to land speculation. One of the indicators of this process was the catastrophic fall in share prices—by 40 per cent between 1961–6—with the steel companies faring particularly badly. In 1966, USINOR shares were only worth one-third of their 1961 value, whereas de Wendel and Lorraine–Escaut shares had fallen to between one-quarter and one-fifth of their 1961 value.

To meet the problem of escalating indebtedness and falling investment, Ferry prepared the steel industrialists and more generally the big business world as a whole for a new type of comprehensive, continuous and contractual relationship with the government, an ambitious and delicate operation. In his capacity as chairman of the CNPF's Commission of Private Enterprise, Ferry made a remarkable speech at the peak organization's General Assembly in June 1962, which indicated how far his own thinking had already gone towards making the transition from a quasi-contractual to a contractual collaboration with the government. He attacked traditional *dirigiste* piecemeal intervention ('*coup par coup statism*') as subordinating business to the arbitrary power of government. The crucial phrase is: 'contract should always be preferred to constraint.' Its significance, in the light of subsequent events is increased when it is supported by another phrase: 'the employer no longer has the right to go bankrupt.'[22] Ferry went on to explain the need to ensure security for both employer and employed, which involved a restriction on the rights of private property and rendered desirable collective action by firms '*sur le plan professionnel*' to organize the readaption of their industry. Short-term economic profitability had to be increasingly sacrificed in certain spheres of action to dictates of a higher order, *raison d'Etat* or public interest. He suggested that a private firm could become an agent of the government, accepting a 'service contract with the state (whereby) it carried out certain tasks which do not use profitability as the decisive criterion.' However, his main message was that in these new types of government–business partnership, *business should take the initiative* and 'deliberately accept the call of convention and contract.'[23]

After a battle inside the CNPF's leadership, the Ferry approach was defeated by those who wished to proclaim a new-found faith in self-reliance and freedom from state intervention in all shapes or forms, expounded in the CNPF doctrinal declaration of January 1965. Ferry resigned from his chairmanship of the Private Enterprise Commission as a non-publicized protest. He devoted himself to securing the triumph of his belief in a 'contractual economy' in the steel industry. Strong enough to swim against the CNPF tide which he had ceased to command, in 1969 Ferry set up his own big business organization, the *Association des Grandes Entreprises Faisant Appel à l'épargne* (AGREF), steel firms providing the backbone of the very large firms willing to work closely with government that composed it.

The Fifth Plan (1966–70) explicitly espoused the Ferry approach, encouraging industrialists and their trade associations to play a more assertive part in industrial policy. 'In a market economy, guided by a plan, the prime responsibility for industrial development belongs to the industrialists. On their initiative depends the success of the policy whose objectives and the means of attaining them have been explained. But these initiatives should be worked out in conjunction with trade associations and the state . . . . It is indispensable that the trade associations keep their member firms informed on the situation by preparing or having prepared economic studies of their industrial structure and that of competing foreign industries. The diagnosis arrived at might subsequently, with the help of the public authorities, provide the basis for defining and implementing a policy of improving structures. Relatively old examples (the cotton industry) and recent ones (steel) confirm the utility of such intervention by trade associations.'[24] The reference to the *Plan Professionnel* being concocted between the CSSF and the government could hardly be clearer.

Months of unofficial negotiation in 1964 culminated in a formal approach by Ferry to Prime Minister Pompidou in January 1965. At the Planning Commissioner's prompting the Ministers of Finance and Industry, in their February 1965 reply to M Ferry's request for public assistance to the steel industry, made clear that: 'The greatest latitude would be left to your *profession* as to the technical or economic application, the state's intervention will nevertheless require as a *quid pro quo* a programme setting out the use to which the money will be put . . . (to be) approved by the government departments concerned, after having examined each case in detail.' Ferry was informed that: 'this plan, worked out by the profession itself and provided with a timetable . . . would receive practical application as soon as the *profession* informs us through you of its willingness to carry out the necessary reorganization. This agreement, which will involve the personal commitment of all your members who subscribe to it, shoud be accompanied by a detailed plan of reorganization and improvement in productivity.' Ferry was to spend the next year in this Herculean task and in the process was to emerge as the self-effacing de Gaulle of the French steel industry.

Michel Debré, Finance Minister at the time of its conclusion, described the Steel Convention as 'the result of more than two years thinking and work in the Ministry of Industry and Planning Commissariat as well as the Treasury Division, not to mention the steel industrialists themselves, under the arbitration of M Jacques Ferry. . . . Discussions began whilst the Plan was being prepared, becoming more precise once the Plan was approved, aimed at enabling the steel industry to overcome its handicaps, to invest, to modernize, to fulfil and attain the Fifth Plan's targets.' How did the leading protagonist from the industry present the agreement which he had done so much to make possible?

Ferry stressed the coherence and continuity, derived from its contractual character, in contrast with piecemeal state intervention. In terms which have a corporatist overtone, he declared: 'the *plan professionnel* is imperative. But instead of the obligation to undertake precise investment projects coming from the external decision of a regal administration, it derives from the schemes of each of these firms, confronted, harmonized and placed in an order of priority, the framework and procedures having been imposed on the industry by itself.' It was 'the industry's own effort towards unity which led to this new style planning. The various official sponsor departments were kept informed of the *plan professionnel*'s preparation at its successive stages. They gave advice and made recommendations. But their remarks, guided by their necessary respect for the principles of the official Plan and by certain regional preoccupations, never had the pretention of replacing the industry's responsibilities by those of the public authorities . . . .'[25]

The Council of Ministers approved the Steel Convention on 27 July 1966—parliament being presented with a *fait accompli*, like the trade unions. The government's contribution was primarily financial, meeting the capital costs of just under 30 per cent of the steel industry's programme and 60 per cent of the cost of the *plan professionnel*. In return, basic steel was to be merged into a duopoly.

For some time the government's encouragement of steel mergers was part of an explicit national policy. The Ministers of Finance and of Industry wrote to the CSSF president on 17 February 1965, recalling that he had on numerous occasions asked for public financial help on behalf of the steel industry. They went on: 'As you have yourself proposed, it is up to the *profession* (i.e. industry) to continue more rapidly and on a bigger scale the necessarily gradual reorganization of its structures to increase the size of its firms, the modernization of its plant and a better use of its equipment.' This policy was one of the most important themes of the Fifth Plan. In the guidelines report, a new industrial strategy was laid down based upon a restructuring of French industry so drastic in character that it appeared to confirm that industrial planning was being conducted in the interests of the 'great monopolies' and as such represented a violation of the preamble to the constitution of the Fourth Republic, which had been reaffirmed in 1958. The report declared: 'In many industries, these mergers should lead to the establishment of a very small number of such (international scale) groups, going in exceptional cases as far as the creation of one dominant group', the government providing whatever legislative or fiscal help as was necessary. It went on to assert: 'It is indispensable that these groups acquire substantial financial resources but also that they have the widest latitude possible to shut down, reorganize and create new factories', the Fifth Plan taking the necessary steps to ensure the mobility and retraining of labour rendered redundant.[26] The text of the Fifth Plan spelled out this policy in slightly greater detail and even more explicitly and forcefully. The primary *objective* of French industrial policy was 'the establishment or reinforcement where they exist already of a small number of *firms or groups of international size*.... In most industrial sectors . . . the number of these groups should be very small, often even reduced to one or two.'[27] This objective was achieved in 1966–7, as is clear from Figure 5.1, subsequent rationalization primarily tidying up the special steels problem.

The International Dimension

However, it was becoming clear that a national champions policy would not suffice. Even before the onset of the 1970s steel recession (whose endemic nature Ferry, along with the other leading members of the steel policy community, was unwilling to acknowledge), Ferry was one of the most farsighted in seeking to extend national patriotism into a European and even world-wide cartel, as the only way of giving enduring protection to the French steel industry.

In 1967, Ferry, realizing that it was not possible to save the French steel industry by planning on a purely national basis, called for an EC steel plan on the French model. 'In a market which has nothing in common except its name, which is in fact, after fourteen years of life, only a free trade area, where certain salutary treaty rules are no longer applied, the current brawl is only a caricature of competition.' The survival of the EC would 'depend on the willingness of the members to discipline their commercial ambitions and master the disorder of their investments. France has set the example with the implementation of a *plan professionnel* which gives the steel industry a greatly increased technical and financial cohesion and better employment guarantees for its workers.'[28] Given that such a proposal to harmonize investments could not be attained in the short run and would in any case not bear fruit for years, Ferry called for immediate EC planning of the 'abnormal' and 'anarchic' trade in steel products, the absence of which had led to a heavy fall in prices. However, given that such a European Steel Convention presupposed the existence of a political authority and source of finance analogous to the French state, Ferry in 1968 proposed 'European' mergers between EC steel firms to achieve a 'rapid and effective coordination through the reduction of the number of EC (steel) decision makers.' Ultimately, Ferry's vision was of a world-wide organization of steel investment, production and sales, finally banishing the scourge of

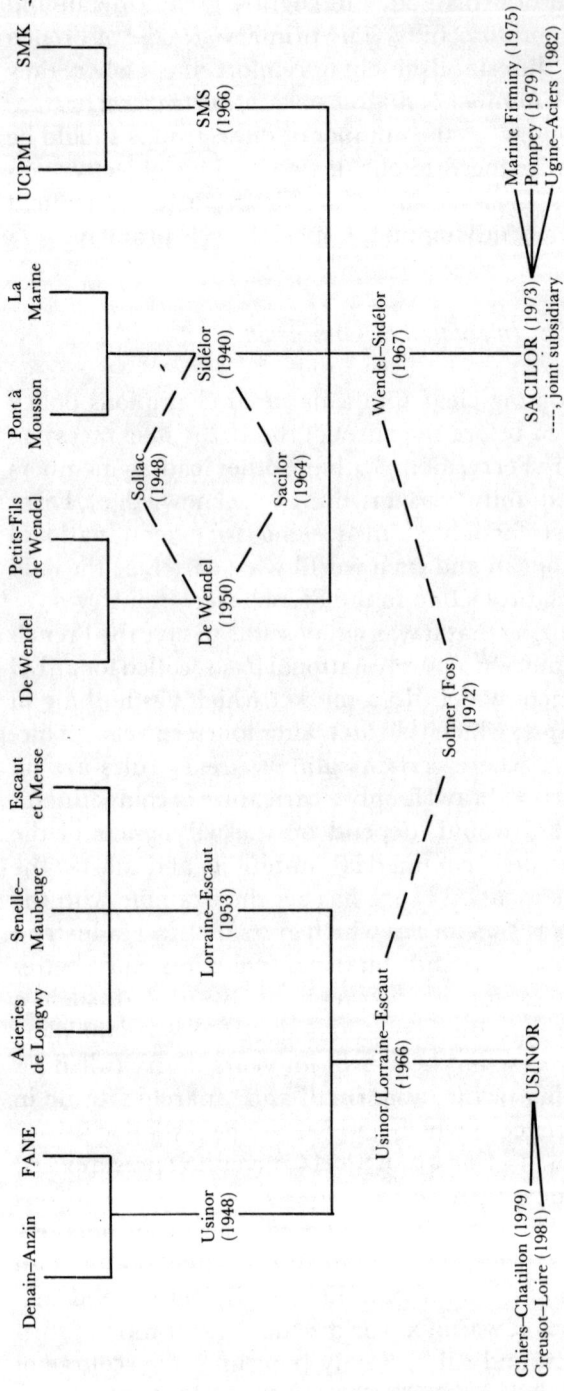

Figure 5.1 *French steel: the transition from oligopoly to duopoly*

Source: based in part on J.E.S. Hayward, 'Steel', in Raymond Vernon (ed.) *Big Business and the State, Changing Relations in Western Europe* (Harvard University Press, Cambridge, Mass., 1974), p.267.

'unlimited competition (which) is an absurd notion in the steel industry.'[29]

Ferry and others issued appeals in favour of the international planning of investment and production capacity in the context of the International Iron and Steel Institute (IISI) meetings which provided an alibi for steel producers to get together to discuss markets and prices informally. At the IISI's 1967 inaugural meeting, Ferry expressed the 'need for more accurate and more widely disseminated advance knowledge of investment programmes and their implications, and their timing. This could be one of the most important tasks of the International Iron and Steel Institute, pending the development in more practical fashion of at least a minimum coordination of large-scale investment decisions. . . . I believe there are limits to competition on the steel market beyond which competition itself ceases to be a healthy stimulant and becomes an agent of destruction. . . . The expansion of any one steel industry must be soundly based, relying initially on the expansion of its own domestic market. In this way, we might well avoid protectionist reactions in some quarters and, in others, the impulse to transfer the burden of their problems to the international market.'[30]

The pressure of Japanese exports in Europe led the ECSC countries and the United Kingdom to secure their voluntary limitation by an agreement in December 1971 covering the three years 1972–4. Under this agreement (in which the European countries were represented by a delegation headed by Ferry as President of the European Steel Club) Japan's six main steel groups would, with their government's approval, form an export cartel. The volume of steel exports (by major categories of product) was fixed for 1972, and in the autumn of 1972 and 1973 export quotas were determined for subsequent years. Ferry also headed the European delegation in extremely tough negotiations with US State Department and Treasury officials which led to more severe restrictions covering 1972–4. Thus, the way in which both the French and European steel policy communities were to respond to the post-1974 recession was clearly foreshadowed in the preceding decade.

From covert to overt nationalization

In his influential study *L'Impératif Industriel* (1969), Lionel Stoleru— a participant–observer of the process of state industrial interventionism that he criticized, both as planner and adviser of Giscard d'Estaing as Finance Minister and President, of the Republic—acknowledged that a collection of improvised, piecemeal interventions did not constitute an industrial policy. The steel industry waited until it was on the verge of financial collapse before it agreed to the 1966 *plan professionnel*. However, having asked the pertinent question: 'is the survival of the steel industry compatible with free competition?', and answered 'the experience of recent years seems to suggest that they are not compatible', he went on to ask a further question: 'If it is agreed that competition must be "organized", should this be done by collaboration between the bosses or by the state?'[31] Despite acknowledging that the vertical compartmentalization of the state administration made it difficult to carry out a consistent and sustained policy, he embraced the need for national mobilization to meet international competition, to be achieved by a semi-corporatist style collaboration between steel businessmen and the state's public servants. This type of joint public–private collaboration had the virtue of excluding nationalization, which might seem the logical consequence for a statist like Michel Debré, Finance Minister at the time the *plan professionnel* was accepted. However, nationalization was unacceptable for ideological and practical reasons to the Right-wing governments of the 1960s and 1970s, and to the senior officials that advised them.

In January 1965, the Minister of Industry and the Planning Commissioner, having written to the Prime Minister that restructuring should be made a precondition of financial assistance, went on: 'If the reform of the steel industry is not spontaneous (sic) and speedy, the situation will degenerate to the point that the government will be compelled to envisage nationalization. Such an extreme and doubtless undesirable solution would nevertheless be preferable to a fragmentation of our steel industry potential.'[32] Steel nationalization had been envisaged by the Left-wing parties at the Liberation, but the break-up of the tripartite coalition in 1947 prevented it from occurring. The Communists, the keenest on nationalization, repeatedly proposed bills (in 1946, 1958, 1963 and 1976), the only point on which they diverged from the steel policy community celebration of the indispensability of a national steel industry being that it should be nationalized. When the steel crisis was coming to a head in 1977, three very senior officials from the Ministries of Finance, Industry, and Labour presented a 'report on the situation and outlook of the steel industry' in which they faced the same issue. 'The sheer volume of the debts owed to the state by the steel industry leads to the issue of whether the state should acquire a shareholding in the steel firms or even take over control. Shareholding seems to be desired by some steel industry leaders, while nationalization is demanded by one of the trade unions (the CGT). From a strictly economic and financial standpoint, even partial nationalization of the steel industry does not seem desirable. It hardly seems worthwhile for the state to own firms whose financial situation is so bad and whose balance sheet is negative. Nationalization would make the state bear the full financial burden of putting the firms back on their feet and free the present shareholders—responsible in part for the present situation—from all financial or industrial responsibility.'[33] They went on to point out that both holding companies, BNEL owning USINOR and especially Wendel, should be compelled to use their non-steel profits to meet their steel obligations (rather than siphoning off into non-steel investment public funds that had been provided for modernization of steel plant). Their final argument against steel nationalization was that it would make reducing overmanning more difficult and thereby make it more difficult to improve competitiveness through increased productivity.

Before we examine the transition from private to public ownership it is important to examine five key questions about the past experience of the French steel industry that have been raised. Firstly, was the mediating role of the CSSF—and of Ferry in particular—tantamount to a semi-corporatist relationship between the state and the steel employers? Secondly, did the way in which steel planning was conducted at the time of the economic crisis demonstrate the weaknesses of such a relationship? Thirdly, did the failure of the steel industry to engage in vertical integration and diversification play a crucial part in its competitive weakness and financial failure? Fourthly, how far did the state subsidies—directly and by cutting costs—compensate the steel industry for the consequences of public control over its prices? Fifthly, how far did political influence, notably for electoral reasons, account for the slowness with which the steel labour force was reduced in the 1970s?

While there was no tripartite corporatist relationship in the steel policy community—from which the trade union leaders were excluded—there was an abandonment of autonomous decision making by the steel firms and a rejection of arm's length remoteness from detailed policy intervention by the various government agencies and political leadership. The corporatist-style collusion that ensued was orchestrated by the CSSF, importing elements of institutionalized formality—notably with the 1966 *plan professionnel*—and based upon an exceptionally pervasive influence. As was argued in an earlier discussion of this body, 'the CSSF provides a rare example of a Trade Association not merely offering traditional services but guiding the strategies of its member firms. It has dealings with the executive, the judiciary, and the legislature on behalf of its members. It exchanges information with the Ministry of Industry's Iron and Steel Division and has frequent dealings with the Finance Ministry's Taxation Divisions. It tests in court tax cases affecting its member firms. It does public relations work with members of Parliament and makes representations to parliamentary groups on its own or with CNPF delegations. Its president frequently gives evidence to the Production Commissions of the Assembly and Senate. The services it offers to member firms include comparative studies of costs, centralized purchasing of raw materials and fuel, common research, and above all collective financing of investment. In 1950 the CSSF set the pattern, followed subsequently and less effectively by the chemicals, electrical engineering, and metalworking industries among others, of joint borrowing through the *Groupement des Industries Sidérurgiques* (GIS), which enabled the CSSF both to know the investment plans of the major steel firms in detail and to influence them. The CSSF was also involved in close dealings with the steel division of the Ministry of Industry—which approves each firm's share in a loan—and with the Finance Ministry—which fixes the total amount that GIS is allowed to raise in the capital market. "This pyramiding of authorizations to borrow money opened the way for negotiations at each level—between company and industrial association, association and (the Ministry of Industry) directorate, and (this) directorate and Ministry of Finance." The CSSF under Ferry's leadership was thereby able to play a pivotal role in shaping the industry's strategy.'[34] It would be tempting to argue that steel nationalization represented a move from 'liberal corporatism' to 'statist corporatism', but this would be misleading. Although the CSSF lost its mediating role, the change is likely to be more one of degree and form than of kind and substance, with the Ministry of Industry playing the role of mediator between the two firms until they are eventually merged.

As far as steel planning was concerned, gross underestimation of the effects of the recession was to provide a disastrous demonstration of the inability of the steel policy community to comprehend the dimension of the break with decades of semi-continuous expansion.

The consequences of delay, owing to the struggle to attain consensus; of ambiguity and contradiction because of the desire to reconcile conflicting pressures; of self-absorption, because of the concern to preserve community, even at the cost of ineffective policy making,[35] all these failings are to be detected in the supposedly rational exercise of medium-term steel planning in France. 'Never was a report by the Steel Commission so succinct, vague and useless as that for the Seventh Plan.'[36] It is easy to make play with the fact that while the planners considered two alternative growth rates of domestic demand for steel between 1974–9—a low rate of 1.9 per cent and a high rate of 3 per cent—what materialized was a decline of 17 per cent. However, the refusal to face the gloomy prospects demonstrated the triumph of consistency within the unquestioned context of institutionalized introvert optimism over external reality, which threatened to rupture a set of relations that had become ends in themselves. Admitting that a target sale of 35 million tonnes of basic steel in 1980 'might seem high ... without even referring to the aberration (sic) of 1975, it is nevertheless consistent with the logic of the substantial investments carried out during the course of the Sixth Plan to increase capacity and those that seem necessary to launch during the Seventh Plan to put present capacity to most productive use and maintain or improve competitiveness.'[37] The clear presumption was that continuity of policy required the expansion of output for which, it was assumed, there would automatically be a market. 'Supply', in the words of Say's law, would 'create its own demand'. A naive statistical optimism is reflected in the steel sectoral planning group observation: 'The search for a restoration of equilibrium may lead the steel industry to fix high export targets, commensurate with its productive capacity.'[38] It came naturally to the steel policy community to emulate their Japanese equivalent, making the *simpliste* identification of Japanese export success with their private–public industrial communitarian practices: 'the conquest of foreign markets is largely due to the permanent symbiosis in Japan between the actions of industrialists and public authorities'.[39] Just as when the United Kingdom imitated French 'indicative' planning in the early 1960s, it self-deceptively tended to believe that tripartite collaboration in planning committees was the secret of success, so the French steel communitarians were attracted by the idea that the answer to their problem was to do more of what they were used to doing already. Unfortunately the remedy was not so palatable.

While in this sanguine frame of mind, the steel 'sectoral planning group' anticipated in 1976 that steel prices would rise by an annual 10 per cent from 1976–80, failing which the industry's medium- and long-term debts—which amounted to 102 per cent of its turnover at the end of 1975—would break the financial backs of the major firms. Proclaiming the reduction of their indebtedness as 'a categorical imperative' was one thing; achieving it was another. Net losses increased from 3.7 billion francs in 1975 to 4 billion francs in 1976 and 6.1 billion francs in 1977. At the same time, medium- and long-term debt grew from 28.3 billion francs in 1975 to 33.9 billion in 1976 and 38 billion in 1977. This rapid exacerbation of the plight of the steel firms led to a breakdown in the semi-corporatist policy community. The Barre Government was undoubtedly tempted ideologically to apply the full rigour of economic liberalism to the steel industry, leaving it to face the competitive realities of the market. However, when faced with yet another 'restructuring plan' from the CSSF in December 1976, the intolerable political cost of such a doctrinaire policy at a time when the Left was posing an increasingly threatening electoral challenge, the former professor of economics who despised politicians was compelled to engage in the economic irrationality of industrial rationalization in the service of electoral expediency.

Deliberately delayed until after the local elections of March 1977—which in any case were disastrous for the government parties—another so-called 'steel plan' was cobbled together in the familiar manner, with Ferry still playing the pivotal role. The 'realistic' assumptions on which this April 1977 programme was based were that demand would recover by the third quarter of 1977 (in fact 1977 was worse than 1976) and reach 28.5 million tonnes in 1980; steel prices would increase by 40 per cent by 1980; the labour force would be reduced by just over 16,000 jobs by April 1979. In presenting his proposals to parliament, Prime Minister Barre explained: 'The government dismissed the possibility of nationalization, which would have transferred to the state—without resolving them—the steel industry's problems, leaving the community to bear the full burden, while the private groups would be freed of their industrial responsibility by the government.'[40] Public ownership having been excluded by the government as a 'sterilizing formula' and workers' participation in shareholding being rejected by the firms because the low stock exchange value of their companies meant that the workers might eventually get control, the provision of financial assistance for investment projects was resorted to yet again, to the tune of 1.3 billion francs.

By 1977 the heady optimism of the Seventh Plan's forecasts had evaporated, at least as far as the government was concerned, and so had its trust in the judgement of Ferry and the CSSF. An interdepartmental economic and financial supervisory committee was established to check that the firms' commitments were honoured, notably the vertical integration 'downstream' and the promotion of new jobs in areas from which the steel industry was retreating. This task was to become a major one for DATAR, responsible for trying to organize a 'retreat in good order' so as to avoid the political consequences of irretrievable regional decline in the steel valleys of Lorraine and in the Nord. Furthermore, Barre insisted that the steel groups should not wash their hands of the consquences of their own failings; the price was that de Wendel and USINOR were to hand over to a state bank, the *Caisse des Dépôts*, part of their shareholdings as a guarantee that they would fulfil their commitments under the 1977 agreement. Furthermore, the profitable holding companies of Denain–Nord–Est–Longwy (DNEL) and CLIF were to be placed under the control of their loss-making steel subsidiaries, USINOR and SACILOR. Despite attempts to counteract manoeuvres by the de Wendel family in particular to separate their profitable activities from SACILOR, the crisis was gathering such speed that the 1977 attempt to bandage a wooden leg quickly proved capable of doing no more than allowing the government to survive the politically delicate pre-electoral period of late 1977 and early 1978.

The hope that the 1977 package would reduce the indebtedness of the steel industry from 104 per cent to 70 per cent of turnover quickly proved illusory, a new plan covering the period up to 1985 was secretly being prepared by the CSSF. Despite Prime Minister Barre's claim that he had been duped by the CSSF and the steel firms, one is inclined to be sceptical, particularly when one learns that when a number of bankers 'made representations to the Ministry of Finance about the (steel) industry's insolvency, they were told to go away until after 19 March (1978).'[41] Living from hand to mouth, thanks to short-term bank loans, escalating losses threatened to drag the nationalized banks that had lent them substantial sums since 1973 down in the wake of USINOR and SACILOR. Having considered in turn and rejected the possibility of amalgamation with other European steel firms, nationalization and a takeover by 'downstream' steel using firms, the Barre government in September 1978 announced a *de facto* takeover of the crude steel duopoly. Even though the complex solution adopted only survived for three years until the outright nationalization of USINOR and SACILOR in 1981, it is worthwhile briefly describing the lengths to which a non-socialist government went to avoid setting the precedent of public ownership as advocated by its political opponents.

While taking majority control of both steel firms by converting part of their debts to the French state (9 billion francs) and other public institutions into debentures, the government's 'rescue plan' pretended that this was only a temporary expedient and that when the firms had recovered their financial viability they would recover their independence, the previous owners retaining a 'blocking minority' shareholding in the new holding companies. The public involvement was dispersed between the state (15 per cent), the *Caisse des Dépôts* (30 per cent), *Crédit National* (10 per cent), GIS (15 per cent) and the banks (30 per cent), with somewhat less involvement in the less insolvent USINOR than in SACILOR. Had USINOR not been nationalized outright in 1981, it might have been possible for it to retrieve its position, owing to its control of the profitable steel tube firm of Vallourec. (We shall return later to the issue of special steel firms.) The state simply wrote off a substantial part of the steel firms' debts to avoid reducing private shareholding to humiliating proportions. It was also recognized that crude steel capacity would have to be reduced by a one-quarter to 24 million tonnes and concentrated in the most modern plants at Dunkirk and Fos.[42]

It is generally recognized that one of the prime reasons for the vulnerability of the French steel industry to the prolonged crisis of the 1970s was its haughty refusal to integrate vertically 'downstream' with more profitable, high-value manufactured products, which were traditionally regarded as of inferior industrial status. A good example of this problem is the relationship of Vallourec—which in 1969 controlled 70 per cent of the French domestic market for steel tubes and was the sixth largest producer in the world—to USINOR, both being subsidiaries of DNEL.[43] The failure to invest efficiently in the potentially high-growth steel tube sector is attributable to the fact that DNEL was dominated by the new steel masters, trained in the technocratic *grandes écoles*, who sacrificed tube investments to steel investments. Furthermore, the two activities were segregated from each other, the reluctance to allow the expanding tube interests to acquire more decision-making influence being rationalized by the choice of a strategy based upon an integrated crude steel complex—just as it had clearly become out of date—instead of a more adaptable, diversified industrial group, which the holding company structure would have allowed and which the big German steel firms were adopting. Declining profits in a highly competitive market, coupled with a reliance upon self-financing, led to a slowing down of investment in the 1960s and 1970s, until the bankruptcy of DNEL led to the absorption of Vallourec first in a state-controlled holding company and then into control by a nationalized USINOR.

The CSSF and the steel masters repeatedly complained that they had been financially crippled by government price control and that state subsidies for their investment programmes were a quid pro quo for their reduced profits. The fact that they continued to complain after they received such assistance simply meant that they had an inordinate appetite for public funds. It is clear that high-level political decisions ensured that the procedure for dealing with their requests for help and for monitoring the use to which the funds were put were formal confirmation of *faits accomplis*. Consequently, 'the Ministry of Finance (particularly its Treasury Division) regards steel policy decisions as given' and until the final crash in 1977–8, the CSSF was relied upon to monitor whether the steel firms were fulfilling their commitments.[44] The French state did not operate its customary financial controls in the special case of steel, a case—perhaps—of industrial patriotism *oblige*?

Finally, before considering how the steel industry has been dealt with since the socialists have come to power, it is necessary to consider the extent to which political—especially electoral—factors explain the poor French productivity record in the steel industry (149 tonnes per head in 1977), compared to Italy (240 tonnes) and Germany (190 tonnes) although not the United Kingdom. For example, whereas the Sixth Plan had expected a fall in steel employment of 4,000 from 1971–5, the number actually increased by 10,000.[45] In 1975, persuaded that the steel crisis was a temporary one and conscious of local elections to come, Prime Minister Chirac asked the steel firms not to declare any redundancies and to engage in counter-cyclical investment in preparation for a resurgence of demand for steel. In its report for 1975, SACILOR tactfully did not allude to this political pressure but declared: 'We abandoned the redundancies that were necessary to reduce our manpower to what was required by the depressed state of the market, a decision taken to avoid the painful human consequences localized in the region and to avoid dismantling our work teams *with a view to the expected revival* (my italics).'[46] With the acceleration of the recession and once the general election of 1978 was over, the government was prepared to envisage

21,750 jobs being sacrificed in eighteen months, 14,000 of the losses being in Lorraine and the bulk being involuntary redundancies rather than early retirements. Violent resistance from the steel workers followed, despite the government's attempt to foster alternative employment in the areas affected, and one of the legacies to the nationalized steel firms was the problem of reducing the labour force, a particularly painful task for a Left-wing government.

Nationalization and Senility: Steel Enters 'Les Invalides'

To fully appreciate the predicament faced by the Mauroy Government and its Ministers of Industry (Pierre Dreyfus 1981–2, succeeded by Chevènement and Fabius) one must remember that after the violence that flared up in 1979 both in the Nord (especially in Denain and Valenciennes) and in Lorraine (at Longwy), François Mitterrand had committed himself to avoiding redundancies unless alternative employment was available beforehand. This dangerous promise was to come home to roost in the Elysée with his election to the presidency of the republic in May 1981. However, at least it did not commit the Left to the belief, fostered by both the steel firms and most of the trade unions, that employment, at the very least, could be preserved. Their arguments were, however, somewhat different. While the steel firms and the CSSF continued to use the preservation of jobs as the justification for securing substantial public funds for investment schemes that would only make sense if the traditional overmanning was drastically curtailed, the CGT line was to deny—until 1978—the need to restructure the steel industry. It was sufficient to blame the French employers and government for an unpatriotic willingness to sacrifice national economic interests in conformity with the requirements of a German-dominated EC cartel. Both the CGT and the CFDT refused to sign the agreement, negotiated with the unrepresentative *Force Ouvrière*, that provided for a loss of 16,200 jobs between April 1977 and April 1979, although in practice over 20,000 jobs were eliminated.

By late 1978 the deterioration in the steel market and changes at the head of the CGT Metalworkers Union led the most representative trade union in the industry to adopt a less demogogically defeatist attitude, while it continued to reiterate the major premise of the traditional policy of industrial patriotism; the need to safeguard France's economic independence. It proposed ways of increasing domestic demand for steel, by stimulating investment in building, shipbuilding, public works and public transport, as well as reducing the supply of labour by reductions in the workweek and the age of retirement. The CGT also suggested that the industry should be diversified, especially towards the higher-value metal-processing products. The CFDT followed suit, although its counterproposals adopted the Mitterrand line that some job losses could be accepted in steel provided that a compensatory job creation programme was vigorously pursued.[47] Such would-be constructive proposals were temporarily swept aside by the burst of rank and file direct action in 1979—factory occupations, road and rail blockades, attacks on police stations—but by 10 March the CGT and Communist Party brought the pitched battles at Denain to an end with a peaceful march, the Socialist contingent in the rear being headed by Pierre Mauroy.[48] (In 1982, as Prime Minister, Mauroy was to be shouted down in Denain when he sought to explain the need for further steel closures in the town.) The July 1979 agreement (not signed by the CGT or the Longwy section of the CFDT) reached after prolonged bargaining between the major firms, the trade unions and the Ministry of Labour provided that—thanks notably to financial assistance from the government and from the EC—the 21,750 job losses planned from 1979–81, would be achieved without anyone actually being sacked. By a combination of resignations, retirements, redeployment within and outside the industry, the edge was taken off the workers' resentment.[49]

Curiously enough, although the number of job losses imposed in the Lorraine-based SACILOR in 1979–81 (12,000) exceeded those in Nord-based USINOR (11,000), industrial relations in the latter case were much more bitter than in the former. Some credit for this must go to the new management installed by Prime Minister Barre at the beginning of 1979. While the new head of USINOR, a *polytechicien* Claude Etchegaray, came from the Chatillon–Neuves–Maison steel group that was absorbed by USINOR[50] and was an 'insider', the head of SACILOR was the financial inspector and successful banker Jacques Mayoux, without any previous connection with the industry, who was given the responsibility for rescuing the financially weaker of the two firms. Etchegaray actually managed in 1980 to get USINOR temporarily out of loss making, thanks in part to higher EC prices, before the further slide into deficit in 1981. Although he did not attain the standing previously held by Ferry, Etchegaray played a key role in Eurofer.

However, with the outright nationalization of steel in the autumn of 1981, both heads were replaced in January 1982, in part because it was necessary to symbolize changes that were more spectacular than substantial. The new head of USINOR was Raymond Lévy, a *polytechnicien* who had managed the public oil group ELF–Aquitaine before in April 1981 becoming president of the USINOR special steels subsidiary, which had absorbed the Creusot–Loire special steels plants. Although the head of SACILOR, Claude Dollé, had been an active Socialist and was briefly a member of Minister of Industry Pierre Dreyfus's *cabinet*, he had previously been the commercial director of a medium-sized firm marketing steel products, linked with the Belgian Cockerill group. So, the choice of management was inspired not so much by partisan criteria as by the need to have men capable of facing the enormous task of rescuing from the scrapyard whatever could be retrieved of these ailing national champions.

The Assembly debate on steel nationalization in October 1981 was conducted before a virtually empty chamber, there being almost as many ministers present as deputies. This confirms the fact that it was by far the least controversial part of the whole nationalization programme of the Mauroy Government. Furthermore, it was decided to convert 14 billion francs of USINOR and SACILOR debts due to the state into shares, securing 86 per cent of the former and 93 per cent of the latter. (The 1972 Common Government Programme had not committed the Left-wing parties to more than majority shareholdings in the major steel concerns.) This imposed only modest additional cost (the major financial burdens being subsequently the cost of keeping these firms in business and meeting their considerable requirements for capital investment) so the parliamentary occasion lacked any tension. The Communist speakers stood out by their effusive combination of an anachronistic elation at the humbling of these bastions of nineteenth-century capitalism with blissfully unrealistic claims that steel production could be expanded in the 1980s.

The ministerial speakers struck rather discordant notes. While the Industry Minister, with prudent scepticism, was concerned to try to preserve the French steel firms' share of the world market, the junior minister for the extension of the public sector, Jean Le Garrec, combined reassurance with optimism. 'For the government, nationalization is neither a punishment nor collectivizing losses but a way of mastering the future.' Having this ambitious end in view, 'all the means necessary to make it more competitive must be provided' by the government, he asserted with the cheerfulness of those who do not have to find the necessary billions of francs. Budget

Minister Laurent Fabius was understandably more preoccupied with the financial burdens that had been bequeathed by the failure of the massive financial gamble to which the steel policy community had collectively committed 40 billion francs of public money, quite apart from the private funds engulfed. To call it, as he did, the 'greatest scandal since Panama' might seem excessive, but the financial collapse of USINOR and SACILOR was undoubtedly so stupendous a failure of private and public industrial policy making and implementation, that it acquired the sinister status of the example *par excellence* of what not to do. In retrospect, there has been at least as much consensus on this negative judgement as there was on the positive assessments of the 1960s, when steel was held up as an example to all industries of what good government–business collaboration should be like.

Nationalization having been almost a formality, it is important to establish whether public policy objectives or the means to achieve them changed significantly as a consequence of the replacement of a would-be 'liberal' by a 'socialist' government. The 1978 move, under the impulse of Prime Minister Barre, 'to reconstitute real undertakings responsible for their decisions' had sought to reduce the role of the CSSF and also of the Ministries of Finance and of Industry because, in the words of two senior officials in the Industry Ministry: 'Only too often no one quite knew where and by whom industrial decisions were taken' in the steel industry.[51] The Barre policy was to give USINOR and SACILOR operational autonomy from public interference, while reaffirming that a steel industry remained essential to France. This meant that the government would lift part of the burden of indebtedness from their backs to prevent USINOR and SACILOR from becoming bankrupt, with the catastrophic effects it would have both on employment and upon the banks which had been induced to lend them money.

The Socialists took office with an embarrassing commitment, made by François Mitterrand in 1979, that far from accepting industrial retreat, a Left-wing government would launch new steel works in the most threatened areas of Denain and Longwy. Whereas such rash promises might make electoral sense, they became redoubtable hostages to fortune when Mitterrand was asked in 1981 to honour them. The problems that arose from an attempt to implement them were belatedly and hastily explored before the new medium-term steel plan was unveiled in June 1982, having been sidestepped in the interim national plan, *Stratégie pour Deux Ans, 1982–83*. After preliminary discussions with the interested parties, four reports were commissioned by the Minister of Industry and the Planning Commissariat, the findings of only one of which have been made public, that by Professor Judet on 'The trends in the steel industry's markets and its medium-term prospects'.[52] The Judet report (commissioned in November 1981 and completed in March 1982) studied the implications of three hypotheses about the evolution of the market for steel in the period up to 1986, projected to the end of the decade. It is the political choice of the least plausible of these three hypotheses that requires explanation, representing the provisional triumph of political over economic rationality.

Using the customary low, medium and high hypotheses to which the French planning process has accustomed us, the Judet report spelled out their quantitative implications. The low-production hypothesis assumed that in 1986 French steel output would amount to about 20 million tonnes necessary to meet a market demand of 17.2 million tonnes (consumption plus net trade balance). This would be the result of a low but non-negative rate of growth, resulting in a reduced demand for steel. The medium-production hypothesis, which had the support of the CSSF, anticipated a national steel output of 21.8 million tonnes, corresponding to a demand of 18.7 million tonnes. The trade association view was that 1982, and especially 1983, would be marked by a major improvement in demand, followed by a downturn in 1984 and 1985, and by a further upturn in 1986. It assumed that there would be a marked increase in both investment and exports in 1983–4. The most optimistic hypothesis envisaged a 1986 output of 24 million tonnes, to meet a market demand of 20.6 million tonnes. This was based upon a policy of economic expansion and a high rate of economic growth, involving a substantial upturn in both the depressed housing market and in industrial investment, especially by the nationalized firms, while exports would increase.

Faced with these alternatives, between which the Judet report made no choice, the minister secured the government's agreement at the 9 June 1982 cabinet meeting to the incredibly ambitious, not to say foolhardy, objective of an output of 24 million tonnes of steel in 1986. The economic unrealism of such a choice was clear at the time the decision was made. Steel production in 1980 had been 23.2 million tonnes (demand of 20 million tonnes) and 21.3 million tonnes (demand of 18.8 million tonnes) in 1981. By mid-1982 the level of production had fallen to 20.5 million tonnes, the lowest level since 1968. So it was a self-deceiving act of faith—based upon a highly problematic upturn in 1983—that became increasingly implausible as successive runs on the French franc in 1982 compelled the Mauroy Government to adopt austerity public expenditure policies that sacrificed the desire to encourage economic growth to the need to preserve the value of the currency, undermined by a growing balance of payments deficit.

In any case, CSSF studies had shown that the domestic demand for steel was made up to only 23 per cent by consumer goods (of which the automobile industry, which alone accounted for 21 per cent, was in great difficulties in 1982) so that attempting to increase consumer demand would not have a substantial effect on the steel industry, even if one could avoid a major leakage of that demand in favour of foreign cars. As for capital goods which accounted for 77 per cent of demand for steel (with the building and public works, mechanical engineering and transport industries being the main clients), the rate of investment had fallen from 5.3 per cent in the period 1970–4 to 0.9 per cent in the years 1974–81.[53] Despite government efforts, this was unlikely to increase appreciably in the coming years. Lastly, exports to the United States were under increasing threat despite EC efforts to secure an agreement to contain US protectionism. With such a bleak economic outlook, coupled with the deficit of 6 billion francs that USINOR and SACILOR had chalked up in 1981, how could the Mauroy Government adopt so offensive a strategy? It recalled the French First World War general who is reputed to have said (or words to that effect): 'My centre is broken, my left is in retreat ... I attack!' Perhaps the sentiments of a French field marshal, watching the charge of the Light Brigade at Balaclava, are more apposite: 'It is magnificent, but it is not war!' Even in the service of industrial patriotism, such a strategy seems to face up to problems by fleeing forwards.

Prior to the 'oil recession' of 1973–4, French governments had little need to bother with the EC about steel matters, but after 1978 the EC Commission became even more closely involved in national decision-making, notably in easing the employment effects of restructuring. This was extended to cover investment programmes and pricing policies, so that the Mauroy Government, jealous like its predecessors of national sovereignty, accepted detailed discussions of its 1982 steel plan with the EC Commission, receiving in return £408 million of aid to USINOR and SACILOR. The French Government was faced by the end of September 1982 deadline, fixed by the EC Commission as the date by which proposals had to be submitted by member governments, setting out the reductions in productive capacity by the end of 1985, by which time national subsidies to steel firms were scheduled to cease. Despite the EC pressures to reduce capacity, because of the prospect of an even larger excess capacity in 1985 (27 per cent) than the crisis year 1980, the Mauroy Government was unwilling to sound the retreat.

The objective was stated on 9 June 1982 to be 'the reestablishment within four years of a strong and competitive steel industry', capable of producing 24 million tonnes. This would be achieved thanks to an 'ambitious programme of modernization' involving an investment programme for 1982–6 costing 15.5 billion francs. An additional sum of about 2 billion francs would be allocated following discussions between the steel firms and their workforce. A further 3.225 billion francs would be used to finance subsidiaries established by USINOR and SACILOR to diversify and redeploy their activities, of which 500 million francs would be used to diversify industrial activity in the areas suffering especially from the restructuring of the steel industry. To honour President Mitterrand's commitment that no collective redundancy would take place without the prior provision of alternative employment, it would be necessary to reduce the workweek substantially and increase early retirement.[54]

Despite these steps to ease the decline of the steel labour force, the 1982 steel plan—the third in five years—would probably involve the loss of 10,000–12,000 jobs, following the previous losses of 16,000 in the 1977 plan and 22,000 in the 1979 plan. This placed the trade unions in a difficult position because, while the CGT and CFDT in particular did not wish to attack the Mauroy Government, they had to retain the support of their members. The younger steel workers in particular, not being able to take advantage of early retirement schemes, felt they had nothing to lose and were inclined to engage in violent protest.

The Mauroy Government, under pressure from the EC Commission to reduce steel capacity and from the trade unions and its own political supporters in the affected areas, kept up appearances in dealing with the EC, while in practice conceding most of the domestic demands. The price is colossal. Quite apart from the investment programme already mentioned, more than 10 billion francs was spent annually up to 1985 by the French Treasury, the lion's share being to cover the losses of USINOR and SACILOR: 6 billion in 1981, over 5 billion in 1982 and 11 billion in 1983. In addition, 2 billion francs would have to be provided to repay the 12 billion francs debt of steel firms taken on by the Barre Government in 1978 and the 3–4 billion francs that the employment agreement with the trade unions would cost. In all, it was estimated that the steel industry will by 1985 have cost the French state 60 billion francs since 1978 (measured in 1978 francs).[55] Steel still absorbed the lion's share of state subsidies to public enterprises in 1985, at the expense of industries of the present and future such as electronics.

Given the substantial debts which the French government is required to bear from some of the newly acquired nationalized firms, the massive losses of EDF coupled with the cost of its electro-nuclear programme, assistance for declining private firms and the need to encourage firms in the 'new technology' sectors (computers, electronics, robotics and so forth) it was unable to continue to sustain the 1982–5 steel plan throughout its duration. The high price of industrial patriotism, rather than the pressure of the EC Commission compelled the French government to speed up the contraction of the steel industry, once the improbable revival failed to materialize. The state representatives, who are in a majority on the boards of USINOR and SACILOR, were the instrument for enforcing financial necessity.

In retrospect, what is especially striking about the post-war behaviour of the principal actors in the French steel industry saga has been the continuity with a misguided past, despite changing economic circumstances and political control. There is the same institutionalized, systematic, congenital optimism that the main problem is securing public funds for an ambitious investment programme, rather than in tackling the fundamental problems of marketing and industrial training, where the German competition has had a marked advantage. Slowly, there has been a move towards a policy of downstream diversification, although this is largely only planned as yet, USINOR's projected 15 per cent shareholding in a merger of France's three shipbuilding companies not being an especially promising venture. The amalgamation of the basic and special steels firms has formally been attained. The politically sensitive issue of overmanning is being faced with humanity and circumspection. A belated shift to electrical furnaces has begun. Yet the fundamental question remained that the European Community would not allow France to continue spending 15 billion francs annually on industrial, financial and social assistance to its steel industry after 1987.

However, change there has been. The pre-nationalization bipartite corporatism of the steel policy community will not be sustained by a substitution of the steel unions for the steel masters. The trade unions refuse to play a collaborative part in the contraction of employment, so what will result is a reliance upon statism and its agents, whatever 'window-dressing' attempts are made to conceal this behind a facade of consultation.[56] Paradoxically, despite the repudiation of any wish to reassert the control of the central government, the 'zero sum' circumstances are forcing the political friends of the steelworkers to impose upon them the ineluctable retreat of an industry that clings on tenaciously to a now specious singularity. The government is irremediably saddled with the problems of this once illustrious invalid, victim of international recession, whose fate was sealed by the obstinate refusal of the steel policy community to recognize in time the 1970s' steel crisis as structural and not conjunctural. Nationalization will not rescue it from its fate. The rearguard battle will be even more bitter because the cause is forlorn. The bulk of the French steel industry, in its years of senile decline, has little to look forward to other than early retirement into the nostalgic discomfort of an industrial equivalent of *Les Invalides*.

Postponement of the inevitable, unpleasant closures of steel plants, with the loss of jobs in regionally sensitive areas, could not go on indefinitely, if only because of EC pressures and the massive injections of scarce public funds necessary to allow USINOR and SACILOR to avoid bankruptcy. The delays were partly due to the fear that these unpopular decisions would provoke a vociferous and violent response from those affected, with damaging electoral consequences that would be exploited both by nominal Communist allies and overt Right-wing enemies. However, a major cause of delay was the inability to take decisions due to the divisions between the two nationalized firms and between the Ministries of Finance and of Industry, which the Prime Minister could not reconcile. The *ad hoc* committee that was to have led to joint planning and coordination between SACILOR and USINOR failed to work because their interests were diametrically opposed. The traditional rivalry of the two firms was exacerbated by the shrinking market for steel and neither would concede that the cuts in productive capacity should lead to the closure of its plants so that a more realistic set of overall targets could be fixed. (One such conflict was resolved in 1984, with the Valenciennes rolling mill at Trith-Saint-Léger being preferred by the government to the Lorraine mill at Gandrange but SACILOR was in 1985 continuing to resist this decision, assisted by the fact that it was left implicit by pusillanimous politicians.) Political and administrative reluctance to force a merger of USINOR and SACILOR was due in part to the wish to avoid the concentration of power that one steel corporation might represent and the belief that perpetuating division would leave the final decision to the state authorities. The opposition between the Ministries of Finance and of Industry also followed traditional lines, with the former being concerned to reduce the ruinous financial demands made upon public funds by the steel firms, while the Industry Minister wished to secure state financial support for its *protégés* without stringent constraints being imposed. The Industry Ministry was told that if it wanted funds for firms with a promising future, it would have to cut back more severely upon the declining industries because meeting their needs was an unavoidable first claim on the national exchequer.

Prolonged procrastination culminated in the cabinet meeting on 29 March 1984 but it was President Mitterrand who had to take the final decisions. He announced his verdict at a press conference on 4 April 1984. Placing the steel problem in the context of the other declining basic industries of coal and shipbuilding (whose 'Trafalgar' was as disastrous, but on a smaller scale) Mitterrand explained that steel had been awaiting an adequate solution for the last eighteen years. From steel plan to steel plan, a process of decline had led to a fall in employment that had been slowed down by successive governments, seeking—in the words of the January 1984 report by the President of the Court of Accounts—to 'buy social peace'. Matters had now come to a head because it was no longer possible to continue the lax policies of the past. While accepting a share in the forecasting errors of his predecessors, who had found futuristic optimism a convenient way of avoiding painful decisions, President Mitterrand proclaimed that his own restructuring programme would give the Industry Ministry 'exceptional powers' to engage in a massive effort at industrial redeployment.[57] In fact, it subsequently transpired that while the Industry Minister would service and carry out the decisions of a cabinet committee, the ultimate power of decision would lie in the hands of the Prime Minister, if not the President of the Republic.[58]

Although the trade unions were consulted, it was made clear that the government's decisions were irrevocable. Despite the damaging regional consequences, notably in Lorraine and even at Fos, it is clear that many of the structural problems of the steel industry have not been resolved. The two enfeebled national champions continue their separate competitive existence, yet they still lack the full autonomy to decide their investment programme or cut their labour force because of the financial and political implications of these issues. Ironically, it was the managing director of USINOR, Raymond Lévy, whose appointment was not renewed in 1984. This was because he had been an early and ardent advocate of revising the unrealistic 1982 steel plan, who proposed the merging or at least the appointment of a coordinator over the two steel corporations and cutting manpower as the only way of preserving the industry's future. Despite support from the CFDT, Lévy encountered the opposition of President Mitterrand's adviser (Alain Boublil) and of the CGT, so although some of his advice was eventually followed, he was made a scapegoat as the purveyor of unwelcome tidings. Through its planning contract with the Lorraine region in 1984, the government sought to deal with the local employment consequences of the decline of the steel industry and the failure to expand the Gandrange plant in Lorraine which was the issue that precipitated Lévy's fall, although it was in line with his advice. It is anticipated that the 160,000 steel workforce of 1974 (the start of the Giscard presidency), which had fallen to 85,700 in 1984, will have to fall to 50,000 by 1988 (the end of the Mitterrand presidency), testing to the full the French state's capacity to conduct this historic retreat without an intolerable amount of demoralization and disorder. In December 1984 the largest bankruptcy in French industrial history occurred with the collapse of the special steel firm of Creusot–Loire, part of whose loss-making activities USINOR was forced to take on. In November 1984, the heads of USINOR and SACILOR, concluding that fratricidal 'coordination' was leading to mutual ruin, wrote to their sponsor Minister of Industrial Redeployment proposing fusion into what would be, after Nippon Steel, the second largest steel firm in the world. They hope that in the process their burden of accumulated debt will be wiped out (including a joint deficit of 8.5 billion francs in 1984 alone) and that the 30 billion francs of further assistance required will more readily be forthcoming. Past experience suggests that the process of decline will not be arrested and that without a revival of capital investment as part of a world-wide economic recovery, the French steel industry will be condemned to *reculer pour mieux reculer*.

6

LOCAL ECONOMIC DECLINE:
Retreating in Good Order?[1]

Having considered how France has sought to deal with the problem of a declining industry in terms of the reactions of the national steel policy community, it is necessary to examine the reactions of the local industrial policy community. The focus is switched from the national and functional aspects of economic decline to its local and community consequences. Rather than confining the discussion to the local consequences of the decline of the steel industry—which would have made a study based upon Lorraine appropriate—a broader framework has been chosen. The Nord, with its more diversified industrial base—including steel as an important constituent—provides a more suitable subject for investigation. However, it is not Dunkirk, the home of USINOR, but the Lille conurbation and the Valenciennes area that will be the foci of our inquiry into how the senior partners in the local industrial policy community manoeuvre between the political, administrative and financial pressures to remain loyal to the locality or take the 'exit' option. The most vociferous actors in this process must not be confused with the most influential, which means that it is behind the scenes, in the gloom of the badly lit backstage rather than under the glaring arc lights of public performance, that we must seek to identify the incentives to which each actor responds and the motives that guide their policy choices.

Just as we have earlier provided a conspectus of the six clusters of actors that make up the global community of economic policy communities and the national economic policy community (see Figs. 1.1 and 2.1), we offer as the context of this discussion of local economic decline a conspectus of the actors that constitute the local and regional economic policy communities. Figure 6.1 is not meant to be an exhaustive enumeration of these sub-national actors but a description of the categories of actor that are involved in the processes of economic policy in general and industrial policy specifically at the

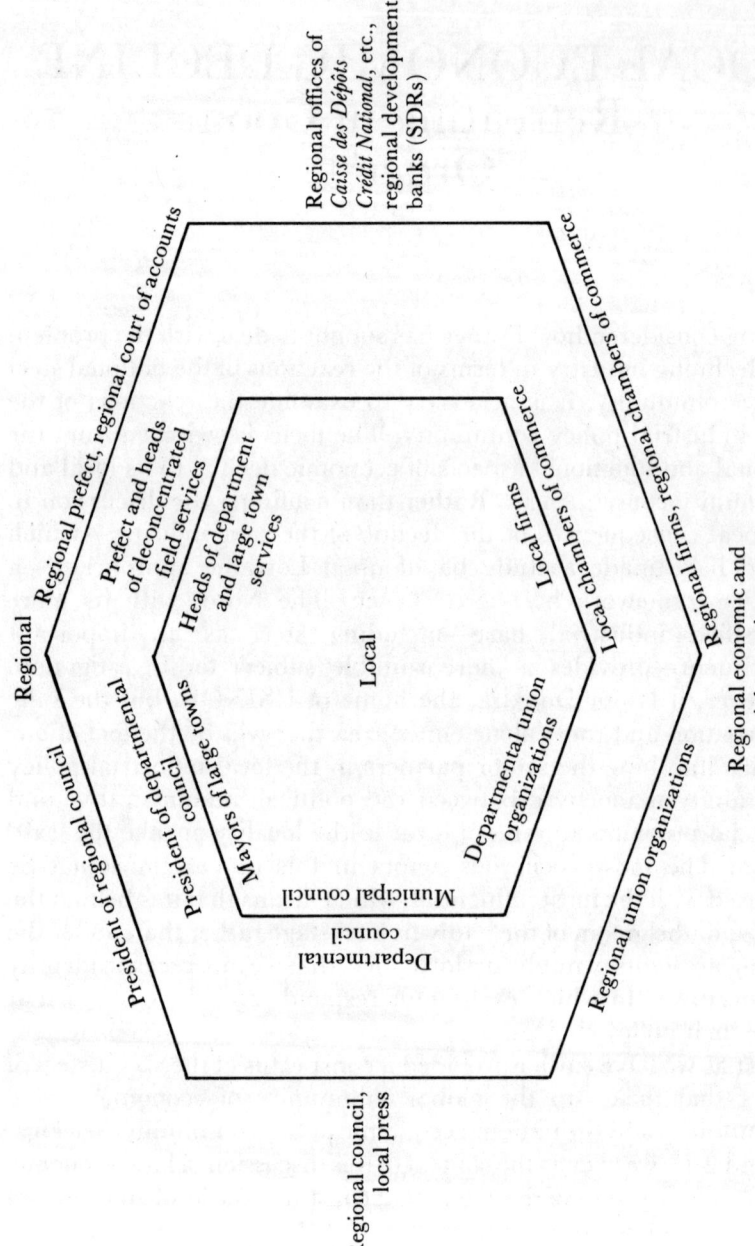

Figure 6.1 The local and regional economic policy communities

local and regional levels. The relative weight of particular actors, in terms of the resources and influence they command, will depend upon their links with actors at the national level and beyond, in addition to the means at their own disposal as will emerge from an examination of the cases of the Lille and Valenciennes areas of northern France.

Lille is the capital of a region with a marked economic and political identity. It has a strong Left-wing tradition, going back to the socialism of Jules Guesde (deputy for Roubaix) in the late nineteenth century, which accounts for the fact that even before the revival of the Socialist Party in the 1970s, it was an area where the party retained its working class roots. The socialist and later Communist anthem, *L'Internationale*, was composed and first sung in Lille. However, it was also the birthplace of Charles de Gaulle and the strength of the paternalistic, Catholic 'divine right' employers has meant that class feeling has been strong in the Nord. In Valenciennes, the Right has predominated over the Left because much of the working class population lived in the 'red belt' of coalmining villages outside the town. The steel industry became the driving force of local industrial development from the end of the nineteenth century. It has been concentrated by a process of amalgamation into the firms of USINOR and Vallourec.

The iron masters of Valenciennes were more effective in exercising local political domination than the textile bosses of Roubaix and Tourcoing in the Lille conurbation. Whereas the traditional role of firms in areas of early industrialization like the Nord and Lorraine was to provide housing and infrastructure as well as employment, these functions were taken over by the local authorities after the Second World War. By the mid-1960s the employers could no longer even ensure full employment, and local authorities were drawn into the business of job protection and attracting new activities to provide jobs for those shed by firms in difficulty. Like much of the national action in the sphere of financial aids to regional development, local actors have operated less in terms of economic rationality than to prevent the eruption of politically damaging conflict. As such, it has as much to do with sustaining the local industrial community as with industrial policy in the strict sense.

The Representative Public Sector

The institutional actors in the local industrial policy community can be grouped into three clusters: the local political community representatives; the local officials of central ministries and agencies; the local managers of the public banks. They are the key democratic, bureaucratic and plutocratic—or more strictly the political, administrative and financial—on the spot actors in the process of public decision making, as it relates to industrial affairs.

THE MUNICIPALITIES

The directly and indirectly elected representatives of the people themselves form an interrelated complex of four main types of relevant institutions: the communes, the urban community, the departmental council and the regional council, together with their satellites. Of these, the only directly elected bodies are the municipalities and the departmental council, and for our purposes it is sufficient to concentrate attention on only four of the former: the three municipalities that make up most of the population of conurbation of Lille–Roubaix–Tourcoing and Valenciennes. Much the most important is Lille, because it is where the main local political, administrative, service and financial—though not the industrial actors—are located. French mayors usually personify political authority in their town and when this was combined with being a deputy, president of the departmental and/or regional council, this cumulation of power increased by geometrical progression. When, as in the case of Pierre Mauroy, the mayor in question is also an influential leader of the Socialist Party nationally, we have an actor capable of taking full advantage of the opportunities that arise from the *cumul des mandats*. Until he became Prime Minister in May 1981, Mauroy usually spent only forty-eight hours a week in Paris, devoting the bulk of his energies to his town and region. Effectively at the head of the fourth largest conurbation in France, Mauroy has utilized to the full (if not exceeded) the economic potentialities provided by relatively strong local finances to develop the economic power of his city. The sharp contrast with his predecessor (until 1973) as Mayor and Deputy of Lille, Augustin Laurent, is due not only to their different personalities and generational change but because of the altered climate—both in terms of the *need* for greater local political intervention in economic matters and the *willingness* to undertake it—has required a new style of municipal leadership and organization. Municipal economic personnel have been appointed, although they usually lack the stamp of *grande école* training enjoyed by the central government officials with whom they have to deal. However, political ties enable specialists from the local university to supplement some forms of expertise in which the municipality is deficient.

By contrast with the Communist Party mayors who are inclined to react to the local consequences of economic recession with a negative rhetoric, blaming international capitalism and the national government, Socialist mayors like Mauroy were prepared, in the long years when their political opponents were in office in Paris, to risk the ambiguity of engaging actively in central–local economic collaboration while remaining firm in their political opposition. In Lille and more generally in the Nord Regional Council, Mauroy experimented with the techniques of decentralized economic development that he was to generalize as Prime Minister from 1981–4. At the local level, this desire to create a capability for economic analysis of the town's economic problems prior to remedial action was reflected institutionally in the establishment in 1977 of an economic development service attached directly to the mayor (that is outside the traditional administrative hierarchy). As time passes, it is likely to be integrated into that structure and lose its initial *administration de mission* style, so useful when trying to develop a flexible, rapid and innovative interventionism. Because Lille has been denied the benefits of the major state financial aids (its difficulties are not regarded to be as serious as the coalmining belt and a steel area like Valenciennes) and although local authorities are, since 1982, allowed to provide direct financial assistance to firms in difficulty or as an attraction to location, they have had to turn to indirect action. They seek to influence the behaviour of firms by fiscal action, by ownership and control over land, by advisory services—working in conjunction with developers—to persuade firms not to leave the town because they have outgrown their existing factory space or attract back those that have left. In old industrialized towns like Lille, Roubaix and Tourcoing, where small workshops and residential areas are irretrievably intermingled, land use planning attempts to exclude industry have been reversed for revenue as well as employment reasons, whereas employers have come to realize the industrial relations dangers of segregating factories in industrial zones on the urban periphery. Even the legal restrictions can be circumvented by political lobbying or agreement between local and central officials about the unacceptable employment or financial consequences of planning regulations ignoring local authority boundaries.

Because Lille cannot be seriously challenged as the commercial, financial and administrative centre of the conurbation (which was conclusively demonstrated by the *Mercure* operation which we shall discuss later, see p. 112), Roubaix and Tourcoing have had to concentrate upon developing their strong points and bolstering their weak ones. Roubaix—thanks to celebrated brand names like La Redoute—has a convincing claim to being the French capital of the mail order business rather than its textile capital. (In 1965 textiles accounted for 50 per cent of Roubaix employment, but this had fallen by 1980 to 30 per cent; the process of decline has continued at the rate of about 2,000 jobs annually out of its 1980 total of 20,000.) La Redoute had considered leaving Roubaix in 1975 for the Lille new town of Villeneuve d'Ascq but was persuaded to stay thanks to provision by the local authority of 10,000 square metres of space for expansion.[2] Unable to attract new firms to the area with its manual working class image, Roubaix and Tourcoing have sought to secure the cooperation of local firms to prevent the dereliction and blight of their central areas at worst, or the loss of jobs by the use of industrial land for housing at best. The natural inclination of local authorities has been to promote such de-industrialization, mainly because they traditionally were not supposed to concern themselves with industrial matters, either because of the belief that this was best left to market forces or because *dirigiste* interventionism ought to be the preserve of the central government and its agents. Urban planning had encouraged the development of peripheral industrial zones in the 1960s, with the result that central areas suffered rapid economic decline. The consequent problems were compounded by the fact that because of the multiplicity of communes that had interpenetrated each other, these industrial zones were often under the jurisdiction of another local authority.

So, both in Roubaix and Tourcoing, a deliberately planned attempt was made in the 1970s to revitalize the old urban setting in which houses and factories were intermingled in a way characteristic of incremental urban development, paradoxical as this may seem. The two towns of Roubaix and Tourcoing armed themselves for this more ambitious, non-traditional role. Roubaix acquired the services of an economist, who had worked for the Regional and Spatial Planning Delegacy (DATAR) in Paris, to head its Development and Economic Action Secretariat, working closely with its mayor and deputy Pierre Prouvost; while the new Socialist team that took control of Tourcoing in 1977 used *Caisse des Dépôts* consultants to back up its own municipal economic and urban action plan.[3] They acquired the knowledge on the basis of which they could prepare a strategy for the management of industrial space, anticipating the decline of particular firms, identifying the land and buildings for which a new use had to be found and then either persuading a firm to step in or finding a non-industrial use for it (for example, the establishment of an eco-museum of the textile industry in Tourcoing). Unfortunately, one needs only one such museum in the area and there are all too many candidates for this vocation!

Roubaix (and to a lesser extent Tourcoing) allied itself with the chamber of commerce of Lille–Roubaix–Tourcoing against the urban community, headed by another Socialist mayor and deputy of the conurbation, Arthur Notebart, who steered industrial development away from the three major towns towards the mass of small communes which gave him electoral support. With the help of the then president of the chamber of commerce, Pierre Prouvost of Roubaix became president of a new *Association pour la Promotion du Versant Nord-Est* in 1978, aimed at correcting the consequences of an east–west urban development axis, reflected in the major public investment decisions of the urban community, notably the metro linking Lille and the new town of Villeneuve d'Ascq. To rejuvenate an area suffering from the secular decline of family textile firms who vied in their incapacity to think innovatively with the old-style SFIO mayors who ruled so many of the local authorities, a new instrument was necessary. The bankruptcy of many of the old firms and the retirement of many of the old mayors tending to coincide with the onset of the 1973 recession, it became possible to move in new directions.

After a laborious two-year gestation, a 'mixed economy company' under the chairmanship of Pierre Prouvost was established in 1979 by the Lille Chamber of Commerce and the municipalities of Roubaix, Tourcoing and Wattrelos, the chamber and the local authorities collectively each providing 42 per cent of the capital, the remainder coming from the Roubaix savings bank (10 per cent) and jointly from the *Caisse des Dépôts* and the *Société Centrale d'Equipment* (6 per cent). (The chamber was specifically and unprecedentedly allowed by the government to increase the tax it levies on its members to cover the cost of this venture!) The company's major function was to buy (and if necessary expropriate) vacant land at use value and not at market price with low cost funds (then being able to borrow from the *Caisse des Dépôts* at a 9 per cent rather than a 14 per cent rate of interest).[4] It enjoyed certain tax advantages in converting property to new uses. It also received financial help from the central Fund for Urban Planning, the local authority and chamber of commerce in making up the substantial difference between the cost of urban land and greenfield sites in the outskirts, which might be three or four times as much. The main aim was to ensure that reutilizing old industrial buildings would be cheaper than building anew, say on industrial estates. It had some success in enabling local firms to extend on the spot and so avoid leaving the area.

However, the most ambitious scheme, masterminded by a former president of the chamber of commerce, was a luxury office tower block—the *Centre d'Affaires Mercure*—built at the 'frontier' between Roubaix and Tourcoing, described euphemistically as 'linking' them. It was intended partially to correct the imbalance between the concentration of high-prestige service functions in the Lille metropolis (although Lille had the lowest service share of the working population of all the provincial *metropoles*) and its unattractive, declining, industrial, poor relation, Roubaix–Tourcoing.[5] (In fact, Tourcoing is a leafy, wide-avenued town, which does not correspond to the annually reiterated 'northern hell' image of the cobblestones of Roubaix, to which the *Tour de France* cycle racing commentators habitually refer.) We shall see shortly that this strategy of promoting a *centre directionnel* to the north of Lille, based on a south–north development axis, was to be decisively undercut by the central government's choice of a new town east of Lille, based upon a west–east development axis, representing a decisive defeat both for Roubaix–Tourcoing and for the chamber of commerce view that there should be a bipolar Nord metropolis. Conceived in 1972, completed in 1978, *Mercure* stands in solitary splendour, a commercial cathedral in an urban desert, compelled to accept tenants that do not correspond to its initial ambitions simply to avoid standing empty. It is estimated that it will take at least twenty years for the Lille Chamber of Commerce to recover the cost of this project.

Valenciennes presents a marked politico-economic contrast with the Lille conurbation in terms of the relative roles of political leadership, represented by the municipality and economic leadership, represented by the chamber of commerce. While Lille, notably in the person of Mauroy, provides an example of maximalist–innovative political intervention in the industrial sphere, Valenciennes suffers from a minimalist–traditional style of political inertia, personified by its Right-wing (RPR) senator/mayor Carous. In the past, the Valenciennes area was able to rely upon a few industrialists, such as the steel firm USINOR, Vallourec or the Northern Coal Corporation, to sustain its local economy, without the local authority concerning itself unduly. This attitude has persisted despite the recession and it has been left to the local chamber of commerce to assume responsibility for economic development, notably through the establishment of industrial estates. Carous himself spent most of his time on parliamentary work in Paris (unlike Mauroy until 1981), yet he refused to delegate authority to take local decisions with the result that little was done and that little very slowly. Thus, when the major local enterprise, the leading French steel tube firm of Vallourec, wanted to sell both some redundant factory space and houses (the firm abandoning its traditional function of providing not merely employment but accommodation for its employees) it had great difficulty in galvanizing the municipality into some semblance of action. The Communist local authorities in the 'red belt' around Valenciennes (the three Communist deputies in the Valenciennes area were re-elected in 1981), while taking a more active interest in the economic development of the area, are divided between their rejection of capitalism and their need to adapt to its logic by doing all they can to attract private-sector jobs. As a local Communist mayor put it: 'The communes prostitute themselves because the demands from the firms necessitate it, otherwise they will go elsewhere.'[6]

THE URBAN COMMUNITY AND LILLE NEW TOWN

To counteract the consequences for town planning of fragmentation of the major conurbations between numerous communes, a 1966 law allowed the French government to insist upon the creation of an urban community. In the case of the Lille conurbation, a March 1967 decree established such a compulsory community, embracing eighty-seven communes, covering 159,000 acres and a population of just over 1 million.[6] Significantly, its most important project was to be planning and financing the development of a new town, initially dubbed East Lille, before the resurgence of local pride and wish for autonomy from Lille led to the choice of the name Villeneuve d'Ascq. The location of the new town, significantly, pre-dated the establishment of the urban community.

The technocratic inspiration behind the venture derived from the belief that town planning was too complex and far-reaching a matter to be left to parochial local politicians, so it was hoped that effective planning would be undertaken by an urban planning agency run by an engineer from the prestigious roads and bridges corps. The land was already being bought by the Ministry before the community was operational. Despite the loss of democratic legitimacy arising from the fact that the council of the Lille urban community was indirectly elected, its president, Notebart, the Socialist mayor of an adjacent, medium-sized commune to the west of Lille, succeeded in wresting effective decision making from the techno-bureaucratic director of the urban planning agency. (The latter was formerly head of the Ministry of Public Works and Housing field service in the Nord, who was placed on secondment for this purpose.) Helped by the fact that the ministry reduced its financial contribution to the agency (from 26 per cent in 1974 to 18 per cent in 1976) and that the latter had provided the northern metropolis with the first detailed medium-term land-use plan (POS) of any urban community in France, Notebart dismissed the director and replaced the agency by one wholly responsible to the urban community. This assertion of local political control—which was to be repeated by Notebart in the case of the new town, as we shall see—was achieved despite the divisions within the community. Of the ninety seats on its council, thirty-six were held by the three largest communes (Lille having seventeen, Roubaix ten and Tourcoing nine) twenty-four other communes were individually represented by at least one councillor, while the fifty-nine smaller communes had to fill sixteen seats between themselves. Notebart prized the immense investment power represented by his pet project of a metro from Lille to Villeneuve d'Ascq (costing 2 billion francs and employing over 2,000 people) which drained funds away from all other schemes and did not come into service until 1983.

The earlier long-term urban development master plan (SDAU) had also been the product of technocratic planning. It had ignored elementary 'irrational' political facts like the commune boundaries and decided that the spinal column of urban development would be along a south–north axis, Lille–Roubaix–Tourcoing. The east–west metro was a logical follow-up to the early 1960s decision to transfer most of Lille University to the future site of Villeneuve d'Ascq. This was done in the ambitious hope that an equivalent to the Boston 128 highway location of a complex of research and advanced technological industry could be achieved and the belief that a channel tunnel would promote west–east commercial traffic. The United Kingdom's membership of the EC and a start on building the approaches to the channel tunnel prompted a speculative boom in luxury building, partly financed by British capital, unfortunately coincided with the onset of the recession. The unilateral abandonment of the tunnel by the British Government seriously weakened the case for a west–east development strategy but by then the community was too firmly committed for it to be abandoned.

The construction of what was initially regarded as a satellite town, East Lille, became (together with the metro with which it was linked) the major concern of the urban community, Notebart being chairman of the new town corporation as well as of the community. Not given any prominence in the original master plan, the new town acquired a dominance thanks to having a precise and overall programme of action and the means of attaining it. It had an implementation team in the new town corporation and state financial commitments in the shape of a special Sixth Plan allocation of funds. Two attempts by the mayor of Lille—in 1972 by Laurent and in 1976 by Mauroy—to absorb Villeneuve d'Ascq, along with four other communes situated between them, which would have increased the 1976 population of Lille proper from 177,000 to 269,000, were both rejected. Let us turn to how Villeneuve d'Ascq, originally intended to be an adjunct of the Lille metropolis, has emerged as its rapidly expanding fourth largest commune and rival centre of attraction.

The creation of the Lille new town was part of the expansionist 1960s' attempt by the French government to develop counter-magnets to Paris. This would allow major conurbations like metropolitan Lille to develop service employment in a major economic redeployment away from the declining industries of mining and textiles. It was initially inspired by a specific desire to persuade university teachers of the expanding University of Lille to live locally rather than commute from Paris. Rector Debeyre (a rector is the educational equivalent of the prefect) was an influential figure in the area, playing a notable part in the Nord's Regional Economic Expansion Committee. Furthermore, the Lille conurbation contained the greatest concentration of slum housing to be found anywhere in France. Now that French industrial revival had generated the resources to tackle the housing backlog and because it was not yet the fashion to restore old houses, building a new town to rehouse the overcrowded inner areas of the northern metropolis seemed an eminently sensible response. (New towns, like teachers living close to their university, were ideas easier to absorb in the Nord because of the close cultural contact with Great Britain, where they had been pioneered and practised.) In a caricature of French 'top–down' decision-making, the Minister of Public Works and Housing in 1966, Edgard Pisani, decided upon the location of the new town as his helicopter flew over the future Villeneuve d'Ascq. After securing the agreement of the Minister of Education, he informed the regional prefect of the decision without local politicians having any say in the matter!⁷

The process of recovering local control came first, through the creation of a new town corporation in 1969. It had equal representation from central ministries and local bodies (mainly the urban community), with as its chairman Notebart, who had a casting vote. To provide a Right-wing counterweight to the Socialist-controlled community and a pliable 'partner' for the administration, the regional prefect and the director of the new town corporation encouraged a fusion in 1970 of the three communes on whose territory the new town was to be built, which took place without the inhabitants being consulted. Although this strategy initially succeeded, the wider manoeuvres to win political control in Lille through the use of ministers (Ortoli in 1971 and Segard in 1977) as electoral locomotives failed. Internal dissensions in Villeneuve d'Ascq, combined with an inflow of Socialist voters from Roubaix in particular, thanks to Notebart's policy of confining most house building to semi-public HLM (low rent housing), rather than speculative builders and coupled with the national swing towards the Socialist Party, led to the Left taking control of the new town in 1977. In the meantime, Notebart won a power struggle with the *grand corps* director of the new town corporation from the Ministry of Public Works and Housing, whose resignation he secured, thereby ensuring the primacy of local political control.

The major disappointment, however, has been that no private research localization has followed in the wake of the Centre for Study and Technological Research into Food Industries and the Centre for Research and Higher Education in Textiles. Villeneuve d'Ascq has had to fall back upon more humdrum office and small/medium firms that have no claim to represent advanced science or technology. Furthermore, by January 1977 seventeen of the first twenty-four industrial firms that located in the new town were transfers from the conurbation, eleven specifically from Lille.⁹ So, although the new town did not attain either the economic or political objectives fixed by the central government and its local agents and called a halt at a 70,000 population by 1984 instead of the planned 100,000, allowing Roubaix–Tourcoing their chance of redevelopment, the dominant Socialist Party was able to demonstrate its local mastery. It was also able—notably through the regional council—to experiment with regional industrial intervention in ways that were to be generalized nationally, following Pierre Mauroy's appointment as Prime Minister in 1981.

DEPARTMENT AND REGION

While in terms of investment expenditure the traditional actors play a predominant part—in 1976 the departmental council spent 1.5 billion francs and the central government 900 million francs in the Nord, as against 700 million francs spent by the urban community and a mere 100 million francs by the regional council—when it comes to calculating the overall impact, one must not neglect the multiplier effect of small sums intelligently used. The regional council's impact may be marginal as measured in money, but not when it comes to initiatives that mobilize resources of those, like the HLM housing authorities, who have funds but do not know how to use them for optimum effect. Second only to Brittany's CELIB (see chapter 7, p. 153), the Nord's CERES Regional Economic Expansion Committee was actively involved from 1953 in promoting the need for planned regional economic development. Decades before this was officially acknowledged, it exposed the myth that the Nord was France's industrial spearhead by showing that its traditional industries, like textiles, were already in difficulties and that it would be difficult to find jobs for its (then) rapidly expanding population. The new regional institutions of the 1960s eliminated CERES as a major actor and by 1974 it became an adjunct of the regional council. The task of attracting industry was left primarily to a joint DATAR–business agency, APEX (to be discussed shortly), which was thought to be more appropriate for the task than a Socialist-dominated body. The regional council—headed until he became Prime Minister by Pierre Mauroy—supported by a very well-staffed (both in numbers and quality) *cabinet régional*, which enabled Mauroy to be by far the best briefed and equipped for his task of any regional council president, adopted a maximalist interpretation of its function. (His closest collaborator, Michel Delebarre, became head of his private staff as Prime Minister and Minister of Labour when Mauroy left office in 1984.) Instead of being confined by the strait jacket of the 1972 regional institutions and limited resources to a residual role by the central agencies and their local agents, Mauroy stepped into the vacuum left by bankrupt businessmen, a vacuum which central intervention was failing to fill. Flying in the face of the traditional view that it was not up to local and regional authorities to intervene when firms were in financial difficulty, Mauroy acted on the belief that when approached either by local trade unions or works committees or by a local councillor proposing a practical solution, he should use his resources as mayor of a large town, president of the regional council and deputy to assess and if possible tackle the problems.

In the mid-1970s, the regional council used to the full the opportunities provided in the context of the Seventh Plan (1976–80) notably through the regionally initiated priority action programmes (see chapter 8), as well as proposing a regional plan (1976) and an emergency plan (1979), which showed that the Nord was one of the few French regions with an economic development strategy. However, this imaginative approach did not meet with a commensurate response from the central government and by the late 1970s the situation had become much more desperate. Short of venturing risk capital—which would be ruled out as illegal by the regional prefect—the regional council could use its experts to investigate whether a particular firm could be saved from bankruptcy and if so how. The main problem is that the region is usually called in when things have gone too far, although occasionally rescues have been effected and the solution has sometimes been to establish a producer cooperative. (The example of Marketube will be discussed below.) However, the Mauroy approach has increasingly been to investigate which sort of industries could be attracted to the area, formulate technically sound schemes backed by suitable financial support and then—the most difficult part—find an industrialist willing to take over. The objective (as expressed by a close collaborator of Mauroy) is 'to stimulate enterprise, not to replace the entrepreneur'. The ambitious aim of making the Nord (after Paris and Lyon-Grenoble) France's third major research centre, with a view to attracting advanced technology industries, has so far met with little success. (Having encouraged the development of Villeneuve d'Ascq, the central government did not steer there any of its advanced technology activities in the aeronautical, computer or nuclear fields.)

The regional council has had to fall back upon sustaining existing industries, like the local railway rolling stock enterprises (accounting for two-thirds of French production) thanks to a regional transport scheme that—in conjunction with the SNCF—rapidly modernized the existing public transport system in the Nord, alongside the construction of the Lille metro. The local building industry—suffering from intense depression due to the recession and the decline in demand because of the end of the rapid increase in population characteristic of the 1950s and 1960s—was helped by renovating old houses and building new ones, thanks to joint action with the central government and the regional HLM organization (conveniently controlled by Mauroy's Socialist friends). The encouragement of new technology was not lost sight of either, some projects being guaranteed a market for houses incorporating heating by solar energy, unlikely as this might seem at first sight in the north of France.

The Bureaucratic Public Sector

In turning from the representative to the administrative public sector local actors, one should note a change in their relative importance as between the 1960s and the 1970s, which was due only in part to the impact of the post-1973 economic recession. The five years from the establishment of the new regional institutions in 1964 until 1969 (failure of de Gaulle's referendum on regionalization) were the hey day of innovative and dynamic *administration de mission*. The innovators were helped by the context of economic expansion and an uninhibited style of economic interventionism by members of the *grand corps* who were convinced they knew what was best for provincial France. Exemplified by the economic sub-prefect who ran the regional prefect's *mission économique* (note the 'missionary' language), they worked on the spot rather than relying, as did traditional French administration, upon sending out a stream of circulars from Paris, purporting to be suitable everywhere and in all circumstances and often regarding such remote control as a substitute for action. The next five years—roughly the period of the Sixth Plan—was transitional. Public investment, whose allocation and coordination gave the regional prefect his main *raison d'être*, was still buoyant. However, the onset of the recession, which dominated the Seventh Plan during the latter half of the 1970s, saw a dramatic drop in public infrastructure expenditure in the Nord. It fell from 1 billion francs to a quarter of this figure in real terms, as the central government reverted from being a 'welfare state' to its traditional 'police state' role.

As the traditional style of prefectoral administration reasserted itself, the life went out of the *mission régionale*. Although, in the Nord, an activist regional prefect like André Chadeau (who in 1978 became head of DATAR before briefly joining Mauroy's prime ministerial *cabinet* and later heading the SNCF railway corporation) attempted to keep up the momentum from 1974–8,[10] the initiative increasingly passed to others—notably APEX (discussed below), the chambers of commerce and those local authorities which had been rejuvenated by an influx of new Socialist leaders. The prefects increasingly reverted to the circumspection summarized in the dictum of a Fourth Republic prime minister renowned for his immobilist inactivity: 'Un préfet qui se mouille se noie'. In the Nord, the prefecture concentrated upon helping small firms in difficulty. Most firms only received temporary respite from bankruptcy through such first aid. More generally, it adopted a sceptical attitude to the task of attracting firms, although the prefecture competed with the chambers of commerce in helping them to prepare their applications. It also sought to simplify the intimidating formalities by developing a *guichet unique* in January 1980 in Lille, a task left to the chamber of commerce in Valenciennes. Finally, when it was necessary to bend the regional assistance rules to attract firms that would be a magnet to others (for example, Rank Xerox in the industrial estate, to the north of Tourcoing), the regional prefecture played a part, but the real decisions were made in Paris, involving the head of DATAR and the Ministry of Finance.

Deconcentrated Industrial Decoys: DATAR and APEX

Whereas it is a gross over-simplification to claim that in France 'regional policy was what DATAR did', the same author is much nearer the mark when he dismissively asserts that: 'The tendency of DATAR to establish a causal relation between its action and actual developments is not well-founded'.[11] As far as public investment decisions are concerned, these are taken either by the central officials or the field services of the Paris ministries, which each have their own priorities and cannot be effectively coordinated, either nationally by the Planning Commissariat and DATAR or locally by the regional prefects. Such effective coordination as occurs tends to be made by standing or *ad hoc* interministerial council and committee meetings in which the DATAR officials seek to influence decisions. During the period of rapid economic expansion, DATAR concentrated upon steering large national and international firms into establishing factories in priority areas. As unemployment increased in the 1970s, the question of whether incoming firms were bringing new technology or would increase exports became less important, as job creation bulked ever larger as the dominant preoccupation. It set up offices in the United States (New York, Chicago and Los Angeles), the United Kingdom, Federal Germany, Japan, Canada, Spain, Sweden and Switzerland, to attract prospective investors. Foreign visits are periodically made by staff from what is in effect its Lille office, using DATAR's foreign missions as their base of operations, as well as making contacts through the head office of foreign firms already established in the area. When Rank Xerox was considering where to locate in France, it was initially encouraged to look at sites in the Ardennes and in Brittany; only later, with the assistance of DATAR's then head, Jérôme Monod, was the Lille area fixed upon and DATAR's local extension, APEX, was left to undertake the detailed local negotiations.

The *Association pour l'Expansion Industrielle de la Région Nord Pas-de-Calais* (APEX) is a hybrid public/private agency. It has come in practice to be identified informally as DATAR-Nord, which explains its treatment as a public/administrative agency. It was launched in 1966 by a consortium consisting of chambers of commerce, the nationalized Northern Coal Corporation, the regional organization of the CNPF (dominated by the textile trade association) and the regional organization of the steel trade association. They did not wish to leave the attraction of firms to the official regional bodies or those controlled by the Socialist Party. The following year, President Pompidou established four posts of Commissioner for Redevelopment (*Commissaires à la Conversion*) since renamed Industrialization Commissioners, the then head of DATAR, Olivier Guichard, deciding that the Nord Pas-de-Calais commissioner would simultaneously be the head of APEX. From 1973–80, the holder of this office was a prefect (former sub-prefect for the mining area of Béthune). DATAR became responsible for 40 per cent of APEX's income, the other main contributors being the chambers of commerce and the Northern Coal Corporation.

APEX deliberately cultivated the opportunities deriving from the duality of its image. When dealing with businessmen, it wanted to avoid being regarded as an arm of the state, although in its dealings with the central ministries and their field services, it was useful to be seen as 'a member of the family', albeit an associate member. It sought to get the best of both worlds by being at the interface between them. The APEX commissioner, as well as being financially accountable to DATAR, owed a dual responsibility to the regional prefect and to the president of APEX (who for many years was Pierre Delmon, former member of Pompidou's personal staff, who became head first of the Northern Coal Corporation—later of the National Coalfields Corporation—and president of the official consultative regional economic and social committee). In keeping with its 'missionary' character, APEX operated in the early 1980s with a small staff of eight *chargés de mission*, who played the role of discreet intermediaries between investing firms and the administrative, financial and political authorities. More specifically, APEX offered to provide potential investors with detailed information about the local industrial environment, with advice and help in choice of location, contacts with suppliers and clients, help in recruitment and training of employees, advice on securing long-term loans, as well as help with obtaining official regional financial assistance and tax concessions.

The record of APEX, measured in terms of the number of people that firms agreed to employ and—more significantly—the number of jobs actually attracted, were 86,000 jobs and 61,000 jobs respectively from 1967 to 1979. The impact of the recession can be observed in Table 6.1, with 1974 seeing a halving in the number of jobs negotiated and actually secured in the region. There was a partial recovery in 1975, followed by a further decline—especially in the number of jobs attracted—which was negative in 1978, prior to the recovery in 1979, mainly in the number of jobs negotiated. The figure of nearly 11,000 jobs negotiated exceeded the attainment in all years since the *annus mirabilis* of 1969, when 26,240 jobs had been negotiated, mainly in the automobile industry (which accounted for 44 per cent of all jobs secured from 1967–79 and 40 per cent in 1979 alone). Of the jobs negotiated in 1979, 6,210 were secured in conjunction with the new Special Industrial Adaptation Fund (FSAI, discussed later), aimed especially at counteracting the unemployment caused by steel closures; 3,884 jobs being due to thirteen new firms and 2,326 jobs being generated by extension of the activities of sixteen existing firms. The pre-existing industrial and service incentives were associated with 4,689 jobs, of which 2,912 were accounted for by thirty-four new firms, while 1,777 jobs were generated by extensions of the activities of thirty-four existing firms.[12]

Table 6.1: Number of jobs negotiated and actually secured by APEX, 1972–9

Jobs	1972	1973	1974	1975	1976	1977	1978	1979
Negotiated	5,550	8,573	4,998	5,180	2,652	4,032	3,819	10,899
Secured	10,190	7,462	3,477	5,679	6,958	3,082	−465	3,020

Source: *Conversion*, no. 27 (March 1980) p.5.

In addition to the resources directly controlled by DATAR (the Regional Intervention Fund which could be used, for example, to speed up the building of a road to service a new factory), APEX could help firms in difficulty to secure assistance from the Interministerial Committee for the Adaptation of Industrial Structures (CIASI), since renamed CIRI. This group of senior civil servants could persuade public creditors not to press demands or it might seek out a prosperous firm with which an ailing firm could be merged. If a firm was judged to be of sufficient technological or strategic interest, CIASI could provide funds and if the firm to be rescued was located in an area with employment problems like the Nord, from 1979 it could receive long-term (fifteen to seventeen-year loans) at favourable interest rates from CIDISE—the Interministerial Committee for Development and Support for Employment. (Since 1983 CIDISE has been absorbed by the FIM—Industrial Modernization Fund.) This directs our attention to the fact that with the onset of the recession, APEX became increasingly concerned with job preservation, notably through the CODEFI in the *département*. APEX claimed that in 1979 it examined fifty-six cases involving 10,000 jobs, of which about 2,300 were 'saved'.[13] Although the role of APEX fits neatly into what may be described as a series of 'fire brigade' sallies, amounting at best to a policy of covering a 'retreat in good order' directed from Paris, it undoubtedly eases the pain of de-industrialization, even if it made a virtue of the excessive redeployment towards the fragile automobile industry from 1969 to 1979.

It is not possible to do more than refer in the sketchiest way to the role of the field services of the ministries involved in matters affecting the decisions of entrepreneurs. While the regional and local officials of the Ministries of Industry, Labour, Public Works and Housing impinge significantly on such decisions, the Finance Ministry officials are of major importance, notably the Treasurer and Paymaster General (TPG), who fixes the rules that other actors spend so much time seeking to circumvent. The fiscal incentives and grants are respectively administered by the field services of the Taxation and Competition Divisions of the Finance Ministry, influenced by the advice of the prefecture, which itself turns for advice to APEX and to the field services of the Bank of France. (The Competition Division was the successor to the old Price Control Division—reactivated in 1981—and had little experience or expertise in industrial aid.) Flexibility in implementing the rules is vital because firms often either do not manage to achieve the number of new jobs they have contracted to establish or only do so over a longer period than stipulated when they received financial assistance. The Treasury Division (Finance Ministry) may impose a reduction in the assistance granted as a penalty for non-attainment of the target number of jobs. However, there is a recognition that such sanctions must not be too severe, otherwise they may be counterproductive, with the whole operation being wound up. At least, that possibility strengthens the hand of businessmen in their negotiations with public officials, but the EC has required greater stringency in administering such subsidies. Sometimes, these officials—particularly the highly 'political' FSAI staff—steer projects away from one maximum aided area to another (for example, from Valenciennes to the nearby mining area of Douai), responding to the pressure of the powerful Northern Coal Corporation, concerned above all to find jobs for redundant miners. Because of the scarcity in the number of new jobs available, there is intense competition between public agencies to ensure that at least their part of the local economy retreats in relatively good order.

Deconcentrated Financial Intermediaries

Turning to the role of public or semi-public banks which provide medium- and long-term loans (private banks concentrating on short-term loans for which they charge very high interest rates to medium-sized firms), the total amount of money available is fixed by the Treasury Division. Until the enforced austerity from 1984, there had apparently never been any overall scarcity of funds for what were judged to be viable projects because the government placed a high priority on encouraging investment and so was willing to provide an unlimited amount of money for this purpose. Originally, there was specialization between the *Crédit National*, which had concentrated on providing loans for the larger, extra-regional industrial firms; the *Crédit Hôtelier* which had lent long term to those building factories and offices (as well as the hotels mentioned in its name) particularly small and medium-sized firms; while the *Société de Développement Régional* (a sort of regional merchant bank, launched in the mid-1950s) used to concentrate upon loans to smaller, more risky local firms. However, these three semi-public banks have increasingly competed with each other, especially on size and duration of loan, rather than interest charged.

Crédit National established a regional office in Lille in 1969, with the authority to make smaller loans to medium-sized firms on the spot. It seeks to lend to small and medium-sized firms that are likely to expand into large firms. The *Crédit Hôtelier* amalgamated in 1981 with the *Caisse Nationale des Marchés de l'Etat* at the instance of President Giscard d'Estaing, under pressure from the small and medium business lobby, which wanted its 'own' bank. The newly entitled *Crédit d'Equipement des Petites et Moyennes Enterprises* was explicitly meant to fulfil this role, with the state owning 51 per cent of its capital. All three banks may lend at an artificially low rate of interest, thanks to the Economic and Social Development Fund (FDES) at the request of the government, to help employment, to increase exports outside the EC or, very occasionally, to investments leading to economies in energy. These banks act as mediators between borrowers and the Treasury when, as often happens, the original commitments are not fulfilled, negotiating on behalf of the borrower. Because firms often combine loans with various forms of regional aid, one of the banks—usually the *Crédit National*—is designated by the Finance Ministry's Treasury Division to put the package together. Frequently—especially in the case of foreign businesses—an incoming firm uses the services of a legal adviser to supervise the whole financial operation, rather than utilizing the chamber of commerce to protect its interests on the spot, because the chamber is itself regarded as an interested party.

Local Economic Intermediaries, Industrial Enticement and Regeneration

THE CHAMBERS OF COMMERCE

Like the semi-public banks we have just discussed, French chambers of commerce (contrasting with their Anglo-American, but like their German and Italian counterparts) are in an intermediate situation between the public and private sectors. Their public law status is not simply a formal matter. They have acquired the right to levy 'additional centimes' to the *taxe professionnelle*. Furthermore, they operate a wide range of public services—sixty-five seaports (not counting forty-eight fishing ports), eighty-four airports, two-hundred industrial estates—not left to chambers of commerce in other countries. Furthermore, they play an important part in industrial and commercial training, which on average accounts for 20 per cent of their expenditure; ports account for a further 20 per cent and airports for 15 per cent. These services yield them a substantial income which, together with their tax revenue, gives them independence of their tutelary Ministry of Industry. Despite its wish in 1963 that the chambers' annual increase in income should be reduced from 25 per cent to 10 per cent from 1960 to 1979 their revenue increased by an annual average of 20 per cent.[14]

The twentieth-century history of the French chambers of commerce had earlier been characterized by an increasing switch from a consultative role (which was being challenged by other channels of advice available to the public authorities) to the provision of expensive infrastructures instead of leaving it to the market or to central/local government. However, the onset of the 1974 recession led to a further change of direction. The difficulties being experienced by many industrial and commercial firms have strengthened resistance to increases in the tax burden, with the result that chambers of commerce have had to rely upon a combination of intellectual ingenuity and inventiveness, backed by research, rather than disbursing substantial sums upon spectacular investment projects. A good example of such ventures was the development of the international airport of Lille–Lesquin, whose annual passenger traffic exceeded 200,000 in 1975. It proved an attraction to businessmen who were interested not only in communications for goods—another sphere in which the chambers of Lille and Valenciennes were active—but also for their top personnel. There was also a deliberate switch from developing large industrial estates on the periphery of towns like Lille, because the estates were regarded as more prone to become centres of industrial conflict. The role of the chamber (as in the so-called 'green plan' to keep industry in the centre of towns like Roubaix and Tourcoing, helped by the fact that modern industry often did not pollute as much and was less demanding in terms of land) was to make up the tenfold difference in the cost of land between the town centres and the suburban industrial estates and do all they could to help dynamic firms expand on the spot. The difficulty in attracting firms from outside the area meant that efforts were concentrated upon developing local firms in the Lille conurbation. By contrast, in Valenciennes, the chamber's industrial estates were not reaching saturation and in any case there was less scope for developing local enterprise, hence the need to attract outside firms to greenfield sites.

Although official attempts have been made to by-pass the chambers of commerce, notably the government's attempt to encourage the long-term modernization of the small and medium-sized industrial firms, an effective ripost was organized through the regional chamber of commerce's *Association pour la Moyenne et Petite Industrie Nord Pas-de-Calais*, which secured a reversion to traditional-style state intervention with a pilot scheme in the North.[15] However, apart from defensive operations like this, the regional chamber was much less significant than the (since 1966) unified chamber of Lille–Roubaix–Tourcoing and the smaller but exceptionally active chamber of Valenciennes. The role of the latter illustrates the fact that the major effort at attracting firms was undertaken by local bodies—whether political, like the local authorities or economic, like the chambers of commerce—that could not disengage because they were irretrievably committed to the area. They were faced with the disastrous consequences for small local sub-contracting firms and shopkeepers, when the two mainstays of Valenciennes economy snapped: coal and steel. (These two industries are now nationalized; the former in 1945 and the latter for all practical purposes in 1978, although this was formalized by the Mauroy Government in 1981.) The chamber's strategy was, on the one hand, to improve transport facilities and on the other to prepare at substantial cost 'bespoke' industrial estates for major firms. However, most of its successes under both headings antedated the onset of the recession. The rerouting of the A2 Paris–Brussels–Bonn motorway and the avoidance of tolls on the Valenciennes section to the Belgian border was a major achievement of the president of the Valenciennes chamber in the late 1960s, although the increased cost was partly shared by the local authorities. When some Left-wing local authorities refused to pay their share, the chamber stepped into the breach.[16]

Unlike the Lille chamber, which, we have seen, switched its effort away from industrial estates in the 1970s (although by 1976 it had equipped nearly 2,000 acres of industrial estates, on which 204 firms employing 10,000 people were located, one-third by transfers of firms, one-third by extension associated with a transfer, with only one-third being new firms[17]), Valenciennes has continued to develop its effort. However, its major catches—the oil firm Antar, the car firm Simca—Chrysler–Talbot and the tube firm Vallourec—all obtained 'their' tailor-made estate before 1973. The chamber was able drastically to reduce the cost of land, thanks to 6 per cent loans from the *Caisse des Dépôts*, further reduced to 3 per cent by the National Land and Urban Planning Fund (known in France by its initials, FNAFU). The cost of equipping these estates with all necessary services was subsidized by the central government, through DATAR, as well as by the *département* of the Nord, the latter providing 20 or 25 per cent of the cost price of the serviced land, depending upon whether fewer or more than 30 'permanent' jobs resulted. A fourth estate was set aside for smaller firms, but when a fifth estate was established in December 1978 it was specifically designed to meet the needs of Peugeot, followed in April–June 1979 by a negotiating marathon between the chamber of commerce, various public authorities and Peugeot to obtain a whole collection of expensive special concessions (to be discussed below) costing the chamber alone 3 million francs. It took the steel industry crisis of 1978–9 to produce the Peugeot acquisition and even this did not compensate for the failure of Talbot to expand to much more than a quarter of the job total (8,000) initially planned. So, despite strenuous efforts to secure an economic future for Valenciennes, the chamber of commerce had largely to content itself with helping local firms to make modest extensions, with workers mainly employed in low-skilled jobs (although it is only fair to add that the jobs being lost were mainly in low-skilled industries like textiles).

To sum up, although some chambers of commerce like Lille and Valenciennes have developed into major actors in the local political economy (unlike the nearby Dunkirk chamber, dominated by USINOR) they cannot effectively secure redeployment and so are condemned in practice to try to organize a 'retreat in good order'.[18]

TRADE ASSOCIATIONS AND INDUSTRIAL RESCUE

As well as the chambers of commerce, the business community is represented at the regional level by an extension of the French peak business organization, the CNPF's Social and Economic Interindustrial Committee (CISE) and by a mass of trade associations. The most comprehensive of the textile associations is the *Groupement Régional des Industries Textiles*, which for a long time had a common head with CISE. The role of such bodies is to counteract the fragmentation of business organizations, both vis à vis the trade unions in collective bargaining and vis à vis the public authorities (covering matters such as foreign trade, taxation, prices and so forth). The textile industry in the Nord is especially fragmented into many distinct, semi-autonomous primary associations, with sometimes, superimposed on them, an especially powerful federal body like the Central Wool Committee. Such organizations have been very effective in defeating attempts by the sponsor Ministry of Industry's Textile Division to establish direct contact with the more dynamic textile firms. One such attempt was made through the Textile Industry Restructuring Committee (CIRIT), established in 1966, whose role was extended in January 1981 to become the Textile and Clothing Industry Restructuring Committee (CIRITH). Instead of the Ministry by-passing the trade associations, these have become the channel *par excellence* through which public funds for restructuring the textile industry have been disbursed. They have been used to eliminate weaker competitors and stimulate investment (which had fallen by two-thirds in 1973–8) among the survivors. It was estimated in 1978 that over two-thirds of the machinery then in use had been installed before 1950,[19] so that modernisation was long overdue.

The post-1974 crisis in the textile industry led to pressure upon the government to take protective and subsidizing measures through a succession of 'Textile and Clothing Plans', which were in fact an assemblage of piecemeal measures masquerading as a consistent, integrated programme of action. The protectionist measures 'including quotas and non-tariff barriers . . . as well as illegal quota arrangements and administrative devices designed to restrict trade', directed less at developing countries than at EC competitors (for example, subjecting Italian sweaters to import licensing under the guise of 'technical visas); or providing 'soft' Treasury loans under the CIASI scheme to 'lame ducks' threatened by bankruptcy. More positive intervention to encourage restructuring, re-equipment, research or exports may be provided directly through long-term low-interest or 'participatory' loans under the FSAI and CIDISE schemes.[20] The 1980 Textile and Clothing Plan, which designated them as 'strategic industries', enabled dynamic firms to secure development contracts from the Strategic Industries Development Committee (CODIS), the latter being absorbed, like CIDISE, by the Industrial Modernization Fund in 1983. Significantly, by January 1981, six of the first eight proposals for such contracts originated from the northern region.[21] The selfsame 'Plan' also increased the funds at the disposal of CIRITH by a quarter, but all these gestures amounted to slowing down the retreat to a socially acceptable speed rather than reversing it.

The Private Sector Proper: Major Firms and Minor Trade Unions

While the north of France is bedevilled by an atavistic and introspective concern with local and family rather than international and corporate business, with production rather than marketing, it is also a region with a tradition of being well organized. The major firms that have emerged are willing to deal directly with the central government. A striking example of this is the woollen textile firm of Prouvost based at Roubaix (the best known constituent being La Lainière, the original 1910 firm) which restructured itself in

December 1980, partly with a view to diversification but mainly to take advantage of the CODIS development contracts promised by President Giscard during his October 1980 visit to the north. It openly asked for low-interest loans to enable it to invest in textiles[22] and improve its productivity by reducing its labour force by wastage rather than redundancy. It has cooperated with the local authorities and the urban community in disposing of its surplus buildings, as well as renting or selling them to expanding local mail order firms like La Redoute or supermarket chains like Les Trois Suisses.

The civilized behaviour of Prouvost can be contrasted with that of the local 'Dalton brothers', the Willots, who from their Lille headquarters built up a ramshackle textile group by a ruthless policy of acquisition and asset-stripping, followed by mass redundancies, until—with the absorption of the cotton textile empire of Boussac—they bit off more than they could chew and were taken over, after government intervention, following bankruptcy in 1981. An example of a more responsible yet dynamic clothing firm is the largest ready-to-wear men's clothes manufacturer in France (and probably Europe), Bidermann, which was persuaded to build a factory close to Valenciennes in 1972 by the chairman of the chamber of commerce and negotiated with many of the various actors we have mentioned—DATAR, the regional prefecture, the tax authorities and the chamber of commerce—to see what aids and exemptions it could secure when deciding how big an extension to make.[23] Ironically, the French Government chose not to support Bidermann (even though it was financially backed by the public Industrial Development Institute) in its 1978 attempt to outbid the Willot brothers in their Boussac takeover.

Another illuminating contrast is afforded between the rival strategies of Prouvost—which has stayed loyal to textiles in the belief that it can survive the prolonged shakeout and profit from the demise of its French competitors—and Auchan, which largely abandoned its textile interests (with one major exception) to become France's second largest hypermarket distribution chain. Like Prouvost, it has remained loyal to the north, while expanding in France and abroad, but it is unusual in that the Mulliez family remains in control, whereas the founding family has been displaced with Prouvost. While its remaining link with textiles is Phildar, claiming to be the world's leading knitting-yarn firm, Auchan had risen from nothing in 1961 to 50 per cent of the Mulliez group's turnover in 1977 and over 70 per cent by 1981. The conversion of a former textile factory into a discount store in Roubaix, following an eye-opening visit to the

United States, with its pioneering mass distribution system, illustrated dramatically the redeployment strategy so successfully carried out by Gérard Mulliez. It was achieved without bothering to join either the CNPF or the chamber of commerce. (The secret of its commercial success appears to be its capacity to buy its goods on three-months credit while achieving a fifteen-day turnover . . . and an imaginatively conceived five-year 'rolling' expansion plan.) Auchan engaged in laborious negotiations with local authorities, from whom it wished to acquire land and whom it had to 'bribe' by agreeing to build infrastructures free of charge, in addition to what it offered them in taxation and employment. Although an upstart by comparison with nationally famous names of long standing like the Roubaix firm of La Redoute (which also has to negotiate with its local authority to expand on the spot), Auchan exemplifies the new balance of power, with the domination of distribution over production.

The contrast with steel is arresting. The prestigious steel masters of USINOR have been humbled and were in the late 1970s committed to trying to avoid bitter industrial strife by a policy of early retirement (at fifty-five or even fifty years of age) and transfer of workers to other firms belonging to the same Denain Nord-Est Longwy group, notably the leading Valenciennes steel tube firm of Vallourec. This latter firm, which by a process of amalgamation had come by the end of the 1970s to control some 70 per cent of the French and 20 per cent of the European tube market, needed to modernize its original Anzin plant in the Valenciennes suburbs and had a tailor-made industrial estate nearby prepared for this purpose by the chamber of commerce. Vallourec took advantage of the facilities—financial and land use—to carry through at low cost a reorganization that was indispensable to its survival. Curiously enough, although it was part of the same group as USINOR, their relations were not good, owing to the resentment of the managers of the tube plants at their financial subordination to the traditionally arrogant steel masters. However, Vallourec was useful in helping USINOR find a home for some of its excess workers, thereby allowing it, with government support, to pursue a policy of 'retreat in good order'. It too faces the problem of running down the workforce in its old Anzin plant, so the help to establish a new plant may ensure the survival of Vallourec, but does not help Valenciennes' overall employment problem.[24]

The attempts at conducting the 'retreat in good order' have been fairly successful, despite outbursts of violence like the bitter confrontations in the steel towns of the Nord and of Lorraine in 1979.[25] The weakness of a divided trade union movement is part of the explanation; the displacement of immigrant workers is another contributory factor. (The discouragement of immigrant worker ghettoes in the cheap and poor housing of parts of Roubaix and Tourcoing has been an important part of their town planning schemes; the urban community, for example, helping to finance the building of middle-class flats in the Alma-Gare district of Roubaix.[25]) However, French employers have followed a deliberate policy of using their installation in new premises to break the hold of the Communist-led CGT, when it exists, or favouring the anti-Communist *Force Ouvrière* when a union is unavoidable. Auchan was exceptional in trying another approach to discouraging trade unionism: by promoting profit sharing, its employees owning 10 per cent of its shares. (One of the consequences appears to be that it has only half the 12 per cent absenteeism rate of the textile industry, which also mainly employs female labour.) It combines this with above average wages and a less hierarchical style of management–worker relations imported from the United States. An outright American incomer like Rank Xerox also pays well above average wages, partly aimed at deliberately 'creaming' the local labour market. Its 'Lille' subsidiary has an impressive 'social package' to maximize its attractiveness in terms of the working conditions and benefits it offers, but pays its way by having a low 'indirect' or non-productive percentage of its labour force. In these various ways, the potential veto power of the workers on the process of redeploying French industry has been nullified, although the need to avoid provoking unrest has led to an extension of the timescale and some sugaring of the pill of unemployment.

A very different inspiration—much more in harmony with the socialist traditions of the Nord—lies behind the establishment of a small worker cooperative in the Lille area, following the failure of a family firm in 1974. Manufacturing plastic tubes, the company (Isotube) employed a labour force of a hundred by the end of the 1960s, but it got into financial difficulties in 1972. The closure was followed by a worker occupation, although after eight months the number installed in the factory had fallen to eight. Thanks to financial assistance from the local authority (which bought the site), a loan from the *Société de Développement Régional* and public subscription, a worker cooperative called Marketube was established. After five years the workforce was twenty-nine, about the number to which it had fallen by 1974 when Isotube went bankrupt. Its productivity record has been excellent, increasing by 60 per cent, thanks notably to a substantial fall in absenteeism: 2–5 per cent compared with the customary 10–12 per cent. Producer cooperatives have increased in number from 1981 to 1983 in the wake of increasing recession bankruptcies and under the benevolent eye of a Left-wing government. In 1981, 255 were established (employing 3,538 people), 299 in 1982 (4,897 employed) with only slightly fewer in 1983, making a grand total at the end of 1983 of 1,269 producer cooperatives employing 40,423, of which 61 per cent were members and not just employees. As 60 per cent of the cooperators are under forty years of age, this is a modest but promising development, although it is a long way from achieving the 'cooperative republic' envisaged by Charles Gide at the turn of the century.[27]

Grants, Loans and Tax Concessions

A striking aspect of the subsidies provided centrally, regionally and locally to influence the locational behaviour of firms is that little is known by the public bodies providing the financial incentives about how effective they are in achieving their objectives. This is not an exceptional feature of public action either in France or in any political system. However, there has been some concern in recent years over public ignorance about the cost of securing jobs as against paying unemployment benefit, although calculating the additional cost of locating the job in certain areas has thus far proved to present insuperable problems. While in 1980 it was estimated that the cost per job created in France averaged about 60,000–70,000 francs, this very approximate guesstimate varied tremendously; for example, in some branches of the chemical industry, involving highly sophisticated capital equipment, the cost per job might rise as high as 2.6 million francs, while in the clothing industry (important in Roubaix and Tourcoing) it might fall to as low as 31,000 francs. This DATAR estimate would also vary between a job created in a new factory compared with an additional job when an existing factory has expanded its labour force, the cost being some 10–20 per cent higher in the case of a new factory.[28]

Because this study was conducted before the May 1982 reform of local and regional financial incentives to investment and job creation, it is important to preface the discussion by an outline of the new arrangements, which essentially consist of a conflation of the previous incentives and an increase in the rates of incentive to restore their real value, eroded by inflation.[29] Two new incentives—a Regional Development Grant and a Regional Employment Grant—have replaced six previous incentive schemes, the first four of which are discussed below. They were the Special Industrial Adaptation Fund, the Regional Development Grant, the Location of Service Activities Grant, the Research Activities Locational Grant, as well as Special Rural Aid and the Decentralization Subsidy. The first four are combined in the post-1982 Regional Development Grant (RDG) covering industry, the service sector and research (although they continue to have different 'maps' of rates of grant), whereas the Regional Employment Grant is available to small firms throughout France. Most applications for the RDG are dealt with by the regional council (which keeps the prefect informed) but the more costly projects are decided by the Minister for Planning and Regional Policy on the advice of the Interministerial Committee for Aid to the Localization of Activities, under the chairmanship of the head of DATAR. On it are also represented the Treasury, Budget, Tax and Competition Divisions of the Finance Ministry, the Ministry of Industry, the Employment Agency (*Délégation à l'Emploi*) and the Planning Commissariat. The Regional Employment Grant (REG) is the responsibility of the president of each of the regional councils, although in many regions decisions are made on the advice of a regional committee on whch are represented the regional field services of ministries that participate in the Interministerial Committee described above, together with the regional and departmental prefects and representatives of the region's economic and social committee. So, despite changes in the organization to give greater weight to the elected regional politicians, to simplify the procedures and to place greater emphasis on the needs of small firms, from whom the greatest prospects of job creation were anticipated, there has been no fundamental change from the pre-1982 arrangements to which we turn.

The Special National Scheme: FSAI

Given the risks involved in taking on more labour and the competition between countries, regions and towns to attract employment, there were a bewildering complex variety of subsidies available. In France, before 1982, about a hundred relatively important ones were identified and there were some twenty-eight bodies responsible for helping businessmen to take advantage of them. At the end of the 1970s, of about 100,000 jobs created annually, 60,000 were directly subsidized by central government grants to the tune of 24,000 francs per job. If the FSAI (Special Industrial Adaptation Fund) loans entitling the state to a share in profits are added, this figure rose to 37,000 francs per job. Whereas firms in the Lille conurbation would only in exceptional circumstances (massive closures in the textile areas of Roubaix and Tourcoing) have been eligible to receive FSAI assistance, those in Valenciennes were fully entitled to benefit from its provisions. In 1979, the national figure of jobs firms had promised to create under the FSAI scheme numbered 16,894 (costing 1.7 billion francs, but resulting in 5.8 billion francs worth of investment), of which 3,968 jobs were to be located in the Valenciennes area. Much the most important single project was the Peugot gear box plant (2,700 jobs) on a Valenciennes industrial estate to which we referred earlier, and it is worth mentioning that the decision to establish the plant as a subsidiary, SMAN (*Société de Mécanique Automobile du Nord*), owned 75 per cent by Peugeot, 20 per cent by Talbot and 5 per cent by Citroën, was the direct result of the financial subsidies received. It was convenient to link the assistance received for the project specifically to the financial management of the plant, even though it worked for all practical purposes as a Peugeot firm.

Although, the FSAI grant/loan scheme was only launched in September 1978, it quickly became disproportionately important in the selected parts of France (especially the Nord and Lorraine) for two reasons. Firstly, it speeded up the process of according subsidies to meet the crisis in the steel and shipbuilding industries. Chrysler France (taken over by Peugeot in August 1978) initially proposed to establish a gear box plant alongside its factory at La Rochelle. However, Peugeot decided in October 1978 to consider other locations partly because it preferred more manageable production units and was interested in going where subsidies were attractive. DATAR quickly steered it towards Longwy and Lille–Valenciennes. In December 1978, five sites proposed by APEX in the Valenciennes area were visited incognito by the director of Peugeot's Industrial Division a few days before the President of the Republic and Prime Minister promised 'important industrial projects for the Nord' generally and Valenciennes in particular, itself followed by USINOR announcing 5,900 redundancies in the area. By the end of December 1978, the chamber of commerce provided an attractive site (see p. 145) and by mid-January 1979 agreement was reached with the Prime Minister to establish a gear box plant employing 2,500 by 1985 in the vicinity of Valenciennes. The preceding month involved intense negotiations between Peugeot and the heads of FSAI, of DATAR and the member of the Treasury Division who was secretary of *Crédit National*. In February and April 1979, discreet visits by a high-level team from Peugeot, headed by the president and managing director, were followed by hard negotiations from 18 April to secure the regulatory, physical and financial concessions on the site chosen, culminating in the 28 June 1979 signature of the purchase of the land by SMAN/Peugeot from the chamber of commerce. A month later, the financial details were settled, the total investment being increased from 1.206 to 1.344 billion francs and the number of jobs by 1985 from 2,500 to 2,700. So, what APEX described as a decision made in 'record time'[30] took ten months from the date when Peugeot became seriously interested in locating its plant in the Nord.

Secondly, the FSAI scheme offered terms that were sufficiently attractive to make the areas selected internationally competitive with the very generous subsidies offered by most other EC countries, although still way behind Ireland. Initially endowed with 3 billion francs, FSAI divided its funds equally to subsidize job creation in areas subjected to massive and concentrated redundancy by making capital grants and offering soft profit-sharing loans. Provided that a minimum of 50 industrial jobs were created either by installation, extension or diversification within three years, the firm could have up to 50 per cent of its investment financed, half in the form of a capital grant, half by a twenty-year profit-sharing soft loan (partly at the very advantageous interest rate of 5 per cent and partly dependent upon the firm's profits, but never as a whole exceeding the prevailing 'normal' long-term rate of interest). Reimbursement could be deferred from three to five years at the start of a project, given the time it would take a firm to 'run in' its new plant. Thus, it was anticipated that the SMAN/Peugeot factory would take some four years to become fully operative.

In the firms in our sample, it is clear that the rules were applied flexibly both in terms of the minimum number of jobs created, the maximum time allowed for the job to materialize and the actual financial package negotiated as well as the imposition of financial penalties. In the case of SMAN/Peugeot, 50 per cent of its investment cost was met by the central government through the FSAI scheme, in addition to which it received a five-year loan of 210 million francs from the EC. (The latter was related to the fact that fifty of the first five hundred of the labour force hired consisted of redundant steelworkers from USINOR.) Although the incoming firm received part of its subsidy at the outset (the customary one-third in the case of SMAN/Peugeot, notably the profit-sharing element), there was usually some time lag between spending and the firm's receipt of its funds, given that the government wished to be sure that the employment commitments will be honoured, so in inflationary times this materially reduces the value of the subsidies. Two smaller firms in our sample that were unable to meet their job creation targets (a small-scale Italian subsidiary manufacturing car radiators and air-conditioning equipment, and a medium-sized French family firm producing household linen) suffered substantial clawbacks because of their failure to fulfil the stipulated conditions. The head of the family firm stated categorically that he had taken the decision to expand his production without worrying about the subsidy offered. Inability to foresee future market conditions had meant that he had been compelled to declare redundant some of the workers he had employed, with expensive consequences that exceeded the subsidies he had received. He was denied two-thirds of his 0.5 million-franc grant and although he received his 1 million-franc profit-sharing loan, he complained about the rate of interest levied. This illustrates a point often made in discussing locational subsidies generally: it is the large firms that take fullest advantage of the capital grant and soft loan schemes offered and that usually benefit most from them. This is partly because they have more room for manoeuvre. They can go abroad if they are not offered the best rate of subsidy and they can lay claim to hold their own in the international market more plausibly, although this is not necessarily true in practice.

Subsidies under the FSAI scheme could not be combined in principle—although they could exceptionally in practice—with those under the more generally available Regional Development Grant (which prior to FSAI accounted for almost half of regional incentives funds) or with the much more modest service and research activities grant schemes. However, it could be combined with all other incentives, notably tax abatements to which we shall turn later. Two firms in our sample illustrate how the two grants could be cumulated. A small to medium-sized aeronautical ball-bearing firm that moved from the Paris suburbs to a Valenciennes industrial estate was able to add a FSAI grant for an extension in 1979 to its initial 1978 Regional Development Grant for start-up, as did a large subsidiary (Corona) of the US firm Pittsburg Paint and Glass that secured maximum grants for two extensions in the Valenciennes area. (It is only fair to point out that the former received the full amount of aid even though it did not quite reach its job creation target on time, when it increased the target to take advantage of the higher FSAI grant.)

The Regional Development Grant

Whereas FSAI was an expedient to assist the areas hit by catastrophic decline of their mono-industrial sources of employment, which like many expedients was extended beyond its initial brief life span, the PDR (*Prime de Développement Régional* or Regional Development Grant) was the mainstay of French regional subsidy policy, dating back to the pre-recession period of rapid economic growth. Nationally, in 1979, 707 million francs were granted to subsidize 47,368 jobs at an average cost of 15,000 francs per job, although in some cases the grant rose to 25,000 francs per job. In the preceding fifteen years, some 7,600 projects had been subsidized involving some 530,000 jobs.[31] The almost exclusive beneficiaries of the PDR were manufacturing firms that were setting up or extending their activities, but firms in declining industries that have been taken over and switched to new products were also eligible, although in those cases it was jobs preserved rather than jobs created that counted.

In the northern region as a whole, over the six years 1972–7, 380 million francs of PDR were provided, with the expectation that 4.5 billion francs would be invested and 28,000 jobs created by the end of the 1970s. The peak years were 1974 and 1977, with large programmes being particularly dominant in 1974, although they have predominated at all times. Another feature of the PDR in the Nord has been the fact that compared with firms setting up, extensions accounted for 73 per cent of job creations and 90 per cent of investments. This contrast has been accentuated in the post-1974 period, with entrepreneurs adopting an increasingly prudent attitude, preferring modest extensions to starting afresh. In terms of the locations favoured by PDR, it is clear that the mining areas received the lion's share of the grants in this period, rather than Lille or even Valenciennes. As far as the industrial spread was concerned, a few automobile firms received nearly two-thirds (65 per cent) in value of all grants made, although they accounted for only fifteen out of the 119 successful projects. They were committed to investing

2,792 million francs and creating 17,000 jobs. There was a marked contrast with two other industries that are prominently represented in the area—textiles and clothing. Textile firms (excluding synthetic and artificial fibres) accounted for only 2.6 per cent of the grants by value and created fewer than 1,000 jobs. Clothing firms also benefitted to a very modest extent, receiving less than 1 per cent of all grants by value. Although these two industries together accounted for thirty-five out of the 119 successful projects, they created relatively few jobs and the amount invested was low (35,000 francs per head compared with 162,000 francs on average for all industries). While it is difficult to make accurate calculations of the rate of attainment of the commitments made by firms because there is unreliable information on projects that failed to materialize, underachieved or—as sometimes occurred—exceeded their targets, it has been estimated that about 75 per cent of the big programmes in the Nord were successfully implemented in 1972–7.[32]

The award of a PDR was semi-automatic provided the conditions were met. However, the size of the grant—decided on the spot by the prefect on the advice of the Departmental Committee for the Encouragement of Employment when investment projects did not exceed 10 million francs and when it did by the Ministry of Finance on the advice of DATAR and a committee of the Economic and Social Development Fund—could be varied *à la tête du client* up to a maximum of 25 per cent of the investment. This was especially the case when the rules are being bent in terms of the award of a PDR to a firm locating outside the zone entitled to a grant. Firms usually resisted attempts by DATAR to steer them into the coalmining areas but sought to get as high a grant as if they had done so. Our ball-bearing firm was able, with the help of the Valenciennes Chamber of Commerce, to persuade DATAR to recommend a capital grant of 17.5 per cent of its investment as against the 20 per cent offered had it agreed to locate in Béthune. It received 25,000 francs per job created. In the case of Rank Xerox, benefitting from the big name magic which might be expected to act as a magnet to other firms (although it was made explicit that location was not influenced by the amount of grant received), it was able to secure a 10 per cent capital grant although just outside Tourcoing (itself not entitled to benefit from PDR) thanks to the head of DATAR using his influence with the Ministry of Finance.

The grant was subsequently reduced to 8 per cent as a penalty for not achieving its job creation target on time. Instead of creating 700 jobs, the target was reduced to 400 and Rank Xerox was allowed an eighteen-month extension in the time allowed to achieve this lower target. The firm's problem was that it had intended to transfer production from its overloaded British subsidiary, but the recession meant that such a transfer would have led to unemployment there, so the plant in the Lille conurbation had to switch provisionally to reconditioning/refurbishing second-hand machines, most of which were exported to second and third world countries. By 1980, Rank Xerox attained its original manpower target of 700 jobs, but this was too late to avoid the clawback of one-fifth of its PDR. Like the earlier reference to two firms penalized for non-fulfilment of stipulated conditions, this confirms Hull's work on this subject, cast in a comparative perspective. 'Although several countries have clawback conditions in their incentive schemes, they often make little use of them. In France, by contrast, the Regional Development Grant clawback provisions are enforced with relative stringency; and indeed in recent years, the amount claimed back in any one year has been as high as 10 per cent of the total value of grants awarded in the same year—a figure far in excess of that found in any other European Community country.'[33] However, the public authorities have to be careful not to threaten the viability of the firm by the penalties imposed, a consideration that is clearly not relevant in the case of a multinational corporation, but is significant when dealing with a small or medium-sized local firm. The holding back of the second and third instalments of the PDR, pending the monitoring of attainments in terms of the capital investment made and jobs created, was thus a serious incentive to fulfil initial commitments (rewarded by payment of one-third of the grant within a month of the favourable decision).

Although we were not able in our small sample to observe the impact of two other regional incentives—the Location of Service Activities Grant (PLAT) and the Research Activities Localization Grant (PLAR)—they are worth mentioning for several reasons. Specific service-sector grants are rare even though this sector provides the main hope of preventing a rapid rise in unemployment consequent upon the shakeout in industry. Whereas service employment had a well below national average increase in the Nord region, it was the only sector that yielded a net increase in jobs in recent years. Provided thirty (or exceptionally fifteen) new jobs were created or greater decision-making autonomy of an industrial plant resulted from the transfer of service staff, 20,000 francs could be awarded per job in PDR areas but only 10,000 francs elsewhere. However, exceptionally (a word that crops up so frequently in

French regulations that one sometimes wonders whether it is not the discretionary exceptions that replace the rules) the grant can be increased by 5,000 or 10,000 francs per job, depending upon the attractiveness of the particular project being considered. Few such grants were made, and it has been suggested that the explanation is that service employment usually grows gradually rather than by discrete jumps.[34] As far as our case study is concerned, the main reason for its ineffectiveness is probably that almost all of the Lille conurbation, which attracts service firms, was only entitled to the lower rate of grant, while Valenciennes, which qualifies for the maximum PLAT was not attractive to service firms. In the case of the PLAR, the fact that the Lille conurbation was designated as a 'research development pole'—third to Paris and Lyon—meant that it qualified for the maximum grant. So far, the Lille area has not succeeded in fulfilling the regional council's ambitions of making its metropolis an effective pole of attraction for industry-related research.

Regional and Local Financial Incentives to Industry

In turning to regional council and local authority incentives, it is worth pointing out that there is a national, French significance in the specific case we are considering. Mauroy, Prime Minister from 1981–4 was undoubtedly influenced by his experience as mayor of Lille (which he remained) and president of the Nord Regional Council (from which he resigned in July 1981) in his Government's decentralization of certain incentives to the regional level and authorizing communes and *départements* to intervene for 'the protection of the economic and social interests' of their inhabitants short of taking shares in a commercial enterprise.[36] In July 1977, a decree authorized regional councils to make a grant, *Prime Régionale à la Création d'Entreprises Industrielles* (PRCEI), to industrial firms that had applied not more than three (later extended to six) months from their date of birth. The aim was to provide assistance to small and medium-sized firms which, it was realized, would have to bear the brunt of job creation, by contrast with the larger firms that tended to reduce employment by modernization and rationalization. The takeover of firms in difficulty could be treated as equivalent to setting up a new firm. Initially, the creation of six permanent jobs within two years secured a grant of 50,000 francs, but in 1980 the minimum number of jobs was reduced to three, while six jobs secured a 'major grant' of 100,000 francs. The applicant had to have a minimum capital of 70,000 francs to secure an ordinary grant and 100,000 francs to secure a major grant. The ordinary grant is payable as soon as the decision is made, whereas the major grant is paid in two instalments: half immediately and half when the fourth employee is hired. If the jobs created do not last at least two years or if the firm moves out of the region, the grant must be restituted.

The Nord Regional Council set aside 2 million francs in 1978 and 1979 to cover the cost and decided that firms from any part of the region could receive grants. In 1979, eighty-three applications were received, of which thirty-three were accepted, thirty-seven rejected and seventeen were pending (two and a half months being on average required to process an application). Predictably, textiles and clothing led the field in terms of the sector to which grants were made, but metallurgical and electronic firms were also well to the fore. Of applications turned down, the main reasons were that the new firm was simply a purchase or extension of an old firm; because it was a subsidiary of another firm; or because it was non-industrial. Whereas in 1978 the beneficiary firms in the Nord were almost exclusively from the Lille area, by 1979 successful applications were much more widely distributed, although Valenciennes managed only one successful applicant firm despite seventeen letters of intent and seven formal applications in 1978–9. The region generally has a below-national-average number of successful applicants, and it would seem clear that before 1981 the PRCEI did not have any significant impact on the setting up of industrial firms.[35]

Maximum exemption from the local business tax (the *taxe professionnelle*, subject of much bitter recrimination by business organizations) is usually automatically given to all industrial and service firms that meet the PDR conditions discussed earlier. It is no longer necessary to secure the agreement of the Budget Division of the Ministry of Finance or local tax officials if the local authority is willing to make the concession. The political complexion of the local authority—whether Communist, Socialist or Right-wing—seems to have no affect on its willingness to exempt business temporarily from local taxes, ideology very definitely taking second place to the need to promote local industry and future tax revenue. The tax exemption runs for five years and is available both from the *département* and from the commune; since 1981 it is also obtainable from the region. The advantage is not as great for a firm like SMAN/Peugeot, which argues that it needs five years to run in and will only just be in full production when it has to face the *taxe professionnelle* bill.

Furthermore, Vallourec claimed that it received exemption only for three years from when the first stone of its new plant was laid, so it too did not feel itself to have been generously treated.

Because of the wide variation in rates of local business tax, it may be more advantageous for a firm to locate where the tax is low, irrespective of whether or not a concession is offered. Within the Lille Urban Community, while at first sight the disparity between the commune with the highest and lowest local tax is 1:40 and is growing, being five times larger in 1977 than it was in 1968, this is misleading. Only very few communes are at the extremes. If one adds the flat-rate *département* and urban community taxes, the disparity shrinks from 1:4. Furthermore, in 1977, the municipal *taxe professionnelle* in Lille was 8.18 compared with 9.04 per cent in Valenciennes, so the difference in practice is not very great.[37] As local business tax can be off-set against corporation profits tax, the value of the temporary exemption is substantially reduced. However, its attraction to the local authorities is twofold: it is psychologically easier to forego income than to spend by making a grant and it gives the local politicians a *feeling* that they can themselves influence the businessmen's location decisions. Whereas it is sometimes argued that France has less of a 'package' approach to regional incentives,[38] this neglects the role of banks, of APEX and of the chambers of commerce in producing a *montage financier* out of the various forms of assistance available, guiding the bewildered entrepreneur through the jungle of grants, loans and tax exemptions, only the most important of which have been mentioned.

Land: Subsidies and Special Treatment

Some attention should also be accorded to the land and labour subsidies to firms when making their locational decisions. The Ministry of the Interior attempted to restrain imprudent local authorities from selling or leasing land on unduly favourable terms—up to 50 per cent subsidy being officially possible in an area eligible for Regional Development Grant, with repayments not normally extending beyond fifteen years[39]—but it was not always successful in doing so with the new generation of activist mayors preoccupied in dealing with the employment problems of their town. The availability and cost of land are major considerations, particularly to a firm located in Paris and seeking to expand its activities. Thus the ball-bearing firm that was refused permission to expand in another part of the Paris area (where it already had a small workshop) was tempted by the fact that land was nearly seven times less expensive in provincial towns like Bourges or Orleans. The cost of land was no lower in Valenciennes than it was in such towns (30 compared with 200 francs per square metre in the Paris region), but the solicitous industrial estate policy pursued by the chamber of commerce was an attraction. It deliberately set aside one industrial estate for smaller firms (by contrast with the tailor-made estates for specific large firms) which were keen not to be too close to plants that might become the focus for contagious industrial disputes. The ball-bearing firm mentioned as a particular merit of the estate on which it was located that most of the land adjacent to it was occupied by warehouses, so it was insulated from potential sources of industrial unrest. Thus, denied the ability to expand its seventy to eighty employees at the workshop in the Paris area (it had only been allowed a maximum of fifty, but DATAR never sent any officials to check) the firm sought a location not too close or too far from Paris, with a local airport that could be used by the managing director who had his own executive aeroplane and by the firm to send its high-value products by air freight. A further reason given by the firm for locating near Valenciennes was the lower cost of building, estimated at only one-half that of the United Kingdom, where it had a small subsidiary and which it contemplated expanding as an alternative, given its Rolls Royce market. However, the firm complained that the authorization to build was slow in coming, taking the maximum three months, but it admitted that construction work commenced even before notification was received.

Both this firm and Rank Xerox mentioned having ample space for expansion as part of the attraction of the site on which they located, the ball-bearing firm having leased the land from the *Crédit National* to which the chamber of commerce had sold it. In the case of Vallourec, although it was tempting for technical production reasons to transfer its new rolling mill to Dunkirk, adjacent to its parent USINOR, it was decided to remain close to its old factory, so that there would be no problem of transferring existing personnel. Furthermore, it preferred to send its tubes for export out through the port of Antwerp—with which it was directly linked by waterway—which was less often strike-bound and to use the excellent motorway links with Germany.

It is not only the cost of land that can entice a firm, obtaining exemption from land-use planning regulations and expensive adaptations to infrastructure are also significant attractions. The

Peugeot plant, which we have already discussed at length, illustrates in exemplary fashion a decision-making process involving political, administrative and industrial actors. Knowing that the gravity of the employment situation and the urgent need of the government and chamber of commerce to find alternative jobs put it in a strong bargaining position, Peugeot was able to dictate advantageous terms. Specifically in the land-use sphere, Peugeot succeeded in winning an impressive list of concessions relating to its preferred site. To meet the firm's requirements, the Valenciennes land-use planning committee agreed, in April 1979, to modify the SDAU, reclassifying 35 hectares of agricultural land as suitable for industry. At the same time, the Peugeot negotiators were able to obtain exemption from regulations covering land formerly occupied by an airfield; special arrangements for road and rail access to the plant; shifting gas and oxygen pipelines; modifications to the SDAU and POS; as well as specially favourable financial terms for the purchase of the 120-hectare site.

For a 'fire brigade' operation on this scale, not only are the negotiations conducted at the highest level but a high price must be paid. Furthermore, dealing quickly with a short-term problem means that the pursuit of a consistent industrial policy takes second place with the result that the declining industries of the present are replaced with firms from a domestic automobile industry whose future itself seems precarious. The need for a speedy response also means that overcoming political or ideological reticence, which would normally require years of discussion, is achieved quickly. In the Peugeot case, all the actors—including the Communist-controlled municipality within whose boundaries the plant was located—cooperated to attract the firm and ease all the difficulties it raised. In a few days, all the official obstacles were eliminated and the red carpet rolled out for the creator of employment! Urban development master plans and land-use plans could not be allowed to stand in the way of several hundred, still less several thousand jobs. Such planning documents can guide the choices made by firms, but they do not constitute a rigid framework once jobs are at stake and the investment is substantial. A feature of the decision-making timetable eloquently illustrates the point. Although all the financial details and the agreement were settled in June 1979, the public inquiry took place after the event from September to November 1979. Its only purpose was to ratify a *fait accompli*.

Labour Cost Subsidies

Although the French government, like other governments, has made a financial effort at directly subsidizing labour as a way of counteracting the particular sectoral and geographical incidence of unemployment, as well as using it unselectively (notably through three successive *Pactes pour l'Emploi*),[40] the evidence from some firms in our sample suggests a number of cautionary remarks. Firstly, it is the least skilled work that is decentralized, both in the sense that it is low-value products that are least demanding of skilled work that are allocated to the relocated plants and that the locally recruited labour force tends to consist of the least skilled workers. Technicians, foremen, etc. are either transferred from the company's other factories or are recruited from outside the area. This was certainly the case in the Vallourec and SMAN/Peugeot cases. Where, as in the case of the ball-bearing firm, it was deliberately decided to make a break with the prevailing acrimonious and conflict-ridden industrial relations, not merely were few people transferred to Valenciennes, but the inexperienced, locally recruited workers (55 per cent female) were not sent for training to the parent factory, for fear of contamination. The price paid, in terms of low productivity, was devastating and not anticipated by the management. It was estimated that initially productivity was at least 30 per cent lower than that of the plant in the Paris suburbs. This was not because of unwillingness to exert effort, the Valenciennes labour force living up to the reputation of *Nordistes* for hard work. Particularly important was the loss of time owing to the lack of dexterity that would only be acquired after two to three years experience, despite the fact that the least sophisticated product was the one transferred.

However—and this is the second cautionary point that puts labour subsidies in a modest light—the wage bill in the Valenciennes plant was estimated to be 30–40 per cent lower than in the plant in the Paris suburbs. So, despite the initially low productivity and even though it was claimed that no attempt was made to exploit the situation of local job scarcity (the average Valenciennes wage rates prevailing being paid, as communicated by the local *Chambre Syndical de la Métallurgie*),[41] it proved to be a profitable move and one that would become increasingly profitable in terms of wage costs in the medium term.

Summing up on financial subsidies, it seems that firms are keen to collect whatever aid they are entitled to receive and are sometimes able unofficially to extract even more than that, without this playing a major part *on its own* in determining their decision to set up as such or even their precise choice of location. Except for the unscrupulous or desperate firm that sees the operation in short-term perspective (getting out as soon as possible once subsidies are pocketed or as a source of cashflow when facing imminent bankruptcy), the factors other than initial or temporary financial assistance are of far more decisive importance. The frequency with which these regional financial incentives have been modified in the quarter of a century since they were first launched in France suggests that, in the absence of an ability to evaluate their effectiveness in attaining their objectives, incremental and expediential improvization is adopted as a series of piecemeal political gestures to persuade the public that their leaders are intervening to protect them. What is clear is that unless linked with a strategy, regional financial incentives cannot be regarded as much more than a dubiously effective panacea. Only when conceived as a set of pump-priming instruments in the service of a grand design—whether 'retreating in good order' or 'redeployment to meet the impact of international competition'—do such incentives take on their full meaning. When the contrast is made between the number of jobs lost and the number of jobs being created (not those proclaimed by bodies like APEX as 'decided', although even these are far below the replacement level) the disparity is arresting. As the Valenciennes Chamber of Commerce put the prospects to a parliamentary committee of inquiry on the steel industry: 'If in the eight years from 1975 to 1983, new industries do not set up offering a massive number of new jobs, the Valenciennes area risks losing directly and indirectly some 25,000 male jobs or 30 per cent of the active masculine population in 1975. As these are the jobs of bread-winning heads of families, this would lead eventually to the departure from the area of 75,000 people, which would be literally intolerable.'[42]

Regional incentive grants in France have, before and after the 1982 reforms, been essentially job-related. More specifically, they have 'tended simply to compensate for the local effects on employment of industrial redeployment'.[43] Particularly at a time when there was a shortage of labour, the main motivation of firms to move into an area was not the offer of a financial incentive. A study by the Paris Chamber of Commerce has showed that the availability of workers was important for 83 per cent of large and 69 per cent of small firms; good transport facilities for 82 per cent of large and 62 per cent of small firms; suitable housing, 60 per cent of large and 42 per cent of small firms; and proximity to head office and Paris, 56 per cent of large and about 45 per cent of small firms.[44] Furthermore, the disparity between the number of jobs that beneficiaries of incentive grants have agreed to offer and those effectively offered has continued to increase. For the major agreements negotiated in Paris, it is estimated that 80 per cent of Regional Development Grants led subsequently to discussions between the firm and the public authorities with the threat of a clawback of part of the grant because of the non-attainment of the job target commitments. At the local level, it was officially estimated in 1978—before the worst of the recession—that the jobs effectively established amounted to 56 per cent of the target in the Puy de Dôme, 50 per cent in Maine et Loire, 35 per cent in Loire-Atlantique and 25 per cent in Ille et Vilaine![45] This alarming gap between the commitments made and their implementation underlines the fact that despite the efforts of political, administrative and banking actors, the managers of firms themselves ultimately determine whether investments are made and jobs are created. It is their success or failure that determines whether the jobs created are ephemeral or simply the first increment of expanding employment. In practice, the public actors have been concerned more with desperate fire-fighting activities to help preserve jobs in firms suffering severe financial difficulties than in stimulating new ventures.

The members of the local industrial policy community are not all on the same footing. As far as certain firms are concerned, partial or total disengagement from the area may be elementary economic sense. For firms like Vallourec, it is rational to use the financial incentives offered to reduce the cost of adapting itself to the new competitive market conditions by modernizing its plant, and it can be influenced—other things being almost equal—into doing so on the spot rather than moving elsewhere. The local political and economic representative bodies, however, are irretrievably committed to the area and cannot regard its fate as a matter of 'indifference' in the sense in which this term is used by economists. Disengagement is not an option available to them except as a corollary of ruin. However, these local actors are not the masters of either their political or economic fate. Whereas major foreign or even French firms can take advantage of the various incentives offered without allowing their behaviour to be manipulated in ways that conflict with their interests as profit-making enterprises, those that offer these incentives have been in a fairly weak bargaining position. Whereas fiscal penalties and licensing controls on firms that wish to locate outside the areas favoured by the public authorities can modify the bargaining context and lend additional support to the incentives offered, as long as the national government was not committed to more than a policy of retreating in good order from old industrial areas like Roubaix in the Lille conurbation or Valenciennes, firms could assume a 'take-it-or-leave-it' attitude. Up to now, most firms would seem to have adopted a 'leave-it' attitude to the incentives, except when they came as optional extras.

The institutionalized partnership within the local industrial policy community does not mean that common interests prevail over conflicting interests. The actors that belong to the 'state' side of the mixed economy usually have a much stronger commitment to the survival and regeneration within the existing locality of the activities that have provided local employment and income than have the predominantly market-oriented actors. In times of economic crisis, more or less footloose firms—particularly when they are subsidiaries of large national or multinational enterprises—can, with or without compunction, disengage on the basis of pecuniary calculation. Even employees can take the option of 'exit' when 'voice' has failed. Only the local political representative bodies are irretrievably committed to 'loyalty' because the 'local' public administrators and semi-public bankers can continue their careers elsewhere in the country. The fight to stem local economic decline must ultimately depend mainly upon the capacity and will of the democratically elected representatives of the local political community, rather than on those members of the industrial community to whom retreat offers an easier way out.

7
INCORPORATING THE PERIPHERY:
From Functionalist Regionalization to Contractual Partnership

If we are to place the post-war *péripéties* of French centre–periphery relations in succinct historical perspective, we must begin by alluding to an ever-instrusive theme whose persistence is indicative of a profound cultural anxiety. Precisely because France has perennially been the arena of more or less abrasive tensions between its society and its state, it has been necessary to emphasize and re-emphasize a spurious unity of the nation which a centuries-old effort at uniformity has failed to induce. This cultural myth, whose great nineteenth-century exponents were Michelet, Taine and—more subtly—the Breton Renan, with Debré and Sanguinetti as its unrepentant twentieth-century rearguard advocates, nationalized France's diverse past to suit present, standardizing modernity. It was expounded between the two world wars (in 1932) with characteristically detached fervour by Julien Benda, the mere title of whose *Esquisse d'une Histoire des Français dans leur Volonté d'être d'une Nation* itself speaks volumes! However, inductively imparting to the will of the people what is in fact deduced from the national requirements of a Parisian universality, it simply ignores the interacting dichotomies not merely between the French state and French society, but within each of these compendious entities. French society subsumes many contradictory forces, of which the urban–rural dichotomy and the capital–labour conflict are only two of those with the most obvious implications for state–society relations. Thus it is no surprise that a historian, who has studied the transformation of *Peasants into Frenchmen*, should argue that: 'patriotism was an urban thought, a handle for an urban conquest of the rural world that looked at times like colonial exploitation'. Broadening his perspective, Eugen Weber concluded his masterly survey of how provincial France was colonized by French officials as the administrative agents of acculturation by asserting that: 'the famous hexagon can itself be seen as a colonial empire shaped over the centuries: a complex of territories conquered, annexed, and integrated in a political and administrative whole, many of them with strongly developed national or regional personalities, some of them with traditions that were specifically un- or anti-French'.[1] While the nation is treated, for reasons of ideological expediency, as an indissoluble and long since integrated entity, Frenchmen remain sub-conscious of the fact that France is a multinational society upon which a unitary state has been superimposed.

The fact that France's periphery may have been incorporated, but has not been fully digested, directs our attention to other interacting dichotomies on the state side of the equation: between politics and administration, territory and function, deconcentration and decentralization. While politics and administration are—especially in France—so closely intermingled that talk of depoliticized, neutral and apolitical decision making is intended surreptitiously to persuade rather than impartially to describe politico-administrative reality, the key question is whether it is competitively elected politicians or competitively examined officials from the *grandes écoles* who are the senior partners at the periphery and the centre. In phrases that recall the internal colonial terminology invoked by Eugen Weber, Ezra Suleiman has explained (in terms that have tactfully disappeared from the French edition of his book) why most of the 'imperialistic' and 'tentacular' administrative elites—whether politically inclined to the Left or to the Right—are irretrievably committed to centralization. 'The elites are fundamentally opposed to greater participation and decentralization, not so much because they are imbued with a Jacobin ideology but because their own interests and positions would be harmed by a more decentralized structure.'[2] Symmetrically, most of the political notables—whether of the Right or of the Left—despite a frequently anti-Jacobin rhetoric, have sought to protect their local power bastions which are a prerequisite of enjoying a privileged collusive relationship with the local and national agents of the central bureaucracy. A salient consequence is what Pierre Grémion has called 'the paradox of centralization: the omnipotent central power is in reality a weak power ... the omnipresence of the central state does not guarantee its omnipotence. Formal centralization is circumvented by other forms of power that develop from the periphery as a result of the extension to it of uniform rules.'[3] It is in this sense of 'centralization', as the linkage between the would-be irresistable force of the French state and the until recently virtually immovable object of French society, that one should understand Hauriou's dictum: 'Do what one will, we will only change from one kind of centralization to another.'[4] Is this profoundly pessimistic assessment of the capacity for self-reform of the French state–society nexus justified? The post-1982 attempt at decentralization is a useful test of this proposition.

Regionalism and Regionalization

Before looking at the twentieth-century rise and fall of functionalist regionalization, it is important to recognize an obvious distinction. The regionalist economic, cultural and political pressures that emanate from the periphery are not to be confused with the regionalizing response from the centre, aimed at transforming the functional relations between central and deconcentrated administration, along with their *administrés*, rather than at territorial decentralization. While the twentieth-century emergence of regionalism suffered from the original sin of being associated with neo-Proudhonian ideas of politico-economic federalism based upon contractual bargains between autonomous regions, the dominant force in France hitherto has been an administrative regionalization of Parisian policies whose main purpose is to reinforce a central control perceived as threatened.[5] This has meant devising ways of disarming the ethnic, political and economic movements asserting an identity and interests separate from those decided upon at the centre, aimed at giving the centre a greater capacity to cope with problems assuming a regional form. The clarity of the discussion is not helped by the fact that in those parts of the French periphery with the strongest and most resilient sense of their own specific identity, the desire for autonomy is combined with an intense feeling of dependence upon the central government. As the remarkable political geographer and pioneer political scientist André Siegfried wrote in 1913, in Brittany 'the state is the *deus ex machina*, whose sovereign intervention is sought as soon as some problem threatens; it dispenses subsidies and assistance, it is the referee called upon to settle the most minor conflict, the rich and powerful protector who provides the money that one needs'.[6] Although at different times the call for increased central aid to the periphery or the desire for greater autonomy attains greater salience, to separate these two manifestations of the attitude of the incorporated towards the incorporator would be to neglect their interdependent character in favour of stressing alternative strategies for remedying a dependent status.

Curiously, the spotlight was focused upon 'functional regionalism', in the early 1960s, precisely at a time when in order to secure the institutionalization of the regions, its techno-bureaucratic protagonists were beginning to beat a prudent retreat. The emergence out of the shadows of a modernizing challenge, of which economic planning had been the main vehicle, was to involve an overt politicization that substantially contributed to the subsequent downfall of what one may describe as functionalist regionalization in opposition to the polemical bogey of politico-economic federalism. The sources of inspiration for this functionalist regionalization, associating 'the represented occupations in the organized regions' (the motto of Jean Hennessy's *Ligue de Représentation Professionnelle et d'Action Régionaliste*, launched in 1913), go back to the start of the twentieth century.[7] However, the person who publicized it after the Second World War was the geographer and regional planner Jean-François Gravier. His arrestingly entitled and influential *Paris et le Désert Français* (1947) was foreshadowed by a 1942 brochure in which he was already arguing that the nation's constituent communities needed to be mobilized to 'colonize' the 'deserts'; 'each of these intermediary bodies should be aroused, defended, represented and thought out'. Gravier went on in corporatist style to assert that interest group notables should be the principal interlocutors of the administration because 'some functions confer the right to incarnate a group better than any vote'.[8] However, it was not at the centre but in the periphery that the link between regional economic revival, functional representation and planned development was first advanced. The pioneer was the *Comité d'Etudes et de Liaison des Intérêts Bretons* (CELIB) in 1950, whose general secretary and driving force until 1967 was Joseph Martray, followed by others, notably the *Comité d'Etudes Régionales Economiques et Sociales* in the Nord in February 1953. Having first secured the support of the main official functionally representative bodies—chambers of commerce, of agriculture and *métiers*—as well as of the members of parliament, local authorities and the trade unions (the CGT did not join until 1961), the CELIB pressed in 1952 for a regional economic plan. The Planning Commissariat responded to the request for official collaboration and the result was the First Breton Plan of July 1953. However, Michel Phlipponneau, a geographer enrolled in the service of Brittany's revival, recognizing that Brittany could not expect privileged treatment, suggested that the national plan would need to be remodelled to become a synthesis of regional plans.

To contain this pressure and prevent the reduction of national planning to a mosaic of regional plans, while recognizing the need to give institutional expression to these regional demands, the Mendès France government gave prefects by decree in December 1954 the right to recognize regional economic expansion committees and specified which organization should be represented in them. This was followed by the June 1955 Edgar Faure–Pflimlin decrees establishing the regional action programmes which marked a recovery of the initiative by the central government, although this was merely a holding operation pending the central counterattack. Regional plans—such as the 1956 Breton Plan, the first to be published—were now prepared by government officials deliberately isolated in Paris, not by the unreliable regional economic expansion committees. Henceforth, 'By integrating the potentially obstreperous, autonomous regional representative organizations into an administratively dominant system, the mediators between regional economic interests and the government could be manipulated and converted into instruments of government policy, purportedly acting in the public interest'.[9] Characterized by a desire to counteract the effects of the Parisian magnet, the financial incentives associated with the 1954-5 regional reforms helped reduce Paris's share of new industrial development from 32 per cent in the early 1950s to 23 per cent in the late 1950s. Although 350,000 jobs were 'decentralized' in the period 1950–64, almost half of them went less than 200 kilometres away from Paris.[10] However, the 1960s were to be characterized by an attempt to shift the traditional centre–periphery altercation to a policy of *aménagement du territoire* in which the political authorities in Paris would formulate a national policy aimed at reconciling the conflicting interests of Paris and the provinces and advancing the projects of the Gaullist state.

The attraction of functional regionalization in the Gaullist decade of the Fifth Republic was that what were regarded as actually disruptive and potentially subversive decentralist regionalist forces might thereby be coopted to the task of modernizing France under the aegis of the principal agent of deconcentrated central authority, the prefect. The preparation for the central counterattack to recentralize regionalism was heralded by the 2 June 1960 decree standardizing administrative areas, followed in 1961 by an integration of national planning with regional economic development plans, and the institution of the administrative instruments of deconcentration embryo regional prefects (initially called 'coordinating prefects') and regional administrative conferences (initially called informally 'regional investment committees' and formally 'interdepartmental conferences'). The preliminary groundwork for the 1964 regional reforms was completed with the creation in February 1963 of the *Délégation à l'Aménagement du Territoire et à l'Action Régionale* (DATAR), the brainchild of Pompidou's *directeur de cabinet* (Ortoli) and a *chargé de mission* in his *cabinet* (Guichard, who was to become the first *délégué* while remaining a member of Pompidou's *cabinet*).[11] Thereafter the bureaucratic and interest group aspects of the 1964 reform went ahead. They were aimed respectively at giving the regional prefect effective control over the coordination of the public investment programmes of the individual spending ministries and substituting planned allocation for incrementalist *saupoudrage* on the one hand and avoiding accountability to elected regional councils, on the other hand, by establishing consultative regional economic development councils that would short-circuit the free regional economic expansion committees.

The equivocal nature of the centralist functional regionalization of the 1960s was not just a matter of utilizing national planning style techniques of 'concerted economy' to implicate trade unionists, along with other interest group representatives, in a Gaullist-style incorporatist 'participation', under the guise of both reducing regional disparities and increasing national-growth-with-moderate-inflation. It involved passing off an exercise in administrative deconcentration as a bold venture in decentralization, in the hope that administrative drive would be reconciled with representative consensus embodied in the new economic notables. This strategy failed because of bureaucratic resistance from within the very prefectoral corps that was supposed to impart the administrative impetus; because of interest group—especially trade union—refusal to go beyond a 'sceptical participation'[12] confined to a non-commital consultative role; because of the resurgence of 'demands for a real "decolonization" of the provinces', which the opposition political notables took up in defence of their threatened local power bases.[13] The 1965 local elections marked a significant early setback to the Gaullist incorporatist strategy, preparatory to its post-1969 reversal by Pompidou. 'The hope of a pro-Gaullist non-party elite yearning to be free of existing political organisms turned out to be a myth. Gaullists did well in those elections only in alliance with the traditional parties, and the CODER, which were to have allowed the new elites to take over French political life, instead fell into the hands of the old ones.'[14]

Prior to the May 'events' of 1968, it seemed that the 1964 reforms might still make headway. A contemporary assessment reached the interim conclusion that: 'whilst bureaucrats and technocrats, political *notables* and interest group leaders are in competition with each other, the former pair have in France succeeded in joining forces to impose a techno-bureaucratic regionalism in the interests of their political masters. For their part, the latter pair—owing particularly to the suspicions of the politicians and the reticence of the interest groups—have failed to create a countervailing force of representative regionalism capable of resisting the reassertion of executive supremacy.'[15] However, even before the May 1968 challenge to authority of all kinds, President de Gaulle had reached the conclusion, expounded in a March 1968 Lyon speech, that 'the centuries-old centralization efforts ... are no longer required' and that regional development would provide the necessary economic power without threatening the unity of the French state. Confronted by a challenge to his personal authority from an unexpected quarter and having successfully mastered it, de Gaulle decided to break the resistance of the old notables ensconced in the Senate and in the town halls by a simultaneous assault in the April 1969 referendum. An elaborate public relations consultation of regional elites preceded the referendum proposals, aimed at manipulating opinion into believing that the decisions on the size and boundaries of the regions, their powers, finance, representative and executive institutions were in conformity with grassroots preferences. The intention to combine territorial and functional representation at the regional level, on the model of an 'economic senate' which had long attracted de Gaulle as it had the early twentieth-century regionalists, was bolstered by the threat that if the referendum proposals were defeated de Gaulle would resign as President of the Republic. Despite substantial public support for the regional reform, the hostility of many interest groups to incorporation and the notables' fear that they might be modernized into impotence, led to a negative vote. This was facilitated by conservative voters, who welcomed rather than feared the prospect of the replacement of de Gaulle by Pompidou, joining the hostile left-wing electors.[16]

De Gaulle's maximalist reform having failed, Pompidou reverted to a minimalist strategy, the latter's instinctive conservatism being reinforced by the disaster that had swept his predecessors away along with his ambitious schemes. Despite the illusions temporarily encouraged by the 'new society' programme of Pompidou's first

Prime Minister, the *Girondin* Chaban-Delmas, it quickly became clear that the President had no intention of using regional reform to promote the modernization of France, a task he allotted to industrialization. In the 1972 legislation, the region was not to be conceived as a threat to the *départements* but as a mere union of *départements* for specialized public investment purposes. It was a framework for allocating public expenditure by *bartering on a departmental basis* between the field services of the central ministries, the departmental prefects and the political notables, refereed by the regional prefect. This was part of the shift away from concentrating upon developing eight large provincial towns towards encouraging a multitude of medium-sized towns. Under the guise of developing contractual relations between the Parisian centre and the provincial periphery, this was in fact returning to old-fashioned *saupoudrage*, motivated by piecemeal improvization in the service of short-term political expediency. The mainly rural, traditional *notables*, who usually could be relied upon, were to be favoured rather than the dynamic, predominantly urban *forces vives*, although the reliance on DATAR to mastermind from the centre the creation of an industrial pole at Fos could be seen as a survival from the pre-Pompidou era. The original regional boundaries were preserved because they were favoured by the local politicians and interest groups, even though DATAR and the Planning Commissariat wanted to halve their number to facilitate economic programming. The result has been that the regional institutions have been surreptitiously by-passed both for forecasting purposes (the 1972 *Régina* five-region model used in the Seventh Plan) or major public investment schemes, entrusted to *ad hoc* agencies. The avoidance of a directly elected regional council in favour of a combination of ex-officio deputies and senators (in flagrant contradiction to the overt desire to avoid politicization, but covertly aimed at guaranteeing the political class a grip over regional representation) and indirectly elected local councillors, denied them the democratic legitimacy to challenge the central administrative will embodied in the regional prefect as head of the pivotally important regional executive. The ridiculously modest financial resources accorded to the regions, denied the status of local authority, completed the 1972 law's achievement of depriving the regions of their capacity to bite, if not to bark. 'The regions which have been created are too small as planning units, too uneven in size, too weak financially and too undemocratic institutionally.'[17] This rebuff to the experiments with the innovative instrumentality of functional regionalization needs to be placed in a wider interpretive framework, prior to speculating about the prospects for a democratic and decentralist regionalism under the Mitterrand presidency.

Giscard d'Estaing's rapid abandonment of his initial enthusiasm for elected regional councils in favour of Pompidou's preference for the *communes* and *départements*, was ironically reflected in his virtually simultaneous (November 1975) rejection of regionalization and creation of a Commission on the Development of Local Responsibilities under the chairmanship of Olivier Guichard architect of the 1964 reforms. In its report, the Guichard Commission frankly admitted: 'It is not so much that France has built its state as that this state has built France . . . the failure of attempts at deconcentration and decentralization are largely due to our confused conception of the state. . . . Every decision aimed at transferring a specific function from the central administration to an elected local authority is felt to be a "dismemberment of the state", a blow to its authority. . . . In French everything tends towards the state.'[18]

Although the report goes on to admit that 'the omnipresent state is not always predominant',[19] it does not face up to the consequences of the breakdown of the bureaucratic–notable system detected by Pierre Grémion. He attributes the main source of the decomposition of the old order to 'the divorce of the nation from the state and the slow dissolution of what the generations have created under the aegis of the state: ambition, the will to exercise power, the belief in reasonable action, the search for a way of settling disputes, the passion and illusion of the general will. . . . There is a crisis because the centrality of the state–nation is questioned at the very time that social groups have increasing recourse to its help.'[20] Using 'corporatist' in the French sense of 'sinister' sectional interest, Grémion describes the action of 'the corporatist centralizing state' as involving the gradual disintegration of the old bureaucratic–notable system under the pressures towards an omnipresent and omnicompetent state regulation that lacks the legitimacy of either the partisan democratic process or the disinterested, state idealist bureaucratic process or an intermediation between them. Functional regionalization has weakened the traditional decision-making process without effectively replacing it. There has been a resurgence of the local politician—especially the mayors of the larger towns—called upon to 'make peace in the corporatist jungle of which the administration has become an integral part and can no longer dominate' owing to 'the diminution in the state's capacity to arbitrate in an impartial way, the weakening in the administration's integrative role (although its pretention to integrate is increasingly proclaimed) and the devaluation of administrative channels when recourse is made to the centre.'[21]

Elsewhere, Grémion has convincingly argued that with 'the region having been transformed into the bulwark of the *départements* and the towns . . . the colonization of the regional level by the *départements* corresponds to the wish of the urban executives to disengage from the regions and have their hands free to negotiate directly with the central state', concluding that 'neither the prefects nor the city mayors have played the game of functional regionalism'.[22] This short-circuiting of functional regionalism, condoned and assisted by DATAR, was resisted by the *Service Régional and Urbain* of the Planning Commissariat. The Plan, as part of its attempt to rescue planning from the increasing discredit into which it was falling, developed the idea of *programmes d'action prioritaires* (PAPs), which as we shall see in the next chapter were to be the hard core of the Seventh Plan (1976–80), enjoying firm budgetary commitments and linking current and capital expenditure. Because an important part of public investment was regionalized, it made sense to develop a regional version of the PAPs, the *programme d'action prioritaires d'initiative régionale et locale* (PAPIR).

At the same time—1973–4—as national planning was being rethought, regional and local planning was being reconsidered in the light of the 1972 regional reform. It was felt that it was not enough to regionalize the national plan, which in terms of the PAPs meant that the regional prefects were asked to suggest how the programmes could be applied in their areas. As the national PAPs did not necessarily correspond to sub-national priorities, it should be possible for towns, *départements* or regions to initiate PAPIRs, for which they might receive state financial support provided they were prepared to contribute towards the cost themselves. In this way, it would be more likely that the real needs of local communities would be met and the programmes rationally administered in a deconcentrated or even a decentralized way. Like the inspiration behind the PAPs, it was hoped to introduce by procedural reform local action programmes that would have three defining characteristics. They would be problems selected as crucial by a political authority (a local or regional council) committed to carrying out the programme through successive budgets. They would cover both capital and current expenditure and have a precise timetable. They should include agreements with both state and non-state actors, such as chambers of commerce and voluntary associations, in the spirit of the 'Plan contracts' launched by the 23 December 1970 decree on urban communities.

Because of a political fear that a general invitation to local authorities to make programme proposals would arouse insatiable expectations and unleash a rash of embarrassing *cahiers de doléances*, it was felt to be safer to entrust the operation to the regional prefects, who chose their own ways of consulting local and regional notables, and selecting programmes to propose, characteristically tending to ensure that there was something for everyone. The Plan's Regional and Urban Service then discussed the proposals with each ministry in turn. This approach favoured mono-ministerial and sectoral rather than spatial projects. Some regions (for example, Languedoc-Roussillon, Provence–Alpes–Côte d'Azur, Auvergne) were so angry at the fate of their proposals—owing either to political resentments of Left-wing regional councils or regional prefects' fury at the changes made—that for all practical purposes they ceased to participate in the exercise. Partly on political grounds, Alsace did particularly well and Limousin especially badly. The end result was very untidy, some agreed programmes being abandoned, other unofficial programmes coming into existence.

A member of the Planning Commissariat's Regional and Urban Service has made a valuable study of the PAPIR experiment as part of a wider regional survey. He has shown that thirty-three of the eighty-nine PAPIRs did not fit the criteria for selection because nine programmes did not correspond to a real priority; ten programmes were priorities but had been imposed upon reluctant regions; five programmes were both imposed upon the regions and they were not priority projects either; nine programmes were too inadequate in scale to provide an 'added value' compared to non-priority programmes. In the event, the government accepted only a few of the programmes proposed by the regions and instead often compelled the regions to finance jointly projects that they did not regard as regional priorities. Only those regions like Nord Pas-de-Calais or Bretagne, which had constituted from their own resources funds that gave them financial room for manoeuvre, were able to *negotiate* in any real sense. The PAPIRs were able to play a part in the region's economic strategy where it existed (notably in Nord, Alsace, Aquitaine and Pays de la Loire). They sometimes took the form of coordinated operations, associating *départements* within a region or collaboration between regions. Last, they promoted planning and a willingness to enter into contracts for the joint financing of medium-term programmes with the central government.[23] However, this forlorn attempt to 'plan from below' did not survive the Seventh Plan; the attempt to graft decentralization upon functionalist regionalization provoked a predictable rejection during the Giscardian centralizing presidency.

The PAPIR fiasco was a striking demonstration that with recentralized regionalism through functional regionalization, the resistance from within the centre itself would prevent genuine deconcentration much less decentralization. Yet the leaders in the more self-assertive peripheral regions became increasingly conscious that: 'Under functional regionalism the outlook for the development of the periphery is that it will remain peripheral i.e. an adjunct to that of the politico-economic–administrative centre(s) of the national and international western capitalist system. As such it will be constantly subject to loss of political and economic vitality and to cultural assimilation . . . . Functional regionalism . . . could, indeed hardly have been expected to challenge political and cultural inequality of status, being itself a product of central dominance.'[24] This led in the 1970s to a resurgence of marginal, peripheral ethno-nationalism. As Grémion put it: 'The cultural crisis revealed and accentuated by the May 1968 "events" led to a rereading of the history of the French nation through the prism of internal colonization . . . . The functional regionalism of the 1960s was replaced by a grievance regionalism.'[25] However, this type of nationalist regionalism made little electoral impact, the political parties even more successfully resisting the challenge from this quarter than they fended off other challenges; notably from economic regionalism, linked with functional representation and democratic planning, championed by heterodox Left-wing politicians like Pierre Mendès France, some of the 1960s' clubs or the leaders of the Left Catholic CFTC on its way to mutating into the CFDT.[26]

For those—the vast majority—who think of regionalism as a subsidiary issue to matters that are regarded as of major concern, the widespread emphasis placed upon the priority need to decentralize through a democratic regionalism is a striking feature of the coming to power of the non-Communist Left in 1981, led by the Socialist Party. Having suffered exclusion for more than two decades from the centre, the Left have appreciated to the full—as did their predecessors under the Second Empire—the need to shake off the incorporatist embrace of the centre by developing more genuinely autonomous regions. This would mean destroying the old bureaucratic–notable system at both ends: ending the prefect's role as regional executive and replacing the old notables by directly elected regional councillors who would not be linked to the centre through the *cumul des mandats*. It would mean a rejection of both the Pompidolian–Giscardian traditionalist defence of the bureaucratic–notable system, based upon the *département*, and the technocratic-interest group functional regionalization experiments of the 1960s aimed at modernization through by-passing the democratic process, seen as bound to resist change. How far have the post-1981 reforms changed the behaviour of salient actors in the regional economic policy community, even before the direct election of regional councils in 1986?

Recentralizing Decentralization or Coordination by Contract?

There have been many discussions of the implications of the Defferre reforms of 1982–3, the more sophisticated among them tending to stress their continuity with the past rather than fundamental breaks with it.[27] Writing before these reforms were adopted, Ashford had pointed to the 'accumulating evidence that central–local relationships will increasingly be mediated through the fiscal and financial links between levels of government', due in part 'to the inability of higher decision-making agencies of government to monitor, guide and adjust policies as the role of the state expands'.[28] It was clearly tempting to see if—through contractual planning—some of the public burden could not be regionalized and localized, when it was not privatized outright. In such a context, it is not surprising that successive French governments since the 1960s, overcoming their legalistic scruples, have extended the techniques of *concertation* and contractual agreements, used first in their dealings with the state's private 'partners', to their dealings with public enterprises and local authorities. What they all have in common is the recognition that sovereignty is a legal fiction and that political and economic realities require governments to negotiate with autonomous or semi-autonomous actors upon whom it would be ill-advised simply to impose constraints. However, what one should not lose sight of is that the agents of the central government are above all concerned to use the contractual device to secure the attainment of their medium-term objectives. So, this choice of policy instruments is aimed at securing the willing collaboration of private and public actors by persuasion, usually supported by financial incentives, not merely in piecemeal decisions but in the implementation of general medium-term programmes, particularly investment projects.[29]

A decade before the post-1981 reforms, a major attempt was made during the Chaban-Delmas Government, inspired by the ideas of Simon Nora (well placed at his right hand to secure the implementation of his aims), to adopt 'more dispersed investment controls . . . to globalize subsidies in order to overcome resistance to globalized investments.'[30] The resistance came mainly and predictably from officials of the Ministry of Finance, operating through its departmental agents, the TPGs, concerned to protect its right to prior approval of local investment projects. However, the urban community and new town use of the contractual device as an instrument of nationally devised urban planning was extended in the early 1970s to medium-sized towns and during the Giscard presidency there was a 'minor explosion' of contractualization schemes. The rural contracts were followed—by a process of 'gradual erosion of the contract as a planning device of the centre, and the proliferation of smaller (-scale) contracts to be arranged by lower-level officials'—with 'contractual agreements for cultural programmes, greenspace, immigrant housing' and towns with a population of less than 20,000.[31] Ashford argues that: 'Each of the proliferating contractual schemes produced another fund and thereby another lever for interministerial bargaining and exchange', quoting in support (following the earlier example of *Fonds National d'Aménagement Foncier et d'Urbanisme*), the 1968 *Fonds d'Action Locale* and the 1975 *Fonds d'Equipement des Collectivités Locales*.[32] The latter became a bone of contention between the Ministries of the Interior and of Finance and raise two kinds of question about the pre-1981 use of the instrument of contractualization. Firstly, rather than diminishing control from Paris as Ashford claims, does the deconcentration of investment decisions not represent a case of dynamic conservatism, with the centre finding a more sophisticated way of exerting control? Secondly, does the Ministry of Finance's capacity to fight back—particularly in times of austerity in matters of public finance—not suggest that the dispersion of decision may belong to the world of appearance rather than reality, due to financial recentralization? We shall return to this latter question in connection with the increasing role of the *Caisse des Dépôts*, but first let us briefly consider the extent to which *contrats de plan* have modified the traditional relationship between the central authorities and the local 'authorities'.

Prior to 1981, one was entitled to be sceptical about the extent to which the overt tutelage by the prefect, intervening in judgements concerning the political and administrative desirability of local decisions, as well as the surreptitious financial tutelage of the TPG, was actually weakened by the development of a system of joint decision making which gave them an oversight of the local authority's development strategy. It was persuasively argued in 1976 that: 'tutelage is no longer the specific supervision over each act of a local authority but a general supervision over its investment policy. Similarly, it is no longer merely a "negative control", arising from a power to prevent but a dynamic power through which the state administration ensures that the local authority formulates its investment policy in conformity with that of the centre.'[33] The prefects traditionally played a pivotal part in the programming of local public investment, an official study of the Sixth Plan's (1971–5) experience roundly declaring: 'the mayors and other elected representatives found themselves bound hand and foot in the so-called debate on the plan which was often reduced to this: they are summoned (by the prefect) to a meeting (chaired by the prefect) where a *dossier* is distributed (prepared by state officials) whose content is known to them (because the prefect has spoken to them about it) and the prefect requests their agreement.'[34] This stress on the techno-bureaucratic *fait accompli* in the 1970s was an over-simplification. Still, the fear that local initiative in matters of ambitious medium-term investment programmes (covering both capital and current expenditure and including joint action by state and non-state actors) would arouse extravagant expectations did, we will see, undermine the imaginative Seventh Plan (1976–80) experiment with Regional Priority Action Programmes.

The 1982 reform of the French planning process, despite its claim that 'the new planning is democratic, contractual and decentralized',[35] has a great measure of continuity with the 1970s' experiments, although they have been taken further and are intended to be implemented with greater commitment. It was argued that 'local mobilization, both in the preparation of regional plans and regionalization of the twelve Priority Implementation Programmes (*Programmes Prioritaires d'Exécution* or PPEs, the new version of the old PAPs) would avoid past subordination of local preferences to central priorities. However, the concern to make local and central objectives compatible through the contractual process in the service of integrated development policies, meant that delicate problems of articulation between national, regional and local investment planning had to be surmounted. In the Second Report on the Ninth Plan, the adversarial potentialities for conflict between politically divergent central, regional and local authorities were to be overcome by a consensus-building process of discussion and commitment to joint financing of precise medium-term objectives. However, the possible bias in the choice of a policy instrument to give expression to what was presented as a balanced and egalitarian relationship, emerges from the official description of the planning contracts to be signed between the central and local authorities. 'The planning contract is an instrument for implementing the national and regional plans. Meeting point between the priorities of the national and regional plans, the planning contract . . . involves reciprocal commitments of two types: actions of particular interest to regions in which the parties are *associated in the implementation of the national plan within the framework of the PPEs*; actions of specifically regional concern which contribute to the attainment of *objectives compatible with those of the National Plan.*' It went on to stress that the association of regional and local authorities was intended to '*reinforce the operational content* of actions envisaged by the PPEs, for whose implementation *the state needed the cooperation of other partners.*'[36] Both the central and local authorities were to commit themselves to support financially the attainment of the objectives on which they had agreed and this will be one of the tests by which their performance will be judged.

Although the detailed negotiations were conducted by each regional commissioner of the republic (ex-prefect) with the president of the regional council, an interministerial committee under the chairmanship of the Prime Minister decided in December 1983 that 30 billion francs would be devoted to regional planning contracts. The detailed work at the centre was done by DATAR and the officials of the minister responsible for national and regional planning, who works in close association with the Prime Minister. While the regions on average devoted half of their budget to their share of funding the planning contracts, they received 1.67 francs from their central government 'partner' for every franc they contributed towards the cost. Those who benefitted most were not necessarily those who were politically close to the central government; for example, the Pays de la Loire, which had the good fortune to have as the president of its regional council the first head of DATAR, Olivier Guichard, used the new system of restructured intergovernmental financial relations to attract central funds. However, Prime Minister Mauroy's region of Nord Pas-de-Calais was only surpassed by the sensitive case of Corsica in securing a disproportionate share of the 6.5 billion francs allocated for 1984, obtaining 900 million francs (13.8 per cent) of the total. The bulk of the funds controlled by the *Fonds Interministériel d'Aménagement du Territoire* and the *Fonds Interministériel de Développement et d'Aménagement Rural* will be devoted to funding the regional planning contracts. All these financial commitments are reported annually in the Finance Act. This not only provides a measure of parliamentary accountability, it also reminds us, that despite the medium-term character of PPEs and planning contracts, they remain at the mercy of the Finance Ministry's capacity to introduce short-term changes of priority by imposing cuts in the central government's forward financial commitments. Furthermore, the government's decision in 1984 to switch the Synchrotron project from Strasbourg to Grenoble—despite the solemn signature of a planning contract with the Alsace region earlier that same year—was a cynical blow to the principle that such contracts were safe from short-sighted political expediency.

The other chosen financial instrument, which combines strategic control over information and money, as well as partially substituting a planning and banking power for prefectoral and ministerial power, is (among its other functions) the local authorities' bank: the *Caisse des Dépôts et Consignations*. Once again, there is an important element of pre and post-1981 continuity. The key change in the *Caisse's* activities occurred in the 1950s, under the aegis of François Bloch-Laîné, leading advocate of the notion of a 'concerted economy' in France, to which we have already alluded. Although the *Caisse's* current head is a former director of Prime Minister Mauroy's *cabinet*, Bloch-Laîné, and his successor (who each served for fifteen years) were former directors of the Treasury Division of the Finance Ministry. As Bloch-Laîné delicately expressed the close relationship with the Treasury: the *Caisse des Dépôts* 'can undertake what the government does not ask it to do, provided that the government is not hostile'.[37] The new style economic interventionism pioneered by Bloch-Laîné in the public entrepreneurial mode, concentrated upon the long-term financing of local authority public works and low-cost housing programmes, especially through joint enterprises with local authorities and private interests in which its subsidiaries, notably the SCET (*Société Centrale pour l'Equipement du Territoire*) was a minority shareholder. Whereas it presented itself as the 'ally' of the local authorities, the *Caisse* was a powerful instrument of central policy when taken in conjunction with the use of capital subsidies, without which local authorities are unlikely to receive a low-interest public loan. As Ashford put it: 'The investment subsidies are attached to the budgets of the various ministries who must then convert them into projects based on local proposals, under the financial supervision of the *Caisse des Dépôts* and the Ministry of Finance, and with the cooperation of the various local and departmental offices of the field services. Whether the subsidy has become the cement which holds the system together or the oppressive instrument of an over centralized government is perhaps the most intense controversy presently affecting French local government.'[38] Ashford makes clear that he takes the more positive view.

However, in the December 1982 report of the Lagrange commission (Roger Lagrange was Socialist mayor of Chalon-sur-Saône) the *Caisse* was severely criticized for its 'excessive centralism' and 'self-absorbed technocratic structures all too often remote from the real concerns of the local authorities' at whose service it was supposed to be. Since the dynamic days of Bloch-Laîné, the secular arms of the *Caisse* (20,000 staff) had lost impetus and efficiency. In addition to SCET and its 140 satellite joint enterprises, the main butt of the Lagrange report's criticism was the *Société Centrale Immobilière* and its 470 subsidiaries, especially in the low-cost housing HLM sector, involving it in the management of some 180,000 housing units and making it the largest building promoter and housing manager in Europe.[39] To bring the *Caisse* closer to its local authority customers and to correspond with the spirit of the new decentralizing legislation, its functional organization should be replaced by regional offices under the aegis of a holding company subsidiary, which was quickly established in March 1983: *Caisse des Dépôts—Développement*, known for short as C3D. Since 1960, regional offices had gradually been developed, numbering eighteen by 1980. Their function was to advise borrower local authorities on the credit facilities available to them, as well as to maintain close contact with the source of the *Caisse*'s funds (the savings banks) and the regional and local agents of the central government. By the end of the 1970s, the larger communes (over 100,000 population), *départements* and regions could receive general loans from the *Caisse* and its associate the *Caisse d'Aide à l'Equipement des Collectivités Locales* (CAECL), provided they negotiated the loan with the regional office after a joint examination of their needs and financial circumstances. These borrowers and the mass of smaller communes could also receive specific loans, but here the prior receipt of a state subsidy was crucial. The borrower was required to provide a variable proportion of the total sum according to whether the investment was subsidized by the state (only 20 per cent need be provided) by local or regional authorities (in which case 30 per cent had to be provided by the borrower). If no subsidy was secured, then the borrower had to provide 35 per cent of the cost of the project.[40]

After the Lagrange report, the *Caisse* was substantially reorganized to meet its criticisms. Significantly, the post of both Assistant Director General and Director General for Regional Development went to a former Director General of Local Authorities at the Ministry of the Interior, Pierre Richard, with a former head of the Plan's Financial Division and Finance Ministry official Jacques Delmas-Marsalet being appointed to take charge of its Finance Division. Richard denied that the *Caisse* was seeking to replace the old administrative tutelage by a new financial tutelage. He stated that as the local authorities' principal banker, the *Caisse*, would not presume to judge whether proposed projects were opportune, but only their financial implications. As two-thirds of central and local government investment is accounted for by the local authorities (with 85 per cent of the 60 per cent borrowed being funded by the *Caisse*, the savings banks and the *CAECL* in 1983), the stated willingness to advise but not impose the regionalized *Caisse*'s will on its local authority 'clients' is promising. However, Richard made clear that financial support for local authority investment schemes would be provided in conformity with the Plan's PPEs, while the *Caisse*'s pivotal role was backed up by its mass of statistical information, which it could use to guide the local authorities in their choice of investment programmes.[41] A powerful potential for financial coordination from the centre still exists to keep local programming in step with central planning, priorities and purposes.

It is tempting to see the 1980s as extending the earlier experiments in the substitution of low-constraint contract for high-constraint law. It could be presented as an approximation to Proudhon's mid-nineteenth-century vision of a decentralized system of autonomous economic associations and local authorities entering into free agreements with each other. 'In place of laws, we will put contracts .... Each citizen, each town, each industrial union will make its own laws. In place of political powers, we will put economic forces.'[42] What would seem to be emerging, more prosaically, is less reliance on a central, bureaucratic uniformity modified by piecemeal bargains between local notables and central officials. In their place, there is an attempt to use the regions to reconcile medium-term financial decision making at the national and local levels, so as to increase its compatibility, effectiveness and acceptability within and outside the economic policy community. The legalistic term 'contract' only partly disengages this new style of activity from the old framework of general law and bureaucratic intervention. To see how this semi-contractual approach can be fitted into the process of national economic planning in a context of endemic economic recession will be a major concern of the rest of this book.

8
REDEPLOYING RESOURCES:
Planning the French Economy or Planning the French State?

Twenty years ago, the importance of planning as an institution and as an activity was probably over-estimated. Although not quite at the summit of its prestige among decision makers and pervasive influence upon leaders of opinion, the Plan fitted well into a period of national economic revival and reinvigorated political ambition, within a context of international economic expansion and political détente. While allowance must be made for the gap between a somewhat pretentious rhetoric (intended to impress, and undoubtedly successful in this objective, partly because it coincided with a generally impressive economic performance) and a reality that was patchy, the claims that were made for the Plan as an institution had an undoubted plausibility. The French Plan won many unlikely friends both at home and abroad because it appeared to combine the virtues of a heroic style of policy making with a rationalistic analysis of the problems to be resolved. It sought to modernize a backward economy and conflict-ridden society without using coercion, by a process of economic policy community building and self-confident public leadership that was breath-taking in its boldness yet prudent in measuring what it was possible to achieve in the medium term.

In 1963, the government's counter-inflationary Stabilisation Plan (which de Gaulle boasted had been 'imposé à Giscard et autre Pompidou') marked the start of a series of reverses that undermined the credibility of the French Plan both inside and outside the public decision-making process; with the May 1968 'events', the oil crisis of 1973 and the election to the presidency in 1974 of Giscard d'Estaing—whose personal disbelief in planning and frequent interventions in decision making were unmistakable signals that henceforth it was enough to 'manage the unforeseeable'—representing some of the decisive steps in the degeneration of the Plan's image as the prime instrument of the national strategy and the programme of action to be implemented in the public and private sectors. Until the Mitterrand victory of 1981, the Plan was widely regarded as discredited but it did not merit the depths of its abasement any more than—in retrospect—it merited the heights of its earlier apotheosis. Much of the difference was the result of the previous 'myth' of the Plan having been dissipated, even though the reality—if only for reasons of political and administrative inertia— had not changed to anything like the same extent. The phrase that caught the imagination in the 1960s was spoken by General de Gaulle but prepared in the Planning Commissariat and amended by the then Prime Minister, Michel Debré to be somewhat less misleading than in its original formulation. As the former Planning Commissioner, Michel Albert, has recalled, the original formula— *'obligation ardente'*—was reversed by the punctilious Michel Debré 'to make clear that the Plan has a political rather than a legal character'.[1] It was still widely misinterpreted and as the ardour of the successive Presidents of the Republic ebbed the planners found it increasingly difficult to secure the high-level support that is essential to impart the necessary impetus to securing the implementation of their plans. Even the sceptical Georges Pompidou and his *cabinet* kept in close touch with the Planning Commissioner—who he made sure was a former close collaborator of his—so that there was a sense that the necessary political backing could be secured for policies connected with the Plan's objectives.

However, as economic policy making was concentrated increasingly in the hands of the President and his staff, it was harder to disguise the fact that the Plan was that of the government rather than of the nation and as circumstances or the government's priorities changed the commitments ceased to be much more than expressions of provisional intentions. So, paradoxically, increased political control was combined with decreased political commitment. The Planning Commissioner's membership of the Central Planning Council, instituted by President Giscard in 1974, provided regular monthly occasions for the concerns of the Planning Commissariat to be ventilated at the highest level, but the Planning Commissioner tended to be informed rather than fully share in decision making. The *ad hoc* and short-term preoccupation of the President, his ministers and their *cabinets* meant that the planners increasingly had to concern themselves at best with piecemeal programming rather than achieving an *overall* strategy. While the day-to-day influence of members of the Planning Commissariat had not necessarily been reduced substantially in the interministerial committees, the decline in the significance of the medium-term, macro-economic framework within which particular decisions had their place, meant that the Plan had to adapt itself to fit the immediate requirements that it was unable to anticipate or bend to its purpose. As a result, the Plan has lost something of its distinctive character; like most innovations it has adapted itself to its environment.

Michel Albert has claimed that the Commissariat's 'mission is to organize the conditions of its own redundancy; the Plan invents and then it leaves it to others to carry out'.[2] This capacity to engage in permanent intellectual revelation and to get one's ideas accepted and acted upon by the economic policy community is compatible with non-vegetative survival only if the planners are able to discover new functions replacing those that have become redundant. Did the Priority Action Programmes (PAPs) of the Seventh Plan, the major positive innovation of the 1970s in terms of French planning methods, allow the Planning Commissariat to overcome the danger that it had all too successfully organized its own dispensability in the context of an economy at the mercy of the international market, whose rigours it had prepared French firms to face? Far from planners in France having sought to impose administrative criteria upon the market, an examination of the PAPs will show that they have tried to import market criteria into an administration which is as allergic to planning and programming as the business world was to competitiveness.

The Plan's enduring prestige is due to its share in the twin achievements of making the internationally competitive industrial firm the reference point of national economic policy and taking the edge off the conflicts that this shift in public priorities was bound to provoke. The much vaunted *concertation* practices, notably through the modernization commissions, but also in the Economic and Social Council, made it possible to test the intensity of opposition to a policy dictated not by the time-honoured preservation of a socio-political equilibrium, but by a deliberate intention to redeploy state support towards the big industrial firms.[3] The planners were not only able to warn political decision makers of the domestic and international constraints upon their choices; they performed an invaluable role of *réducteurs d'intransigeance* as Léo Hamon put it, helped notably by the leaders of the CFDT trade union, who in the late 1950s and early 1960s believed that planning could be made democratic both in its procedures and in its objectives. Yet, by the mid and late 1960s, policy priorities like full employment were being abandoned in favour of what a planner and future minister popularized as an industrial imperative based above all upon competitiveness, the economic policy of the government becoming an extension of this industrial policy.[4]

The commitment to this strategy was to culminate in the late 1970s under the premiership of Raymond Barre when, with the additional stimulant of the world economic crisis, everything was done to promote the profitability of firms to whom the fate of the nation and state was entrusted. This meant abandoning instruments of state intervention like price control and tolerating rates of unemployment that were previously unacceptable, temporarily cushioning the firms, the regions and the families that felt the full brunt of the shock. This would allow the country's industrial champions to take up the cudgels on a solid, self-financed foundation, albeit with financial assistance from state banks and public funds. Such a policy is not to be confused with the doctrinaire *anti-dirigisme* preached across the Channel; rather than a withdrawal of government, it involves a new approach, in which planning, and the state machine generally, has to be adapted to fulfil its subsidiary role in the service of industrial competitiveness. The attempt to combine an increasingly selective policy with one that sought to retain an overall consistency of public action had, furthermore, to be introduced in a situation in which it was desired to reduce the share of public expenditure within the gross national product, while expanding the share of military relative to civil expenditure. (The increase in military expenditure, for 1976–80, was three times that over the period of 1970–5, and 60 per cent greater than the increase in civil expenditure, the military share of the budget being due to rise to 19 per cent in 1980 and 20 per cent in 1982.) To overcome the inertia of institutions well experienced in the arts of self-preservation, redeployment of public expenditure provides an attractive instrument for bringing about the desired changes, particularly when the idea of extending to the state sector a theory of investment decisions inspired by the most advanced US firms seems to offer the appropriate management technique: the *rationalisation des choix budgétaires* (RCB).

Rethinking French Planning in the Early 1970s

The medium-term programming of public expenditure became an active issue in the late 1960s and early 1970s, when the desire to resist the further increases in taxation which had inspired the pioneer US PPBS ventures encountered the planners' desire to combine programming capital investment with that of current expenditure. Even before they became conscious that the era of big public investment projects was on the wane, the period between Plans (which has always been the occasion for reconsideration of the methods and objectives of the Plan) was put by the planners to especially intensive use in the years 1971–3. Why did this period, between the start of the Sixth Plan's implementation and the preparation of the Seventh Plan, give rise to a particularly searching rethink of the function of planning in France, including consideration of whether it should be abandoned altogether? The Plan's dependence on the personal role of the Planning Commissioner had meant that the extended illness of René Montjoie, who was to be followed by a conscript, Jean Ripert, seriously weakened its standing. Many of the old ailments had become worse. Forecasting was increasingly difficult, with an increasingly unpredictable international and domestic situation. It was possible to mobilize a divided French society only to a limited extent, particularly when the planners were so closely identified with the government. The pursuit of overall consistency made innovation difficult, while the attempt simultaneously to make a large number of choices meant that they were not made in the best conditions. The credibility of the Sixth Plan was in question: the two major trade unions had dissociated themselves from it, the senior civil servants seemed to have less commitment to it and the government was reluctant to face the criticism that would result from openly disclosing its policy. To avoid the Seventh Plan being reduced to general rhetoric that would be received with increasing scepticism, it was regarded as essential for there to be a 'hard core' of precise programmes, to be fitted into a precisely specified financial framework. In the event, with the coming of Giscard to the presidency in 1974, the planners had to consider themselves lucky to have survived the new dispensation. They were compelled to prepare their Priority Action Programmes without benefit of the detailed overall allocation of resources between ministries and between regions, the former to be based upon medium-term plans that never saw the light of day.

However, the ministry programme budgets that formed the core of the exercise in rationalizing budgetary decisions, launched by Michel Debré as Finance Minister in 1968, offered the prospect that programming might not only be linked forward to budgeting but backward to planning. Not only would it be possible to relate the programming of means to the objectives planned, but through a decentralized management by objectives and indicators of the results to be achieved, it would be possible to check intentions against performance. The fact was that this would require not merely a revolution in planning methods, but a revolution in budgetary processes and in administrative practice. In 1973, a former Budget Division official who moved to the Planning Commissariat to realize this extraordinarily ambitious series of innovations declared: 'all programming implies prior planning. When the Seventh Plan is prepared, which it would be judicious to base, as far as possible, upon the programming ideas advanced by the ministries that have experimented with programme budgets, it seems timely to move towards the integration of a general planning, with a five-year fixed timescale in terms of objectives and impact and a set of rolling partial programmes in terms of achievements and costs. The new system will be characterized by a greater reciprocal flexibility of the present annual structure of budgetary expenditure and the structure of State objectives', the plan and the budget each influencing the other.[5]

The head of the Finance Ministry's RCB *mission* recognized that if these ambitious objectives were to be attained, it would be necessary to overcome the semi-feudal compartmentalization within and between ministries and that present methods of coordination were inadequate. Reliance upon interministerial committees and working parties meant that: 'the communication of data is only conceded late, incompletely and with reticence, the discussion becomes conflict even before it has been fully informed and an arbitrated compromise based upon pleadings replaces the desirable synthesis, whose constituent elements have not been brought together by a common search for alternative solutions'.[6] Furthermore, another prerequisite of successful programme budgeting was deconcentrated decision making. 'Attempts at deconcentration have not hitherto succeeded owing from the start to the lack of an adequate system of information of those to whom powers are delegated. They are ill-informed about the objectives pursued; they do not receive the information that is indispensable if they are to carry out public action; lastly, they have no latitude to adapt the means and their use to the specific requirements of their field of responsibility.'[7] The rigidity of public expenditure was due to the related fact that 'little is known, if anything at all, about the use made of administrative resources; the product of administrative activity remains undefined, *a fortiori* not measured, and the relationship between this product and the objective to which it corresponds is all the less clear because the objective itself, the practical result to be achieved, has often never been clearly settled or communicated to an administrative authority, which would be accountable for it.'[8] Now although most ministries produce three-year programme budgets, they are usually mere projections that have contributed to the ministry's internal budgetary discussion but are used neither for its discussions with the Budget Ministry nor for measuring the efficiency of management within the ministry.

While the development of programme budgeting seems to have led to some improvement in intraministry collaboration, the attempt to substitute rational allocation for political bargaining quickly ran into difficulties, especially because 'it is not so much the objectives of ministerial programmes which tend to be contentious, as the *priorities* attached to the respective programmes ... in terms of funding.'[9] The Seventh Plan Priority Action Programmes (PAPs), which sought to grasp this nettle, had been preceded by Sixth Plan innovations that did not attract much attention. Firstly, 20 per cent of the public investment projects were declared to have priority over the others in that the funds allocated to them would be guaranteed unless the Plan was formally revised. Secondly, six 'finalized programmes' were selected, involving only 3 per cent of public investment funds, to undertake a more ambitious RCB-like operation. Precise objectives were to be fixed, with indicators so that results could be accurately monitored. Not only would the funding cover both capital and current costs, but these programmes would be necessary to attain their targets. Two of these six experimental programmes—those concerning helping old people to remain in their own homes and road safety—were to reappear among the Seventh Plan PAPs.

The problems of implementation encountered in the Sixth Plan and the consequent loss of credibility in medium-term public investment planning led the team that was re-thinking the strategy for the Seventh Plan to the conclusion that it was vital to secure stronger links both with the budget and the spending ministries, backed up by the top-level political support necessary to overcome the traditional administrative reluctance to engage in medium-term planning. The political commitment accorded to anti-inflationary balanced budgets and the avoidance of increases in taxation and social security contributions, coupled with the increasing cost of social and economic transfer payments and of the civil service which (along with military expenditure) were not programmed by the

Plan, 'led almost inevitably to the abandonment of the other objectives', notably the planned public investment programmes. As the former head of the Commissariat's Economic Service put it: 'experience has shown that the Plan's participation in the annual budgetary discussions are not sufficient to change the direction of the decisions made year by year . . . . The lack of a real medium-term programming in most spending ministries, the inadequate integration of the Plan's programmes with the plans prepared by the ministries, can lead in the course of the Plan's implementation to budgetary decisions that are contrary to the Plan's guidelines or priorities. In the annual budgetary negotiations with the Ministry of Finance, the ministries may propose, often rightly, an allocation of funds favouring current as against capital expenditure, leading to the non-implementation of the Plan's programmes which are confined to investment projects. Similarly, the low rate of implementation of some of the Plan's priorities shows that even within capital expenditure, the *de facto* choices of the ministries at the centre or in the regions do not conform to the Plan's guidelines.'[10] As we shall see, the PAPs were—following the Sixth Plan *programmes finalisés*—to try to ensure that current and capital expenditures were treated as complementary parts of a single project.

However, the other main weakness was that despite the Finance–Plan collaboration developed in connection with the preparatory stage of the Sixth Plan, the Budget Division officials (in the pre-Barre era) could not rely upon the ministers to hold the anti-inflationary line and as a result regarded 'commitments entered into in the planning context as being excessively ambitious. It is as though, when the Plan is prepared, the planners, relying upon the spending ministries and the concertation bodies, forced the hand of the Finance Ministry so that subsequently, when the Plan is implemented, the budgetary authorities reduce the effective commitments to the level that they consider . . . to be more realistic.'[11] Such realism implied that medium-term planning of public finance should include programmed decreases as well as increases in public expenditure, an attitude that—whatever its logic—was bound not to commend itself to the spending ministries. Yet in hard financial times an insistence upon redeployment rather than simply increasing public expenditure was inevitable and became the price of protecting medium-term priority projects from being abandoned *en cours de route*, under short-term pressures.

While an emphasis on the consensus-building role of the modernization commissions had always been accorded a disproportionately large place relative to their importance in decision making, in the new arrangements envisaged for the Seventh Plan their role was to be scaled down dramatically, especially in the second programming phase of the process. The commissions would continue to be consulted during the first guidelines phase of the planning process, when the secretive ministries could be induced to disgorge some information; but once the government had made its major policy choices, the detailed programming would be left to the ministries and agreed with the Budget Division. The major shift in the subject matter of the planning process away from planning the whole economy towards programming part of public expenditure was thus accompanied by a shift away from the emphasis upon the 'social partners'—always prone to make excessive demands—towards an increased stress on the public administrators with no mean appetites of their own. In turn, this presupposed that the ministries would be willing to engage in an exhaustive medium-term programming of their activities of an entirely novel kind, and the PAPs were to be the instrument of bringing this major change about.

The PAPs: Vicissitudes of Conception and Application

In the anti-planning climate of 1974–5, it was only possible to put into operation part of the strategy worked out within the Planning Commissariat in 1973. It was not possible either to get the ministries to engage seriously in detailed medium-term planning or to fit their plans into an overall rolling public expenditure plan. However, on 30 June 1975, Prime Minister Chirac asked each minister, working on the assumption of a standstill total budget, to send to the Planning Commissioner by 1 October 1975 a ten-page document setting out the 'main guidelines of the action of your ministry for the period of the Seventh Plan . . . indicating the strategic direction of your action and what modifications you propose to make to it in the light of the priority objectives and the preliminary guidelines of the Plan.' Given the fact that this exercise had to be performed in the 'deadest' three months of the year, it is even less surprising that the results were more a testimony to the rhetorical skills of the authors than anything like the serious medium-term planning effort which it had been hoped to promote.

However, doubtless in the belief that precise proposals would yield increased allocations, the ministries came up with numerous schemes. In addition, because it was hoped to overcome the irrational effects of compartmentalized administrative responsibilities, twenty-eight interministerial study groups were established to report by the beginning of October 1975 on themes inspired by the Seventh Plan guidelines that the Planning Commissariat believed might suggest appropriate PAPs. In the event, these groups made relatively few practical suggestions. Most of the PAPs were inspired by proposals from the ministries, a fact that was to make it subsequently even more difficult to promote the interministerial collaboration that was an important objective of the whole exercise. Lastly, the regional dimension—which was to be covered by the PAPIRs, the PAPs that were to be based upon *initiative régionale (et locale)* and were alluded to in the previous chapter—was included in the form of information from the regional prefects about the policy preferences of their areas. These naturally varied but indicated a general priority for health and transport, with environment somewhat behind and education bringing up the rear.

The criteria which the planners had in mind, with a view to selecting from among the 132 programmes proposed, involving a cost of 432 billion francs (of which 262 billion francs would not involve either new or redeployed funds) were subject to two overriding considerations. It was, firstly, felt desirable to have rather more than the six 'finalized programmes' of the Sixth Plan to ensure a sufficient coverage and impact, yet not so many that the whole exercise would become fragmented into a multitude of miniprogrammes. Furthermore, the amount of money that could be devoted to the PAPs—after prolonged and heated bargaining with the Budget Division—was agreed to be about 200 billion francs (of which nearly half would go to one superpriority directly attributable to a presidential decision, the development of the telephone system). Within these constraints, it was felt that politically, the PAPs needed to be related to both the government's objectives and the Plan's guidelines, as well as being capable of mobilizing public support. (Apparently, the reinforcement of the 'struggle against tax fraud' proposal was ruled out on this latter ground.) Administratively, it was hoped that the PAPs chosen would promote interministerial coordination. Procedurally, a RCB-style linkage between clearly specified objectives, the means to achieve them and the capacity to monitor the physical as well as the financial results of the actions undertaken was rather optimistically required, necessitating formulating operational indicators for each action contemplated. Financially, the programmes were not normally intended to last beyond the life of the Plan, thereby overcoming the built-in tendency of public expenditure to accretion by inertia and were to fulfil a pump-priming role for innovative programmes. Lastly, the hope was that despite the exclusively administrative character of the PAP preparation, the programmes would be accepted by the non-administrative 'partners' in public action, notably the local authorities and social security organizations, with whom it might be possible to enter into contracts.

Some ministries, instead of selecting priorities from among their activities, tried to cover all aspects of their work. This was often due to the fact that in terms of intra-administrative politics it was 'not possible' for the minister or his cabinet to choose between the proposals of the various *directions*. This meant that, in addition to their inadequacy as a basis for medium-term planning of public expenditure, there were too many proposals most of which were only remotely related to the Seventh Plan's preliminary guidelines. For these reasons, and because the financial implications exceeded by far the amount of money set aside to cover the PAPs, the Planning Commissariat excluded or conflated many of these proposals to about a quarter of the initial number. Small working parties of from three to seven officials from the various ministries concerned (but always including representatives of the Plan and the Budget Division) then worked out the details. The selection was hammered out by interministerial meetings at Matignon chaired by a member of the *cabinet* of the Prime Minister, composed of other members of the Prime Minister's *cabinet*, the Director of the Budget Division and his staff, the Planning Commissioner and his staff, and a member of the *cabinet* of the President of the Republic and of the Finance Minister.

The Budget representatives made no secret of their scepticism about the whole exercise. They were prepared to take on board questionable proposals such as the Rhine–Rhône waterway (which was inserted at the express request of the President of the Republic, following a personal commitment he had given to the *Conférence Interrégionale pour la Liaison Rhin-Rhône* at Dijon on 24 November 1975) despite the fact that it was not supported as a priority either by the Ministries of Equipment or of Transport and that the Plan was unenthusiastic to put it mildly.[12] They argued that most of the proposed PAPs should simply be abandoned as threatening insoluble financial problems and that as a matter of 'realism' they should concentrate on a very few genuine priorities like the EDF electro-nuclear programme. However, this onslaught was beaten back by the Planning Commissioner who argued that the number, content and cost of the PAPs was for the government rather than the Finance Ministry to decide. As for the electro-nuclear programme, the Minister of Industry did not want it included among the PAPs as this would involve entering into public commitments further ahead than the government was politically prepared to go on this sensitive issue at the time. Having failed to avoid what was seen as an attempt to allow the spending ministries to have guarantees for their non-priority projects—their real priorities being financed anyway—the Budget officials refused to regard the PAPs as anything more than empty financial *enveloppes* that could be filled from year to year as circumstances permitted. This was why the Budget Division (successfully) resisted the idea that there should be commitment to a precise timetable of the sums to be spent in each of the five years. The prime concern was to avoid building medium-term constraints into the budget procedure that would hamper the flexibility needed to deal with short-term problems and changing priorities.

The initial enthusiasm of the spending ministries for the PAPs waned once they realized that if the new procedures worked as was intended, they would have to redeploy their existing funds—admittedly easier over five years than annually—rather than obtain additional resources and would be more rigorously accountable than they had been previously. Unlike the blank cheques for public investment of the past, the PAPs might allow the Plan and the Budget Division to check for the first time on the efficiency with which the ministries utilized their existing resources. It was particularly the ministries like Health, that had weak bargaining power in the traditional budgetary process, which threw themselves most wholeheartedly into the PAP innovation. When it became clear that the Ministry of Health would receive little extra money (for example, by redeployment from other ministries) and was expected to redeploy within its own exiguous existing funds, it felt that it had been misled. The process of redeployment became especially difficult for a ministry when a large part of its estimates were covered by PAPs, as was the case with Health and another small ministry, that of Trade and Craft Industries.

Even in large ministries, the same problem could occur in particular divisions when most of the money went to those activities concerned by a PAP. In the Roads Division of the Ministry of Equipment, this led to a massive *de facto* redeployment away from the Paris region. However, whereas most ministries managed to take the RCB sting out of the PAPs and submerge their operation in the bureaucratic inertia of routine administration, departments like the

Ministry of Justice, which had hitherto escaped the potentially revivifying effects of involvement in planning, were affected for the first time.

A major failure of the partial programming innovation was in the practical arrangements for ensuring a proper implementation of the PAPs. This was to be done firstly by preparing confidential *dossiers administratifs*, only extracts of which were published in the second part of the text of the Seventh Plan, where the objectives, content, organization and finance of each PAP were succinctly set out. Partly because of the speed at which the work was done—even though many of them were not completed until well into July 1977—but mainly because they had no official status, they failed to provide the intended basis for interministerial collaboration and joint action. The programme indicators[13] were usually inadequate or overambitious, with the result that it became impossible to check up on their implementation when annual reports were prepared for publication each year in the *Rapport d'Exécution* appended to the Finance Act. The lack of a formally signed agreement, which meant that it was not always possible to know which document was the final version, enabled the Budget Division to refuse to be bound by it, although it was unofficially used. Somewhat more surprising is that the other ministries did not consider themselves bound either, so that little procedural pressure was exerted to break down the barriers of mutual suspicion between them.

Predictably, in the absence of pressure to coordinate, habitual departmentalism quickly reasserted itself. Each PAP had a designated ministry as programme leader (*chef de file*), the minister selecting—after consulting the other ministries concerned—a project leader (*chef de projet*) who was responsible for supervising the programme's implementation and calling regular meetings of a coordination group. Because of the heterogeneous character of some of the PAPs and the reluctance of ministries to concede the leadership in any matter in which they were involved to another ministry, what happened in practice was that each ministry managed its own piece of the PAP, thereby circumventing entirely a major purpose of the whole venture: coordinated implementation. The ministry formally in charge naturally tended to favour those actions that were its own primary responsibility. More serious, ministries appear often to have had only a single copy of the *dossier administratif* and to have taken no steps to ensure that its contents were communicated at all relevant administrative levels through a circular or by meetings of the officials concerned. Implementation went best when for all practical purposes one bureau in a single ministry was responsible. The hope that it would be possible to start by rationalizing a small part of a ministry's activities and that its effects would spread—part of the logic of partial planning—turns out in practice to be much too optimistic. Frequent changes of minister (four at the Ministry of Labour during the Seventh Plan) or of project leader did not help. Coordination groups often either did not meet at all or were attended by junior officials without the authority to give joint action the necessary impetus. Ministries sometimes would have been prepared for Planning Commissariat officials to play the coordinating role, but they were reluctant to take on this task, which would have probably been beyond the capacity of a very small staff that was not intended to involve itself in detailed management and lacked the authority to impose coordination on unwilling partners. Ministries were also reluctant to enter into formal contracts with non-administrative bodies and even when arrangements existed for an annual conference of all those concerned with carrying out a PAP, as was the case with one concerning 'helping old people to remain in their own homes', it never met.

If the attempt to use the PAPs to teach the ministries new administrative tricks and to modify their traditional behaviour would seem to have made little headway, did they work better in terms of guaranteeing the priority in budgetary terms of certain programmes as reflected in the extent to which they were financially and physically implemented? The bare figures suggest quite a good overall performance, reflected in an implementation rate of 93.5 per cent, with the telephone maxi PAP's 92 per cent concealing the welcome fact that it proved possible to meet the physical targets at lower cost.[14] However, the 95.1 per cent implementation rate for the other twenty-four PAPs covered very variable results, with the general rule being that those of an economic character were better implemented than those that did not directly serve the dominant industrial strategy. Some of the figures were also very misleading. The 78 per cent implementation rate for the Rhine–Rhône PAP did not take into account the fact that the target had been halved by the mid-term adaptation of the Seventh Plan, so that the real implementation rate was more like 39 per cent! The 88.5 per cent implementation rate for the Manpower Agency (*Agence Nationale pour l'Emploi*, ANPE) PAP looked good in quantitative terms, but in fact many of the new posts were given to unemployed managerial staff under the government's *Pactes pour l'Emploi*. This recruitment was not calculated to improve the quality of the staff, which was one of the PAP's objectives in an attempt to make the ANPE a more attractive and effective employment service at a time of increasing unemployment. After two years, in which the PAPs explicitly received priority in the Finance Acts of 1977 and 1978, they had to take their chance in the annual budgetary meetings. The planners had envisaged that the PAPs would be dealt with preferentially at the start of the budgetary process, following a go ahead from the Central Planning Council ensuring that they would not compete directly with other expenditures, but this guarantee did not survive the harsher situation once Prime Minister Barre's more stringent policy prevailed.

Planning and Political Decision Making

What captured the imagination of so many people, beyond as well as within her borders, about French planning was not so much the rationality of its techniques as the sweep and boldness of its ambitions and achievements. So that when, during the Giscard presidency, there was a retreat from this 'heroic' conception of national economic and social planning, the somewhat mythical primacy of the Plan was questioned. Perhaps, after all, the emperor had no clothes! Although it might be demonstrated that: 'The vast exercise of putting more than a hundred of the most promising "variantes" through the (Dynamic Multisectoral) DMS model (involved) one of the most ambitious exercises in measuring the trade-off between vastly complicated policy options which has ever been undertaken',[15] still there was a disheartening disproportion between technical skills and the political will to use them. It was all too evident in the Eighth Plan that these increasingly refined techniques were used too little and too late, being at the service of what appeared to be an accommodating defeatism that deferred to external market constraints in the name of classical economic orthodoxy. Gone was the indomitable and tenacious political will that united Monnet and de Gaulle in their view that rebuilding national power and influence were the prime objectives; a view that Pierre Massé still shares, when he argues that a strong and *solidaire* France is essential, even if isolated salvation is no longer possible.[16] The protagonists of a plan based upon a calculated assertion of political will, whether from the political Right like Michel Debré or Jacques Chirac or from the Left-wing as embodied in the varied views of the leaders of the Socialist and Communist Parties, were out of power and appeared destined to stay there indefinitely.

Jacques Delors, former head of Social Affairs at the Planning Commissariat (CGP) who in 1981 became Minister of Finance in the Mauroy government, argued that from the start 'The Plan existed alongside but parallel to the State' and had problems in achieving consistency with day-to-day government decision making, notably budgetary decisions.[17] Whereas decisions had always largely been taken outside the planning process, the more recent tendency has been for ministers, senior civil servants and the heads of meso-economic firms to free themselves from such constraints upon their freedom of action as planning might impose. In the case of the preparation of the Eighth Plan, the proximity in time of the launching of the Plan and the start of the presidential election campaign, made all concerned especially sensitive to the fact that controversial issues like the increasing unemployment and remedies such as increasing public investment or reducing working hours, might be embarrassingly spotlighted. Yet, at the same time, the President and Prime Minister wished to utilize the fund of public goodwill still attaching to the CGP as an institution, owing to its past reputation for relative autonomy from the government, to provide a spurious appearance of consensus about its policies. This kind of 'virtue by association' has meant that although 'the work undertaken by the *Commissariat du Plan* has been relegated to secondary status by decisions taken in the Central Planning Council . . . by talking of the Plan without actually planning, one can attach the reputation and authority of the Plan to whatever particular initiative has been decided on by the government.'[18]

The extent to which the politicization of planning involved the direct intervention of the Prime Minister and his personal staff in the text of the Plan became clear in the final report of the Eighth Plan, whereas the refusal to debate it before the 1981 presidential election underlined the explosiveness of the issues that were to be postponed until after the decisive moment of political choice. It transpired in extracts from a confidential letter on 14 August 1980 from the Planning Commissioner to the Prime Minister, that he considered it both unusual and undesirable that the 'text of the Plan should be used by the government to award itself congratulations on its performance and that this innovation risks being criticized because of the political timetable.'[19] This letter also frankly admitted that the draft plan 'attempted to elude' the problem of increasing unemployment and 'presented as a risk what is a certainty', as well as declaring that the increased public investment proposed in the plan was not consistent with the 1981 budget decisions.

Such an open disclosure of the extent to which national planning strategy was being subordinated to the government and President of the Republic's tactical convenience was crowned by the postponement of the parliamentary debate on the Eighth Plan until after the presidential election. This was because Chirac's RPR was highly critical of the Eighth Plan's priorities and threatened to vote against them if they came to a vote. Also, it would not have been helpful to a Giscard candidacy to focus attention upon the medium-term sacrifice of employment to the defence of the currency and the balance of payments. An occasion on which the Plan might, owing to the coincidence of timing, have become the centrepiece of a presidential election campaign, in the way envisaged by Pierre Mendès France in *A Modern French Republic*, was deliberately evaded, incidentally stressing Giscard's unwillingness to subordinate political improvization to the constraints of planning. So the Eighth Plan, while including twelve PAPs[20]—without any precise financial commitments and short of the ambitious objectives that had marked their Seventh Plan predecessors—in practice concentrated upon the development of France's much-envied electro-nuclear programme and the need to increase the country's birth-rate. After all, Giscard having been criticized for stating that France would soon account for only 1 per cent of the world population, it became a great national priority to exhort the people to procreate and stem if not reverse the demographic tide that threatened to submerge France.

The Priority Implementation Programmes of the Ninth Plan

Whereas the defeat of Giscard at the presidential election was to have as one of its by-products the advance of economic planning, if not to the centre at least to the spotlighted forefront of the stage, its immediate effect was to paralyse the Eighth Plan. The year 1981 became a hiatus in the planning process because it took Michel Rocard, the new Minister for National and Regional Planning, several months to prepare a two-year interim plan to cover 1982–3. This transitional arrangement was intended to serve the twofold function of getting France back onto the path of pre-recession economic growth and fuller employment, as well as to enable a drastic change in planning methods to be adopted for the return to medium-term planning covering 1984–8, the last five years of President Mitterrand's term of office. However, the increasingly adverse situation in 1982 quickly dissipated the optimism of the Interim Plan. The Socialists repeated in a milder form the initial mistake of the Giscard presidency; the belief that the international recession would be short-lived prevented the French state from facing the harsh realities of the market. By the time it came to preparing the Ninth Plan (1984–8), it was clear that despite the scorn poured upon the still-born Giscardian Eighth Plan, its Socialist successor was condemned to follow it closely, both in form and in substance. After the claims that the only figures in the Eighth Plan were the page numbers, it is ironic that macro-economic figures were even more conspicuous by their absence from the Ninth Plan's forecasts and objectives. The political wish to avoid being committed to achieve hazardous targets prevailed.[21]

The one aspect of the Ninth Plan where such a negative judgement would not be true concerns the renamed PAPs, the Priority Implementation Programmes (PIPs). Despite their clear continuity with the PAPs, the PIPs could claim to be more detailed programmes, with precise financial allocations, frequently quantified indicators and arrangements for monitoring and evaluating the extent to which they were being carried out during the duration of the Ninth Plan. Table 7.1 sets out the twelve programmes given priority in the period 1984–8. As in the case of the PAPs, there is the claim that they constitute the hard core of the Plan, based upon close collaboration between the Planning Commissariat and the Budget Division of the Finance Ministry, with the planners represented at all the annual budgetary discussions with each spending department. The items included in one or other of the PIPs are specifically mentioned in the appendices to the annual Finance Act so that parliament and the National Planning Commission can monitor their progress each year as part of the budgetary process. What Table 8.1 indicates is that by far the largest programme is item 2 on education and industrial training, especially on the current expenditure side, where it accounts for nearly 40 per cent of the total allocated to all PIPs. Conversely, programme 4, encouraging innovation, developing services to firms and training in the new technologies—the second largest programme—is almost entirely concentrated upon capital expenditure, amounting to some 37 per cent of the total allocated to all PIP capital expenditure. Significantly, both these programmes have an important industrial training element, whereas the third largest programme (item 6) is also concerned with promoting employment.

Table 8.1 also shows the allocation for the first year of the Ninth

Plan, providing 59.4 billion francs out of the total five-year PIP 'envelope' of 350.5 billion francs. So, in the 1984 financial year, 6.4 per cent of all state expenditure was devoted to the PIPs, an increase of 16 per cent compared to an average budgetary increase of 6.3 per cent.[22] Clearly, they were at least initially receiving priority and so living up to their name. The PIPs are planned to increase on average by 7.1 per cent in *real terms* over the period 1984–8, and it is here that trouble is most likely to arise, on the precedent of the PAPs. As long as the annual budgetary process continues, the pressure of circumstances may lead the government to withdraw promised funds at the cost of abandoning priorities fixed in a non-crisis context on the basis of more congenial assumptions. It will be possible to

Table 8.1 The twelve priority programmes of the Ninth Plan (1984–8)

Priority Implementation Programme	1st year 1984		Total 1984–8	
	Expenditure		Expenditure	
	Current	Capital	Current	Capital
	(millions of francs)			
1. Modernize industry by introducing new technologies and mobilizing savings	499	2,677	3,871	16,009
2. Modernizing the educational system and youth industrial training	12,970	3,584	70,135	21,102
3. Encouraging innovation, developing services to firms and training in the new technologies	519	10,164	3,342	60,963
4. Developing the communications industries	3,318	276	19,462	1,729
5. Reducing energy dependence	672	2,095	3,403	12,059
6. Active employment policy, especially in the organization of the workweek	5,140	216	34,980	1,298
7. Better marketing at home and abroad	3,611	1,165	20,308	7,882
8. Providing an environment favourable to the family and the birth rate	187	39	1,084	225
9. Decentralization, deconcentration and regional balance	213	3,083	2,357	18,685
10. Improving urban life	75	2,501	534	14,552
11. Modernizing the health system and control over health expenditure	3,745	1,362	20,767	7,931
12. Improving justice and personal security	567	708	3,562	4,299
Total	31,516	27,850	183,805	166,735

Source: *Journal Officiel*, 30 Dec. 1983, p.3849, article 2 of The Law 83–1180 of 24 Dec. 1983 on the application of the Ninth Plan.

verify precisely, thanks to the very detailed performance indicators, quantified in physical or financial terms, whether the priorities are being abandoned in practice. In a context in which public expenditure is to be reduced rather than continue to grow, redeployment into priority programmes is both difficult and essential. The many specific sub-programmes, each with their own little policy sub-community, provide a plurality of rallying points for the members of particular fragments of the national expenditure community, as they strive to protect their medium-term priority from the depredations of inflation-preoccupied budgetary officials. Each year, the Prime Minister hovers in the background, with the capacity to 'arbitrate' either for or against honouring each PIP commitment. They are only as firm as he is steadfast in their support.

9
SWITCHING TO THE STRATEGIC MANAGEMENT OF COLLECTIVE IMPOVERISHMENT

While the National Plan has long since ceased to be the framework within which the French government fits both its own medium-term policy decisions and attempts to coordinate in a comprehensive way the activities of the public and private sectors, it nevertheless still offers the best source from which one may discover how the government of the day quinquennially perceives the current economic situation and the prospects facing the country. Consequently, if we wish to understand the state of mind of the official decision makers, confronted by the post-recession problems of the 1970s, an indispensable starting point and permanent point of reference is the 1978 *Report on the Adaptation of the Seventh Plan*. Published in September 1978, just halfway through the duration of the Seventh Plan (1976–80), it helps us to understand the considered response of the tandem of President Giscard d'Estaing and Prime Minister Barre, drastically modifying the over-optimistic Seventh Plan's presuppositions of 1975–6 and preparing the way for the Eighth Plan's stoic summons to batten down the hatches for a stormy long haul. Although the Planning Commissariat (CGP) documents pay some passing attention to the views of other economic actors, we shall have to go beyond their increasingly governmentalized confines to consider how these other political and economic actors responded both to the 1970s' recession and to the French government's own attempts to cope with its consequences.

The opening chapter of the 1978 Adaptation Report wryly recalled that in 1976, when the Seventh Plan was officially approved, the widely held view was that 'France was emerging from the crisis and that it would soon return to conditions of growth similar to those that had prevailed prior to 1974. We have to admit today that at the time all the consequences of the crisis were not appreciated, especially with respect to the growth, changes and disequilibria of the world economy, of which the oil crisis and the recession of 1974–75 were only a *révélateur*.'[1] The increasing exposure of France to the constraints of international developments that were beyond its control dated from the late 1950s, once its traditional protectionism was replaced by an acceptance of the competitive consequences of membership of the EC. As its own industrial expansion gathered pace in the 1960s and as the volume of its international trade expanded, the domestic impact of fluctuations in its external environment became ever more imperative in their effects. The government, whatever its desire to assert its own independent strategy—such a will was undoubted in the period 1958–69, when General de Gaulle was at the helm—found itself increasingly compelled to adapt to foreign forces that it could not compel, cajole or induce to conform with the schemes devised in Paris. Even when the inflationary pressures were in the first instance domestic—as in 1963, with the Stabilization Plan following the coalminer's strike or in 1969, with the devaluation of the franc by Pompidou after de Gaulle had refused to do so in the wake of the massive 1969 wage concessions to buy off the extended general strike—it was the inability to sustain their balance of payments and international monetary consequences that led to the corrective action taken.

Because France had managed to sustain a steady, high rate of growth for most of the 1950s and 1960s, its citizens and leaders had become accustomed to the idea that this cumulation of wealth would continue indefinitely. They were not prepared for the increase in inflation following the escalation in oil prices (after twenty years in which the real cost of oil had been halved) to be accompanied by a dumbfounding descent into deflation throughout the industrially developed world, from which there was no separate escape for France. Although less prone to stagflation than most other countries, France shared the overcapacity in basic steel, chemicals and shipbuilding that afflicted her major competitors and like them was ill-equipped to face competition from the newly industrialized countries of the third world. Just as the so-called developing countries were being dramatically differentiated into two categories—those condemned to grinding poverty and those who had managed to make the breakthrough into certain areas of industrial specialization where they could supersede the old industrialized countries—a similar dualism was developing among the latter. Some, like Federal Germany, thanks to their technical and commercial mastery in particular industries, due to the innovative drive and efficiency of their national champion firms, would enjoy a secure balance of payments and a strong currency, aided by a financially orthodox monetary policy. Others, like the United Kingdom, would sink into an industrial decline rendered all the more spectacular by its former dominance; a decline which its oil revenues would cushion but not of themselves correct. France was seen as not firmly among the front-runners, even if it had left the laggards well behind it. The salient ambition of French planning since Jean Monnet had been to steer France into a position in which it could triumphantly sustain the pressures of European and then international competition. In the grim circumstances of the late 1970s and early 1980s, without its own national oil resources, France would have to redeploy its industry to take on the challenge of conquering foreign markets and defending its home market.[2]

Goodbye to Full Employment

Whereas in 1976 it was still possible to harbour the illusion that a rapid return to full employment was attainable, by 1978 it was possible openly and officially to assert that for the foreseeable future mass unemployment would endure in France, particularly because of the 'external constraint' on which we have dwelt. The choice offered to the French people was between general impoverishment and the reinforcement of the competitive capacity of French firms. 'Thus employment is linked to growth. Growth is linked to the balance of payments, which in turn is linked to the adaptation of our industry.'[3] This chain of reasoning, subsequently reiterated *ad nauseam*, was intended to compel those who believed that it was a prime duty of the state to ensure conditions conducive to full employment that this could only be achieved *indirectly*—through and subsequent to the prior concentration upon combating inflation and promoting industrial redeployment. By 1980, the Employment Commission of the Eighth Plan could regret that the concentration upon competitiveness had made the fight against unemployment a secondary concern. This was true not only of employers (whose pursuit of profitability required them to reduce manpower costs), but also of state economic policy makers. However the trade unions were a conspicuous exception: 'There seems to be a sort of general acceptance of unemployment within French society. Consequently, when the main economic, social and political forces attach greater importance (sometimes unconsciously) to other objectives, the growth of unemployment becomes, after inflation, a way of regulating an economy confronted by serious problems of structural adaptation.'[4]

It is important, if one is to see the employment problems caused by the mid-1970s' recession in perspective, to be aware of the fact that in France the number of people unsuccessfully seeking employment had already doubled in the preceding decade (1965–74), despite the rapid rate of economic growth. This domestic increase in unutilized labour was due to three main factors, only the first of which had a particularly marked incidence in France. The post-Second World War population boom meant that there was a rapid increase in the active population in the 1960s and 1970s, the high birth-rate coinciding with a low death-rate among the cohort of survivors from the First World War. Thus the average annual rate of active population growth increased from 20,000 in the years 1954–62 to 132,000 in 1962–8, 170,000 in 1968–75 and an estimated 200,000 in 1975–80. Secondly, the regular growth in the number of women seeking employment has meant that the average annual increase has risen from 18,000 in 1954–8 to 90,000 since 1974. Thirdly, there has been a marked change in the role of immigrant labour in the workforce; from a probably underestimated annual net inflow of 70,000 in 1968–73, there appears to have been a significant net outflow, estimated at a total of about 160,000 for the years 1973–6.[5] Unlike the first two factors, the outflow of foreign labour can be directly attributed to the economic recession, coupled with a change in government policy.

The second half of the 1970s was characterized by two other changes that had an important bearing upon unemployment. Firstly, there was a marked decline in the average annual increase in productivity: from 5.1 per cent in 1969–74 to 3.6 per cent in 1974–9 (and even 3.3 per cent in 1977–9). Such a decline was evident in all the OECD countries—smaller in Federal Germany, greater in the United Kingdom. The reduction in working hours—which became a prominent controversial issue in the debate on remedies for unemployment and so merits more extended treatment—has had a more specifically French evolution. Because of the chronic shortage of labour and low hourly wages in the period up to the 1960s, working hours *increased* slightly—on average one hour over the whole period 1945–60. Then, until the 1968 'events', working hours were stable, thereafter commencing an average annual decline of 1 per cent, thanks to legislation and collective bargaining, which has continued since 1974, although at the slower rate of 0.7 per cent from 1977 to 1979. As an increasing number of people reached the forty-hour workweek (48 per cent in 1979 as against 18 per cent in 1974 for manual workers and 69 per cent in 1979, compared with 47 per cent in 1974 for white-collar employees) there was a tendency to cut back on overtime working. Prior to the 1974 recession, the reduction of the workweek was most marked in the large firms in the most dynamic industries, with high rates of productivity and wages; whereas since the recession the reduction has occurred mainly in small firms in the declining industries, with low productivity and pay, as a way of adjusting to falling demand.[6]

This difference in behaviour as between the expanding and declining sectors leads us to a pre-recession cause of unemployment that has since been accentuated: the restructuring of production under the influence of technical change and the pressure of foreign competition. Agriculture, which had been characterized by a rapid reduction in its workforce in the decade 1963–73 (annual fall of 128,000, mainly among farmers rather than farm labourers) has since experienced a slowdown to 72,000 per annum (even lower since 1975 at 60,000 to under *half* the pre-1974 rate) playing its traditional role as a rural refuge from the full impact of industrial slump. Whereas industrial employment had been increasing annually by 64,000 in the period 1968–73, from 1973–79 it was falling by an average of 68,000 each year, the fall first being registered in the last quarter of 1976. Over half the jobs lost in the period from 1973–8 were in industries—notably textiles, iron and steel—that had been declining even before the recession. However, the mainstay of growth in industrial employment in the 1970s, motor cars, itself went into recession in 1980.[7]

Before turning to the regional dimension and to the rapid growth in service sector employment (the principal source of new jobs both before and since the recession), the building and public works sector merits special mention. This is because its decline, which pre-dated 1973 but was severely accentuated thereafter, owing to a fall in industrial investment added to the decline in house building, had a very widespread impact, notably in areas with almost no other secondary sources of employment. Prior to 1974, industrial expansion had helped somewhat to reduce the disparities in employment opportunities between regions but the 1.5 per cent annual fall in the number of industrial wage-earners had levelled downwards, hitting hardest those regions that had expanded fastest in the period 1968–74, although they continue to have the least unfavourable rates of growth in industrial employment. Services (which like building have helped correct regional employment imbalance) expanded the number of jobs by an annual average of 170,000 in 1962–8, 240,000 in 1968–73 and 223,000 in 1973–9. However, this overall growth conceals a change in the type of tertiary employment, from an emphasis on trade prior to 1968, to public service employment since then, especially health services in the most recent period. Since 1977, there has been a rapid expansion in non-food retail shops, stimulated in part by the same 'refuge' factors that account for the slowdown in migration from farming. Finally, there has been steady growth in the number of white-collar employees, managers and members of the liberal professions, which is consistent with the expansion in the service sector despite the dire predictions for the future arising from foreseeable technological advance, notably in electronics.[8]

Quite apart from the incalculable human costs of unemployment, the probability of becoming unemployed, which in 1970 was less than 5 per cent and exceeded 12 per cent ten years later, has had important financial implications, it being estimated in 1977 that for every 100,000 people unemployed the cost to the community was 4 billion francs (shared equally between transfer payments made and social security contributions not received). Despite the official 'smokescreen' spread about the diversity of types of unemployment, it was calculated in 1978 that unemployment in the singular had nearly doubled between 1974 and 1978, rising from 2.7 per cent to 5.2 per cent.[9] The staccato stress upon the competitiveness of French firms as a precondition of permanent employment, should not distract us from the fact that since 1974 employers have taken advantage of this stronger bargaining position to reverse the 1960s' trend towards unified and stable conditions of employment. This has been done notably by multiplying the number of special types of fixed-term and temporary contracts to increase managerial capacity to reduce manpower costs and facilitate management's freedom of action. Whereas only 2.5 per cent of the wage-earners were in 1970 covered by such precarious forms of employment, this number has rapidly increased since the recession. While the end of fixed-term contracts accounted for 25 per cent of those registering as seeking employment in 1976, the number had risen to over 35 per cent in 1980, the under-twenty-five year olds, women and white-collar employees being particularly affected by this increasing job insecurity. The number of full-time, permanent jobs offered through the National Employment Agency (at a time when it was receiving priority budgetary funds to extend and improve its services) fell from 1.4 million in 1974 to just under 800,000 in 1979. This decline coincided with an increase in the number of part-time jobs *offered* through the agency from 24 per cent of all jobs in 1974 to 33 per cent in 1977, whereas those *seeking* full-time jobs increased from 75 per cent in 1974 to 87 per cent in 1977. The underground economy generally and 'moonlighting' in particular also appear to have notably increased since the recession, and have softened the impact of short-time working and unemployment.

The duration of unemployment has continued to increase—from an average of 8.9 months in March 1976 to 11.1 months in March 1979—but the number of those registered as unemployed for over a year nearly doubled from 145,000 in the same three-year period to 270,000, of which 47 per cent were under forty years of age. However, those worse affected seem to be people who combine at least two of three characteristics: being over fifty years old, suffering from illness, being unskilled. Although the probability of becoming unemployed falls with age, the young have predictably found it easier to find a job; once the older become unemployed, they are more inclined to retire from the labour market. The recession seems to have especially affected male manual workers; the rate of unemployment among men rising from under half to over half the rate of jobless women: 3.1 per cent as against 6.7 per cent in March 1976, compared with 4.1 per cent and 7.9 per cent in March 1979, whereas the number of jobless manual workers rose from 4.7 per cent to 6.4 per cent over these three years.

Regionally, the rate of unemployment (those seeking employment as a percentage of wage earners) was in the 1970s highest in south-east France, (11–12 per cent in 1978 compared to 4.7 per cent in 1973) followed by the south-west, Nord Pas-de-Calais and Brittany—all approximately 9.5 per cent in 1978 as against 3–4 per cent in 1973—with Alsace continuing to be best placed with 4.3 per cent compared with 1 per cent. The Paris region was somewhat better off than the national average with 2.6 per cent compared with 2.7 per cent in 1973 and 5.8 per cent as against 7.6 per cent for France as a whole in 1978.[10] Lorraine—severely affected by closures in the steel industry—did not do much worse than triple its rate of unemployment by 1978, which was broadly in line with the national figures.[11] Since 1978, the lugubrious process of running down the steel industry has continued in Lorraine and the Nord.

The high and sustained French rate of economic growth—the pride and joy of its governments under the Fifth Republic—took a very sharp knock in 1975. Table 9.1 shows that after a good recovery in 1976, thanks to expansionist policies at home and abroad, it fell back to a modest rate of about 3 per cent in 1977–8. France did better than most of its EC competitor countries, but whereas it had managed to sustain a favourable margin over them of 1.5 per cent in its gross domestic product in the period 1960–74, this gap had now been halved to 0.7 per cent, in line with the fall in GDP. One of the French government's objectives was to open up the gap at least to 1 per cent, but it was concerned to stress that with its dependence upon international trade and the state of the world economy 'growth cannot be decreed'.[12] In particular, it was aware of the need to curb the inflationary pressures that pre-dated the oil crisis. These go back to the 1960s' cost-push to prices, due particularly to the increasingly capital-intensive nature of production (investment necessary to improve productivity to overcome international competition) and the rise in real wages at the expense of profits. However, since the mid-1970s' recession, the major preoccupation has been the rapid growth in public expenditure, due especially to the sharp rise in disbursements and fall in revenue consequent upon the rapid increase in unemployment.

Table 9.1 The comparative percentage increase in gross domestic product, 1974–8

	1974	1975	1976	1977	1978
France	+2.8	+0.3	+4.6	+2.9	+3.2
EC	+1.7	−1.6	+4.7	+2.2	+2.5
OECD	+0.3	−0.6	+5.2	+3.4	+3.5

Source: *Rapport sur les Principales Options du Huitième Plan*, p.31.

The French record in the matter of developing its public services without recourse either to substantial increases in taxation or to budget deficits was an enviable one, prior to the oil crisis. Table 9.2 makes clear that from 1965 to 1973 the French share of the Gross Domestic Product taken in national and local taxation and social security contributions, while high, remained virtually unchanged, whereas they increased rapidly in Sweden and the Netherlands, somewhat more moderately in Federal Germany and only slightly faster in the United Kingdom. However, by 1976, while Federal Germany was able to hold its charges almost steady, France and the United Kingdom both increased theirs by 4 per cent, whereas the Italian increase amounted to 7.2 per cent and the Swedish to 7.9 per cent! As far as the government's borrowing requirement is concerned, Table 9.3 indicates that France in the 1970s kept its public finance under control far more effectively than its major EC partners, even if the days of the balanced budget, dear to Giscard d'Estaing when he was de Gaulle's Finance Minister, are now merely a memory.

Table 9.2 Tax and social security charges as a percentage of gross domestic product

Country	1965	1973	1976
Sweden	35.6	43.0	50.9
Netherlands	35.5	43.7	46.2
France	35.0	35.5	39.5
United Kingdom	31.0	32.6	36.7
Federal Germany	31.6	36.3	36.7
Italy	29.2	28.6	35.8
All OECD	28	32	36

Source: OECD, reprinted in *Rapport sur les Principales Options du Huitième Plan*, p.38.

Table 9.3 Government borrowing requirement as percentage of gross national product

Country	1975	1976	1977	1978
Italy	14.6	9.9	9.8	12.6
United Kingdom	4.8	5.0	3.2	4.0
Federal Germany	5.7	3.6	2.5	3.0
France	2.2	0.4	1.3	1.9

Source: OECD, reprinted in *Rapport sur les Principales Options du Huitième Plan*, p.31.

However, the French Government was especially conscious of the fact that from 1974 to 1978 public and social security expenditure had grown annually 1 per cent faster than revenues and 3 per cent faster than the gross domestic product. Table 9.4 reveals that because social transfer payments were growing annually at 7.9 per cent on average, compared with all other public expenditure, by 1978 they accounted for over half of the total. (It is worth noting that despite talk of government 'disengagement' and although 'economic transfers' were only one-seventh the size of 'social transfers', they expanded almost as fast—7.6 per cent—from 1971 to 1978, owing to the recession.) The government's anxiety was that by the mid-1980s taxation and social security charges would need to rise towards 50 per cent of GDP, so the Eighth Plan suggested that they should not be allowed to expand, on pain of 'discouraging initiative and leading to inertia and irresponsibility'.[13] This liberal–conservative language should not surprise us and we shall have occasion to explore more fully the theory and practice of the French Government that expounded it, as well as its adoption by the Socialists when in office in the 1980s.

Table 9.4 French public expenditure, 1971–8

	Billions of francs (current)		1978 (%)	Rate of average annual growth, % (constant francs)
	1971	1978		
Wages	61.6	169.8	18.8	5.8
Consumption	41.1	95.3	10.5	3.2
Investment	29.2	65.8	7.3	2.8
Social transfers	145.6	460.5	50.8	7.9
Economic transfers	21.6	67.2	7.4	7.6
Other public expenditure	19.7	47.4	5.2	3.7
Total public expenditure	318.8	906.0	100.0	6.2

Source: French National Accounts, reprinted in *Rapport sue les Principales Options du Huitième Plan*, p.39.

Turning to the changes that occurred in the constituent elements of final demand—consumption, investment and exports—Table 9.5 provides us with a comprehensive view of the trends in the French economy on the demand side over the 1960s and 1970s, showing that investment bore the brunt of the halving in the pre-1974 rate of economic growth.

Table 9.5 Average percentage annual growth rates in French final demand, 1960–79

Constant Prices	1960–9	1964–74	1974–9
Consumption:	4.6	3.8	3.8
Households	4.9	4.2	3.7
Public administration	5.2	3.2	3.9
Gross Investment:	6.9	4.2	0.4
Firms	7.8	5.2	0.7
Public administration	–	1.0	0.4
Households	9.8	7.5	0
Exports	7.5	9.6	5.7

Source: INSEE, reprinted in *Commission de l'Emploi, Huitième Plan op cit.* p.30.

We have already discussed the fall in house building, which helps explain the collapse in investment by households, so we shall concentrate upon the effects of the recession upon investment by firms. Table 9.6 shows the impact of the slump upon competitive private sector investment, which did not recover to the 1972 figure until 1978, while the rate of self-financing also made a comeback in 1978 and again in 1979. Further explanatory factors account for the sharp decline in investment by firms, which fell as a percentage of sales from 4.9 in 1972 to 3.5 in 1976. Between 1972 and 1976, their long-term debt increased by 79 per cent and short-term bank loans by 96 per cent, while profits suffered from the growth of wages and consumption.[14] Fortunately, the nationalized industries increased their investments by 75 per cent in volume between 1973–8 and by an annual rate of 10.4 per cent in volume over the period of the Seventh Plan (1976–80) although by 1979 investment was down to 9 per cent. This generally good record was due particularly to two major public investment programmes: the modernization and doubling in capacity of the telephone system (which alone accounted for over half the 200 billion francs set aside for the Seventh Plan Priority Action Programmes) and the controversial electro-nuclear programme of EDF which is the largest effort by any nation in the world to substitute nuclear power for other sources of energy.[15] The Barre Government refused to continue boosting public enterprise investment to avoid threatening the private sector's place within the mixed economy.

Table 9.6 Investment and self-financing by non-nationalized firms, 1972–8

	1972	1973	1974	1975	1976	1977	1978
Investment (1970=100)	118.7	124.1	120.8	108.3	117.9	115.4	118.6
Rate of self-financing	74.5	69.0	57.7	62.3	64.0	61.6	78.4

Source: INSEE, reprinted Commissariat Général du Plan (CGP) Service Economique (28 Feb. 1979) p.17.

The government's desire to promote investment in the competitive sector was frustrated on the cost side by the increase in real wages in the early 1970s and by the increasing share of the wage bill represented by employers' social security contributions—22.7 per cent in 1972 and 25.6 per cent in 1978—which encourage the substitution of capital for labour. Consumption was sustained by the rapid growth in social transfer payments already noted and by the increase in the minimum wage, which grew in real terms by 7 per cent between 1970 and 1975 and by 3.5 per cent from 1975 to 1978. This increase in the minimum wage represented a modest reduction in differentials between wage-earners, which also occurred as between the less and more skilled.[16] Table 9.7 shows the slowdown in the increase in the purchasing power of wages from 1974, although it was not until 1979–80 that this fell to zero and then led to an actual fall in workers' purchasing power. Although Prime Minister Barre continued to assert in 1979–80 that the purchasing power of wages would be maintained—itself a regression—this claim rapidly lost credibility but a context of growing unemployment and a politically and industrially divided Left has meant that the trade union capacity to resist has been more vociferous than effective. However, the French Government would point to the fact that wage-earners in other EC countries had suffered a fall in real wages even earlier. By 1978, the Barre Government had become sufficiently confident in the political and industrial weakness of the Left to dismantle most of the price controls that had provided an instrument of indirect wage control since the failure to secure an agreed incomes policy in 1964.

Table 9.7 Annual percentage growth of prices, real wages and social security receipts, 1972–8

Annual growth rate	1972	1973	1974	1975	1976	1977	1978
Household consumption prices	6.0	6.8	13.3	11.6	9.8	9.1	9.4
Purchasing power of the *per capita* wage	4.1	5.5	2.6	3.7	3.4	2.3	2.3
Purchasing power of households' social security receipts	7.2	8.1	4.8	13.8	6.0	6.4	7.2

Source: INSEE, reprinted *CGP, Service Economique*, (28 Feb. 1979) p.17.

The oil crisis of 1973–4 marked the end of a period, going back twenty years, when the falling real cost of raw materials and energy ensured very favourable terms of trade for the industrially developed countries, whose manufactured goods were increasing in price. 'On the basis of the French minimum hourly wage, it cost eight hours work in 1950 to pay for 100 litres of unrefined petrol, but only 2.25 hours work in 1970.'[17] To meet the balance of payments deficit of 28 billion francs in 1974 and 22 billion francs in 1976 (after a year in balance thanks to negligible economic growth in 1975) there was a spectacular growth of exports (6.6 per cent in volume in the difficult world market of 1977), whereas invisible exports doubled in 1977 their 5 billion francs surplus of 1976. In 1978 there was a balance of payments surplus of 6 billion francs, but the renewed increases in oil prices from mid-1979 put France back into increasing deficit in 1980. On capital account, France continued to have one of the lowest debt burdens in the world calculated as a percentage of gross national product.[18] So, despite the intractable choices France had to face in the late 1970s, they posed less insuperable problems to its political and economic elites than some of its European competitors faced.

Conflicting Policy Prescriptions

French public opinion was not favourably impressed by the French

Government's attempts to cope with the consequences of the oil crisis and there can be little doubt that had the various national electoral confrontations between Left and Right been focused exclusively upon socio-economic issues the Left would have won power before 1981. In a poll conducted at the end of August 1979, only 25 per cent thought that the government's policy would deal successfully with the country's difficulties, whereas 63 per cent thought that the government was improvising without any sense of direction.[19] In April 1980, when asked about the success of the President of the Republic's policies over a wide range of issues, the public's response was very negative on all economic issues (see Table 9.8). This was true even of President Giscard's own partisans, between 61–76 per cent of UDF voters admitting that his policies to deal with unemployment and price increases had been failures.

Table 9.8 *Public assessment of Giscard d'Estaing's record in the previous six years*

Issue	Success (%)	Failure (%)	Difference (%)	No opinion (%)
Energy policy	31	41	−10	18
Strengthening French industry	25	42	−17	33
Reduction of differentials in standards of living	20	65	−45	15
Struggle against unemployment	12	78	−66	10
Struggle against price increases	5	88	−83	7

Source: *L'Express* (10 May 1980) p.113 (Louis Harris-France Poll).

Although the President and (especially) the Prime Minister's popularity sagged markedly between elections, at the decisive moments of choice—in the 1974 presidential election and the 1978 general election—the fact that the French public were presented with a *choix de société* rather than a choice of economic policies to deal with the international crisis meant that discontented voters swung over to the Right because they were not willing to face what was presented to them as a dramatic and possibly irreversible change in the character of France's socio-economic system. The effects of the economic recession upon the popularity of President Giscard were reflected in the collapse in public satisfaction with him, from a peak of 59 per cent in May 1975, to 57 per cent in January 1976, down to 39 per cent in December 1976. This was the lowest level to which a President had sunk since the inception of the Fifth Republic. The period 1976–7 was also a time when the Union of the Left was winning sweeping local electoral victories, but it is significant that presidential popularity began its steady recovery in May 1977—before the open split—overtaking the number of discontented in June. However, it was not until the September 1977 break between the Communists and Socialists that a nine-point excess of the satisfied over the discontented opened up, growing to an eighteen-point gap just before the March 1978 general election (56 per cent as against 38 per cent). In the wake of the victory of his supporters, Giscard's popularity returned briefly to its peak of 59 per cent in April as against 30 per cent discontented, but the gap closed over the next seventeen months and by September 1979 the number of discontented (44 per cent) again exceeded those satisfied (40 per cent).[20]

The much greater and semi-permanent unpopularity of Prime Minister Barre (1976–81)—in which he seemed positively to revel, regarding it as a measure of public incomprehension of his severe commitment to the austerities of classical economic orthodoxy or at least their desire to protest at the sacrifices they realized had to be made—was much more directly related to the public's perception of the government's handling of the world recession. Chosen by Giscard as France's best economist (whereas he only merited the title of the author of France's most widely used elementary economics textbook) specifically to exert a grip upon an economic situation that his predecessor Jacques Chirac had failed to master, the President deliberately utilized the formal, institutional duality of the French political executive to shift on to the broad and willing shoulders of the anti-populist Prime Minister the burden of hostility which his own policies provoked. Although at the beginning of 1977—shortly after Barre took office—his rating was close to that of Giscard, the number of the discontented quickly exceeded the satisfied by margins far in excess of the President's rating. Thus in May 1977, Barre's 'deficit' was 16 per cent as against Giscard's 6 per cent, and the dissatisfied consistently exceeded the contented right up to the 1978 general election (3 per cent in February), falling briefly below the contented in April, only to recommence the ascent to new heights of unpopularity. In September 1978 and June 1979 Barre's 'deficit' was 29 per cent, whereas Giscard had a 'surplus' of 12 per cent and 4 per cent. By the time the President had plummeted to a 4 per cent 'deficit' in September 1979, dissatisfaction with the Prime Minister had reached the record deficit for the Fifth Republic of 31 per cent (57 per cent dissatisfied as against 26 per cent satisfied)! If one takes the average quarterly figures, the popularity gap between President and Prime Minister significantly widened. In

1977 they were 4, 5, 7 and 11 per cent, in 1978 they increased to 11, 15, 19 and 16, modestly continuing this late 1978 reversal in early 1979 with percentages of 15 and 14.[21] This seems to confirm the earlier poll data that indicated that Barre's Government was held directly responsible for increasing inflation and unemployment, even though the voters were not prepared to dislodge his political master from presidential office until 1981.

When Prime Minister Barre introduced his 'Stabilization Plan' in September 1976 (recalling the similar 1963 Plan which de Gaulle claimed he 'imposed' upon his Prime Minister Pompidou and Finance Minister Giscard d'Estaing) he had to face not merely the intra and extra-parliamentary opposition of the Left but also the constant sniping of more than half his parliamentary majority, the RPR deputies, led by his disgruntled predecessor Jacques Chirac. The initial reaction to the crisis had been to concentrate upon fighting inflation, reducing energy consumption and developing exports. The anti-inflationary measures consisted of a combination of tight money, increased interest rates and balanced budgets with the accentuation of price control, especially from October 1974. However, the initial concentration on controlling industrial prices was not consistent with the Seventh Plan's priority for industrial development. Following a period of hesitancy over the future of planning, the preparation of the Seventh Plan in 1975–6 was characterized by an ephemeral revival of optimism in the possibilities of returning to the pre-crisis expansion and a growth rate of 5.5 per cent (7.2 per cent for industry) was envisaged, based notably on a high rate of investment.[22] This return to 'go' after 'stop' quickly caused France to run into balance of payments deficit, and Raymond Barre was called upon to carry out a more consistently deflationary policy in August 1976, following a conflict between President Giscard and Prime Minister Chirac that was broader and more political than their differences over how to tackle the economic recession.

Despite the temptation to follow a more 'soft-sell' policy with a view to the 1978 general election which, it was generally assumed, would be won by the then United Left, Barre's 'Stabilization Plan'— which made nonsense of the Seventh Plan and foreshadowed its mid-term 'adaptation' after the 1978 election—sought not merely to improvise a short-term anti-inflationary set of measures, but to prepare the way for a switch towards a less *dirigiste* policy which we shall consider later. Whether the German social market model was appropriate to France is a central issue. The spectacular start in 1978 to the reversal of decades of price control was accompanied by the claim that because Federal Germany had successfully curbed inflation without price control, it could be abandoned with equanimity; whereas it is arguable that it was *because* Federal Germany had mastered inflation that 'medieval price control' (Barre dixit)[23] was unnecessary. The Seventh Plan's commitment to full employment was tacitly abandoned and the stability of the currency was presented as a pre-condition of containing the growth in unemployment. Membership of the European Monetary System had the virtue of making the parity of the franc a matter of international commitment, restraining domestic propensities to laxness. Those on the Left and in the RPR who took a different view were peremptorily dismissed as economic illiterates. The *Guidelines Report of the Eighth Plan* (in whose redrafting Barre and his staff took a direct hand) made a virtue of 'rejecting the mirages of a "general expansion" that would certainly reduce unemployment temporarily but would make inflation and the balance of payments deficit and consequently, in the longer term, unemployment, worse'.[24] Not content with dismissing as unrealistic Chirac's view that public investment should be rapidly expanded and the threatened social security deficit painlessly avoided thanks to a fall in unemployment, Barre disingenuously engaged in his own brand of provocative unrealism when he declared: 'Why should the unemployed not solve their difficulties by setting up as artisans or creating a small industrial or commercial firm; not only for their own sake but for the community, which will profit from their success and will not have to carry the burden of providing them with benefits?'[25] This Guizot-like summons to social-through-self-enrichment carried the implication that it was not just the fortunate and bustling few that had the entrepreneurial equivalent of a field marshall's baton in the private's knapsack but that creating one's own small business was a solution to mass unemployment, not simply a private refuge from recession, with many aspirants rapidly joining the swelling ranks of the bankrupt. The public outcry at his reiteration of this Panglossian precept indicated that Barre could not get away entirely unscathed as a politician with sentiments that can usually be proffered by a professor of economics to his students with impunity. In 1979 9,200 firms were established and 6,200 were started in the first half of 1980 by the unemployed, helped by some modest financial assistance. This gives a measure of the element of truth in Barre's contention.

The divided French Left sought to fight the 1978 general election on the basis of its pre-crisis 1972 Common Programme and thereby provided an easy target for criticisms of its economic unrealism. Attempts by those in the Socialist Party, such as Michel Rocard, to adopt a more realistic stance, were attacked by the Communists and a section of his own party as defecting to the enemy and veering towards the defeatism attributed unilaterally to advocates of social democracy. Barre scored an early victory in a pre-electoral debate with François Mitterrand because whatever the Socialist leader's talents as a politician, he was definitely an economic novice. So, armed with a programme lacking economic credibility, advertising their mutual suspicions and inability to govern together so that they also lacked political credibility, the Left contrived to snatch defeat from the jaws of victory. The all-or-nothing line of argument—'nothing will change unless everything changes'—embodied in the view that the electors were really (rather than rhetorically) faced by a 'choice of society', meant in practice that even modest improvements were not made; rather, things changed for the worse! One of Barre's electoral arguments had been that if the Left won office the purchasing power of the workers would fall because of the resurgence of inflation, whereas if the Right were returned to power they would preserve the workers' living standards. As we have seen, although this was true for about a year afterwards, the French workers had followed in the wake of workers in adjacent countries by the end of the decade. This was not easy medicine to swallow in a country where living standards had tripled in the preceding thirty years.

Many planners and senior officials in the ministries, who had looked forward with enthusiasm to a change of government and policy (some, out of idealism or *arrivisme*, had even rallied to the rejuvenated Socialist Party and become active members) were very disgruntled at the retention, in an exacerbated form, of the previous men and measures. The overt scepticism towards forecasting and hostility towards planning of Giscard and Barre naturally led the practitioners of these arts to regret the Gaullist past and the provisionally lost Socialist future. However, the more ambitious and cynical sought to swim with the international market economy tide, which brought with it not merely the need to restructure French industry to face the intensified competitive pressure, but also the need to protect electorally important small businesses from the full impact of the recession. The Chirac government had created in November 1974 the *Comité Interministériel pour l'Aménagement des Structures Industrielles* (CIASI), but it quickly lost its initial function of pump-priming the provision of funds for purposes of restructuring industry and instead became a small business and job-preserving operation, under the pressure of circumstances. CIASI came under the control of the *Direction Général de l'Industrie* (DGI was established in July 1974) to enable the Ministry of Industrial Development to change from being a clientele-dominated, sectoralized ministry, left to look after small firms, into one dedicated to restructuring French firms into large multisectoral groups that wanted more than the public financial assistance obtainable through the Finance Ministry (for example, the negotiation of large export contracts). As the instrument *par excellence* of the government's industrial policy, DGI could carry out the selective approach of deciding which industries—such as machine tools and microprocessors—should receive priority help and which firms would be favoured, especially important in the placing of large public contracts such as those in the electro-nuclear field.[26] CIASI was renamed CIRI (Interministerial Committee for Industrial Restructuring) under Mitterrand.

The intra-bureaucratic implications of the recession can be seen to advantage in two aspects of the increased exposure to international pressures in the 1970s. The fragile nature of France's trade surplus in the years immediately preceding the oil crisis—the favourable balance in car sales exceeded that of French industry as a whole—meant that the Ministries of Industrial Development and (especially) Foreign Trade became commercial travellers for French goods. Financial assistance for exports was stepped up at a time when credit was being restricted and the Finance Ministry's Foreign Relations Division wanted to make all financial assistance to firms conditional upon their increasing exports. This division has played an increasing role in industrial decision making since 1974, including decisions on French overseas investment, having a vested interest in policies that will reinforce its place within the industrial policy-making process.

On the sensitive issue of the inflow of foreign investment—it was estimated by the Industry Ministry in 1971 that one-fifth of French industrial jobs and one-quarter of sales were due to foreign firms, which were concentrated in large firms, especially in the oil, electrical and electrical engineering, chemical and automobile industries—there continued to be policy confusion because of the different priorities of the various public agencies. The Ministry of Finance, through its Treasury Division, which is generally unfavourable to overseas investment by French firms because this involves a drain on the balance of payments and involves expensive guarantees, is primarily concerned with the short-term balance of payments advantages of foreign investment in France. The Regional Planning Agency (DATAR) is always favourable to investment inflows because of its desire to create jobs in areas that are under-industrialized or suffering from recession. On the other hand, the Ministries of Industry and of Defence usually champion 'national solutions' so that foreign firms may be amazed at their inconsistent treatment—invited in by DATAR yet repulsed by the Ministry of Industry—although the Treasury Division will have the last word[27] if the issue does not escalate to prime ministerial or presidential level. So national policy can become the plaything of intra-bureaucratic battles between various parts of the state apparatus, subject to the superimposition of a decision at the highest levels in the light of political considerations.

The attitudes towards public economic policy of business interests present a sharp contrast with that of the major trade unions. Big business never felt closer to the government under the Fifth Republic until 1981, witness the harmony between François Ceyrac, President of the CNPF peak business organization with first Jacques Chirac and then Raymond Barre. (This identification with the Right did not only occur when the Left threatened, if elected, to implement an extensive nationalization programme.) The unions, the Communist-dominated CGT and the Socialist-aligned CFDT, effectively represented about half of the workers. The intransigent opposition to private business and their political allies of these two unions, not just on matters of short or medium-term economic policy but on the very existence of the capitalist system of production as such, can be contrasted with the reformist-to-quietist unions—FO, CGC and CFTC—that are usually willing to accept the modest concessions offered by business organizations and government both during collective bargaining over wages and working conditions, as well as in the forums for consultation on general economic policy matters: the Economic and Social Council and the commissions connected with planning at the national level, as well as the economic and social committees at the regional level. Despite their intense distrust of the right-wing governments of the Fifth Republic, even the CGT and CFDT were inclined to accept the official view that: 'The role of the State is essential if negotiations between employers and employed are to take place satisfactorily';[28] an acknowledgement that they were too weak to rely upon collective bargaining alone to achieve their objectives. The 1970s' recession has increased this weakness by reducing the demand for labour and—rather than the fiasco of the 'united left' in 1977–8—led to a serious fall in trade union membership. Desperately seeking for a way out of their predicament, the unions have sought to mobilize their remaining strength to pressure the government into persuading the employers to reduce working hours · which, in addition to helping to deal with unemployment, would restore workers support for their unions.

France shared with Britain in the post-war period the position of having the longest working hours, despite the nominal achievement of the forty-hour workweek in 1936, thanks to the Popular Front electoral victory and subsequent general strike. We discussed earlier the steady movement towards an effective forty-hour workweek in the 1970s commencing before the onset of the recession and leading on average to a reduction of five hours over ten years or half an hour annually. This was achieved thanks to a combination of collective bargaining and the reduction of the maximum legal workweek. However, the resistance of employers increased at a time of falling profits, when they were particularly reluctant to accept any increase in labour costs and any reduction in the utilization of capital equipment. The Plan's Employment Commission had in 1978 circumspectly considered the issue of 'work sharing' prior to the report adapting the Seventh Plan, but made clear that the official view was hostile to a general reduction of the workweek with full wage compensation, as demanded by the trade unions, on the grounds that it would lead to an *increase* in unemployment. In its Eighth Plan report, the Employment Commission stressed that unemployment would only be significantly reduced if wage increases were moderate and if businessmen considered it worthwhile to invest. This meant that the reduction had to be gradual, diversified and negotiated to fit special circumstances; 'the gradual fall in working hours would only be the result of a variety of reductions carried out in the firms'.[29]

This was very much the line taken by the business organizations, and prompted sharp criticism from the trade unions who looked to the reduction of the workweek to thirty-five hours by 1985 as an indispensable element in their struggle to return to full employment. While the Employment Commission did envisage an average annual reduction of a half an hour to an hour over the period of the Eighth Plan (1981–5), it was left to the government-appointed conciliator, Pierre Giraudet, to make precise proposals. Giraudet, who had been at work from January 1980, following the breakdown in the prolonged government-prompted negotiations between the CNPF and the trade unions, made his proposals in April of the same year. They failed to secure acceptance because there was an insistence by employers that in return for reduced working hours, there should be greater flexibility. While this was agreeable to some workers, the trade unions were bitterly opposed to what they saw as a loss of control over a standard workweek. The unions—particularly the CFDT—had belatedly managed to persuade the Planning Commissariat to calculate in detail the effects of a substantial reduction in the workweek, thereby placing increasing employment at the centre of policy rather than treating it—as Barre certainly conceived it—as a mere by-product of competitive business. In the spring of 1980, twenty-seven scenarios—involving ninety economic variables and essentially comparing the effects of concentrating upon protecting the balance of payments (A), upon a high rate of investment (B) and upon a reduction to a thirty-five and a half hour workweek (C)—were presented by the Planning Commissariat, showing that genuine alternative priorities to those of the Government existed. However, they came too late and the Government was too firmly committed to its policies for these alternatives to provide more than debating points in the arguments in the press, planning commissions, Economic and Social Council and in parliament. Although the CFDT and CGT did not boycott the final phase of the preparation of the Eighth Plan—as they had done in the case of the Seventh Plan—they vehemently made clear their general rejection of the policies envisaged in a thoroughly governmentalized Plan.[30]

The Barre Government—despite frequent protestations of its wish to seek concerted views with all interested parties—made clear in practice that its real 'partners' were the heads of big businesses and the CNPF. This was obvious not merely from its policy statements but from its behaviour over issues like ending price controls, tax concessions for investment in shares and the reduction of the workweek. In the latter case, it was not prepared to go further than encourage firms to pursue their own interests, which were envisaged as broadly synonymous with the national interest. As a Ministry of the Economy report on 'Public aid to industry' put it: 'Out of 40,000 industrial firms, only 1,500 employ more than 500 people. Many of them are financially linked, which further reduces the number of wholly independent entities. These 1,500 firms make 80 per cent of the investments, account for 90 per cent of all exports and employ almost all the research staff. So it is not abnormal that actions aimed at strengthening the complete freedom of our economy should, at least in the first instance, concentrate upon this "hard core" of French industry.'[31] It conceded—in the wake of the leaked Hannoun report—that 56 per cent of all public financial aid to industry in 1976 (3.3 per cent of industrial added value compared with 3.2 per cent in 1972) went to nine firms: 31 per cent to public corporations or agencies dealing with aerospace, coal and atomic energy; 7 per cent to a Franco-American computer firm, CII–Honeywell–Bull with a minority public holding and 18 per cent to five private firms—Dassault (aircraft), CGE (electrical engineering), Thomson–Brandt (electronics, etc), Creusot–Loire (nuclear reactors, etc.) and Alsthom–Atlantique (turbines, etc). These nine firms received 80 per cent of aid to dynamic industries and 70 per cent of aid to industries undergoing rapid change but only 43 per cent of export aid. The three headings accounted for 83 per cent of public aid, so the fact that the 'big nine' received little aid towards restructuring (11 per cent of the total) and for employment and regional development (6 per cent of the total) is not significant. Despite assertions that there would be closer public supervision of the extent to which assisted firms invested and exported, the whole atmosphere of the post-1978 period was suffused with the desire to restore the confidence of businessmen and was irradiated by the confidence of an entrepreneur–minister like René Monory (Minister of Industry from 1977–8 and Minister of the Economy thereafter) and of Raymond Barre in the profit-making businessman.

The advent of the Mitterrand presidency brought about a temporary reversal of this policy. However, as we shall see in the next chapter, it was—under pressure of economic necessity rather than from political preference—resumed and extended under Socialist auspices from 1983.

10
CHANGING DIRECTION AND SOCIALIST CRISIS MISMANAGEMENT

In January 1985, the French Socialist Party, conscious that its stringent economic policies, aimed at restoring the medium-term competitiveness of French industry as well as dealing with the immediate problems of inflation and an adverse balance of payments was making it very unpopular, sought to take remedial action. Facing the daunting prospect of electoral disaster in 1986 on a scale equal to its triumph of 1981, it sought to win over public opinion by launching a three-week, multi-media campaign entitled *En direct avec vous*. It started with a 'phone-in' message recorded by the actor Michel Piccoli which touchingly hoped to make an impact with the statement: 'Did you know that out of the 110 proposals made in 1981 by François Mitterrand, 98 have already been carried out? That's not so bad for the half-way stage in a seven-year term of office, is it?'

This preoccupation with the need to demonstrate that one was worthy of support because electoral promises had been kept was not new, Mitterrand's first Prime Minister Pierre Mauroy having appended a checklist of the extent to which the 110 proposals had been implemented to his book after the first year in office of the new majority.[1] It is reminiscent of Harold Wilson's obsession with the scrupulous respect of Labour Party manifestos in Britain. What is not recognized is that the voters are less interested than professional politicians or academic observers in the precise coincidence between specific pre-electoral promises and post-electoral performance than in the success or failure of the policies pursued. If what appear to be the 'results' of the policies faithfully applied are repellant, it is merely an additional irritant to be reminded that these policies had been previously accepted as appropriate ways of dealing with the country's problems. It would be rather tedious to adopt a balance sheet approach to an assessment of the manner in which the French Left sought to reverse previous policies. Rather, our concern will be to concentrate upon the problems of changing direction and the reluctant acceptance of an invidious situation. A systemic, structural crisis has to be managed because it cannot be willed out of existence.

On the relatively rare previous occasions, such as 1936 or 1968, when the Left has briefly occupied or approached power in France, there has been a romantic tendency to consider the 'everything is possible'. This is one variant of an assertive and active French policy style which emphasizes the will of the actor rather than the inertial constraints that inhibit innovation. Its pretensions may and often do exceed its capacity to attain its ambitious objectives, leading to humiliation when the gap between them is publicly exposed. Although President Mitterrand proudly asserted at his June 1982 press conference that the French state which he personified would not yield to international market forces—'I will here express a will, a political will, a personal will, a national will'—he was forced a week later to devalue the franc ... against his will. Proposal 20 of his 1981 presidential programme had declared: 'The franc will be protected from speculation', only to have to accept three 'readjustments' in 1981, 1982 and 1983! The same proposal went on to stress the need to reduce import penetration and promised: 'By 1990, the share of foreign trade in the gross domestic product will be reduced to under 20 per cent'. The protectionist implications of this promise are evident if it is traced to its source in the 1980 *Projet Socialiste pour la France des Années 80*. The objective was not merely the 'indispensable reconquest of the internal market' but a reversal of the post-war trend towards becoming part of the world market in the course of which the share of international trade in the gross national product had increased from 10 to 22 per cent between 1960 and 1978. The *Projet* explicitly stated that it was the Socialist objective that by 1990 the 'mad chase between imports and exports will have ceased' and the share of trade will have fallen below 20 per cent of the gross national product.[2] However, this belief that France's dependence upon world trade could be reversed by an act of political will owed too much to the most 'wilful' and mercantilist, minority faction of the Socialist Party (the CERES, led by Jean-Pierre Chevènement) to survive the test of office. President Mitterrand, advised by his then Finance Minister and future President of the EC Commission, Jacques Delors, turned instead to his European Monetary System allies (and especially the Federal German Republic) for the assistance that would enable France to avoid opting out of the international market economy.

The heroic, assertive posture adopted by the Socialists just prior to coming to power in 1981 affirmed its adoption of 'a logic of rupture' with capitalism.[3] 'The socialist *Projet* has as its prime objective to get France out of the crisis. What our country lacks today is the will and mobilization' to reverse the trends that had led France into recession. 'To escape from the crisis, we must escape from capitalism in crisis. Since the crisis is capitalism's strategy for restoring its profits and its power, we have to invent another development logic directed at other objectives and with different incentives. We cannot escape from the economic crisis that is making France a subsidiary of the United States of America without radically changing present trends. Profit seeking must no longer sovereignly determine decisions about investment and goods. It must give place to the rationality of citizens democratically stating their needs through planning and the market.'[4] This peremptory rejection of the crisis management of a capitalist economy—which in part accounts for subsequent failures when such crisis management was accepted as unavoidable—was implicit in the pre-crisis Socialist–Communist Common Programme of 1972 belief that a high rate of planned economic growth would make full employment and increased public expenditure unproblematic. Explicitly rejecting the Giscardian attempt 'to make the French people accept austerity', the 1980 *Projet Socialiste* declared: 'We want equal, autonomous and creative growth'.[5] To avoid market forces preventing the attainment of these aspirations, it was essential to 'restore' and 'rejuvenate' the economic planning processes: 'The Plan must become the instrument of collective ambition and a mobilization of energies that are at present discouraged'. Such hortatory rhetoric was supposed to have a magical capacity to galvanize the nation. 'One thing is certain: nothing is possible without effort, without will, without mobilization and it is the main contrast between the policy of the right and the one proposed by the *Projet Socialiste*.'[6]

These sentiments, Promethean in their inordinate conception of what can be achieved by political will and planning, may be contrasted with the circumspect and chastened remarks of Michel Rocard, Socialist Minister of National and Regional Planning (1981–3), when he launched the National Planning Commission, created as part of the reform of the planning process carried out in 1982. When he talked of the context of economic crisis, it was not qualified by the epithet 'capitalist' as in the *Projet Socialiste* or by many of those on the Left who had discussed the problem in the 1970s. One must bear in mind the context. The year 1973 was not only the time of the oil crisis; it was also the year in which two influential books focused upon contemporary crises in capitalist states and societies: James O'Connor's polemical *The Fiscal Crisis of the State* and Jürgen Habermas's broader and more profound *Legitimation Crisis*, conceived in the period of continuous economic growth immediately preceding the oil-induced recession. It was argued that the failure of the 'steering performances of a self-regulated *system*', in particular the state's capacity to complement, supplement or substitute for functions inadequately or not performed by the market, was what gave meaning to 'crisis' as an external constraint that deprived policy actors of their discretionary power.[7] Nearly a decade later and with the benefit of hindsight, Rocard argued with lucid pessimism that the 'crisis' was structural, cultural and global; that 'the very use of the word "crisis" has put many an analysis off track. This word, which the economists have borrowed from medical vocabulary, describes the acute phase of a disease which either kills the patient or, if he pulls through, announces a progressive return to good health. The use of this word thus brings to mind a temporary situation seen as abnormal compared to a state of so-called good health . . . to which we shall return after the crisis is over. But both these hypotheses, i.e. the temporary nature of the present situation and the end of the crisis in the form of a return to an earlier condition, appear more and more detached from reality. We are not in the throes of a crisis but rather in those of a gigantic process of change. The only thing that is more or less certain, and that we are aware of today, is that we are moving towards a new state of world affairs where the rate of economic growth will be low or non-existent, where the quantitative aspects of social protection will stagnate, where international competition will be keener and keener, and where instability and even insecurity will become more general.'[8]

After explaining the over-optimism of the 1982–3 Interim Plan (which had quickly gone off course) by the Left's prolonged exclusion from office and its consequent failure fully to understand the constraints on political power, Rocard sought to dissipate illusions about the capacity through planning to change direction substantially or quickly. With Chevènement, then seeking to 'mobilize' the Ministry of Industry and the newly nationalized industries to carry out the ambitious industrial policy that he and his CERES friends had worked out in opposition, particularly in mind, Rocard confessed: 'I have recently come to the conviction that *volontarisme* is sometimes the worst enemy of *volonté* (determination) . . . . *Volontarisme* consists in thinking that one can, by multiplying the sums (of money) and manpower allocated to a project by, say, three, reduce the time it takes to reap the benefits by a factor of, say, two or three . . . . Discouragement follows, the decision is made to change direction and the result is a massive waste of both human and financial resources.'[9] Rocard concluded that France needed the courage to adopt 'long-term, sustained, persevering policies, the patience and the tenacity, in a word, the steadfastness and the determination, in the face of the hyperboles and precipitation of *volontarisme*' that would carry it through the purgatory of increasing unemployment.[10] Under the pressure of forces beyond his control, President Mitterrand was compelled to accept this view in 1983 after having rejected Rocard's first draft of the Ninth Plan as too pessimistic! How has France measured up to this 1980s' challenge?

Choice and Constraints in Macro-Economic Management

In France, accustomed for most of the life of the Fifth Republic to the persistence of broadly the same presidential and parliamentary majority, political change in either majority amounts to a crisis. In the United Kingdom, accustomed to the undramatic swing of the pendulum from one parliamentary majority to another, such a change is accepted as the normal working of the political system. However, in recent years both countries have become preoccupied with the problem of a change in the partisan majority formally monopolizing legitimate control over the government machine and the public policies for which it is responsible. The process of bipolarization in France between two rival political coalitions, both of which were credible contenders for government office, meant that a change in the political majority not only became feasible; it threatened to bring about an adversarial reversal of many of the institutions, practices and policies that had remained intact following the 1958 upheaval in the Fourth Republic stalemate, based upon a centrist Third Force majority. Would the techno-bureaucratic continuity of policy that had remained largely immune to partisan political change since the Second World War and which was credited with relative success, notably in the economic sphere, survive?

Let us briefly consider two alternative models of public macro-economic management, leaving aside consensus or neo-corporatist models which do not fit past or present French experience with any approximation to plausibility.

1. *Adversarial Reversal* places the emphasis upon ideological partisan choice and assumes a malleability of macro-economic management that allows political preferences speedily to prevail. One set of sectional interests will be satisfied at the expense of the others. In terms of ideology, one would assume that a market-oriented economic liberalism would provide the economic policy inspiration of the parties of the Right, while the parties of the Left would be committed to either a state interventionist or planned socialism. Public spending and public ownership would be increasing with the Left in power and diminishing with the Right in power. In fact, the economic policy discontinuities do not correspond to such a straightforward ideological split for reasons ranging from national political culture, through the requirements of cooperation within the economic policy community, to the pressure of political and economic circumstances. Furthermore, 'The rapid oscillation of public policy is not what committed partisans have in mind when they advocate greater differences between political parties. They usually assume a "great and irreversible change". But a change can be irreversible only under very limiting and special circumstances . . . . Twentieth century history suggest that great changes in public policy are as likely to arise by accident or as a by-product of other events as they are to arise from the intent of political parties' Richard Rose points out.[11] Major policy innovations have been more frequently a by-product of war—most recently the Second World War—rather than party-mediated ideological preference or the pressure of organized interests.

2. *Techno-bureaucratic Continuity* has been as favoured an explanation of French economic policy success for most of the post-war period as adversary politics reversals have been of British economic policy failures. Particularly since Andrew Shonfield's *Modern Capitalism*, it has been widely held that the French meritocratic elite of senior economic bureaucrats were the pragmatic instrument *par excellence* of sustained and consistent national economic effort, immune to piecemeal intrusions of short-sighted sectional interests and partisan dogma. When this group is widened to include the other—predominantly public and private business—members of the economic policy community, we have the actors that adapt to the consequences of secular trends and conjunctural fluctuations in domestic and international economic conditions or endeavour to master them.

Before we examine more closely the collision between both ideologically inspired alternatives and techno-bureaucratic imperatives and politico-economic behaviour, so that we can separate the rhetoric from reality, a brief review of the recent macroeconomic experience of France and the United Kingdom will help to place French experience in comparative perspective. The two economies are broadly similar in structure, despite the very contrasting records. In 1981, Britain had nearly three million more people in civilian employment, with fewer employed in agriculture, more in public employment and just over 35 per cent (but declining) in industry in the two countries. Whereas the French saved and invested more, the total outlay of the French government as a share of GDP (gross domestic product) was only slightly higher than that of the British government (49.2 as against 48 per cent). British *per capita* GDP was only 84 per cent of that of France, while annual output per employed worker was over 50 per cent higher in France, especially in industry although in agriculture the British had an approximately 25 per cent advantage. Both countries traded about a quarter of their GDP abroad, so that exposure to the competitive constraints of the international market is wholly comparable.[12]

From Table 10.1 it is possible to draw some significant contrasts in the performance of the two economies in the period 1971–83. Whereas the French economy expanded at double the rate of the British economy from 1955–68, thereafter—especially since 1973—the gap between them has fallen to 1 per cent on average, owing mainly to a fall in the French growth rate. Nevertheless, whereas the United Kingdom suffered negative growth in four years, France managed a positive rate in all thirteen years, although fluctuations in industrial production have been similar. Despite France's reputation as a country that tolerates a relatively high rate of inflation, the British fared worse over this period and the margin of fluctuation was much greater. Unemployment rose more steadily in France, but accelerated from 1981 in the United Kingdom, whereas it was temporarily steady in France in 1983. Increasing unemployment is due in part to increasing productivity and real wages, although real wages in the United Kingdom actually fell in four out of the thirteen years whereas in France it rose continuously, thanks in no small measure to indexation of wages, abandoned in 1984. France's increasing involvement in foreign trade and her greater exposure to the oil price shocks of the 1970s account for the greater occurrence of current account deficits on the balance of payments. Finally, the general government financial balance has been in deficit in the United Kingdom since 1972 and in France (with the exception of 1980) since 1975. Raymond Barre made play

Table 10.1 The performance of the French and UK economies, 1971–83

	GDP (growth rate)		Industrial production (growth rate)		Unemployment (%)		Inflation rate		Real wages (growth rate)		Labour costs (1980=100)		Current balance payments (as % of GDP)		General government balance (as % of GDP)	
	F	UK	F	UK	F	UK	F	UK	F	UK	F	UK	F	UK	F	UK
1971	5.4	2.6	4.5	0.0	2.6	3.9	5.5	9.4	5.4	2.8	106.2	75.8	0.3	2.0	0.7	1.5
1972	5.9	2.1	7.5	2.1	2.7	4.3	6.2	7.1	4.9	6.2	102.6	74.9	0.1	0.4	0.8	-1.2
1973	5.4	7.6	7.0	9.1	2.6	3.3	7.3	9.2	6.7	3.4	112.4	67.4	0.6	-1.4	0.9	-2.7
1974	3.2	-0.9	2.9	-2.8	2.8	3.1	13.7	16.0	4.9	1.0	116.0	68.1	-1.5	-4.0	0.6	-3.8
1975	0.2	-0.9	-7.4	-4.8	4.1	4.6	11.8	24.2	4.9	4.7	116.8	73.9	0.8	-1.5	-2.2	-4.6
1976	5.2	3.7	9.0	3.0	4.4	6.0	9.6	16.5	4.1	2.8	116.3	67.5	-1.0	-0.7	-0.5	-4.9
1977	3.1	1.2	0.9	4.9	4.7	6.4	9.4	15.8	3.0	-9.6	113.0	65.9	-0.1	0.0	-0.8	-3.2
1978	3.8	3.5	2.7	3.7	5.2	6.3	9.1	8.3	3.6	9.2	110.3	71.1	1.5	0.7	-1.9	-4.2
1979	3.3	2.0	4.4	3.6	5.9	5.6	10.8	13.4	2.1	1.4	110.1	82.5	0.9	-0.3	-0.7	-3.2
1980	1.1	-2.6	0.0	-6.9	6.3	6.9	13.6	18.0	1.3	-0.7	100.0	100.0	-0.6	1.4	0.2	-3.5
1981	0.3	-1.3	-0.8	-3.7	7.3	10.6	13.4	11.9	0.9	-1.9	94.4	105.1	-0.8	2.6	-1.8	-2.8
1982	1.6	2.3	-2.6	1.0	8.0	12.3	11.8	8.6	3.0	-1.4	90.9	101.3	-2.2	2.0	-2.6	-2.1
1983	0.7	3.3	1.8	2.9	8.0	13.1	9.6	4.6	1.5	1.0	89.6	93.7	-0.8	0.7	-3.2	-3.7

Source: Kate Barker et al., 'Macroeconomic policy in France and Britain', *National Institute Economic Review* (Nov. 1984) p. 69.

with this fact by comparing the performance in 1980 (the last full year when he was Prime Minister) with the subsequent French performance and that of the United States, the United Kingdom, Federal Germany and Japan in 1983. All the others were in deficit both in 1980 and in 1983.[13] Whereas this seems to reflect credit on the performance of the Barre government, he failed to point out that in the four preceding years when he was Prime Minister France was also in deficit, ranging from 0.5 to 1.9 of GDP.

Raymond Barre has also made great play with the rapid increase in the public debt from 418 billion francs at the end of 1980 to in excess of 1,000 billion francs in 1985. However, although serious, this development should be placed in Franco-British perspective. Writing in 1983, a National Institute team declared: 'The ratio of general government debt to GDP ten years ago was very much higher in Britain than in France. Britain, with a ratio of 70 per cent was far above the average of major industrial countries and France at 25 per cent was well below. The contrast is not nearly so extreme today. The debt ratio in Britain was eroded by inflation in the 1970s and then maintained at a reduced level by the stringency of fiscal policy; in France despite the smaller size of the recorded deficit the debt ratio was constant up to 1980. Since that date it has risen quite fast, at a rate which has been regarded with deep concern in France. The UK debt to GDP ratio is now only a little above the average for a major industrial country, which has itself risen sharply in recent years, whilst in France the ratio is still well below average.'[14] Opening the 1985 budget debate, the Finance Minister declared that France's internal public debt at 870 billion francs was only 18 per cent of GNP compared with over 20 per cent in Federal Germany, 43 per cent in the United States and nearly 50 per cent in the United Kingdom and Japan.[15] While the relatively underdeveloped state of the market for public-sector debt in France and high interest rates accentuate its problem of debt financing, the situation may be described as desperate but not serious.

In view of the Anglo-American tendency to regard the economic policy debate as one between Keynesians and monetarists, it is important to stress that the French tradition in economic management was a combination of Rueff-style traditional monetarist credit control, balanced budgets and stable exchange rates, with piecemeal state intervention in resource allocation and industrial development. 'The use of budget deficits to stabilise aggregate demand, which was of the essence of Keynesianism . . . was foreign to France.'[16] Such counter-cyclical action, based upon the assumption that state intervention was subsidiary to the operations of the market, was not typical of French interventionism which in the post-war period was concerned with rapid and sustained growth rather than with stabilization. The French emphasis upon monetary policy was combined with greater success in approximating to targets than that achieved in the United Kingdom, despite the conversion of the Labour Government (under IMF pressure) in 1976 and the enthusiastic embrace of monetarism by the Conservative Government since 1979. As Table 9.2 shows, the worst failure occurred in 1980, when the British outcome was more than double the target, whereas in France the achievement was— unusually—below target. So although the United Kingdom preached monetarism, France practised it more effectively, one of many examples of the divergence between rhetoric and reality.

Table 10.2 Monetary targets and actual percentage growth in France and the United Kingdom, 1977–83

Year	France (M2)		UK (M3)	
	Target	Outcome	Target	Outcome
1977	12.5	13.9	9–13	16.0
1978	12	12.2	8–12	10.9
1979	11	14.4	7–11	10.3
1980	11	9.8	7–11	22.2
1981	10	11.4	6–10	13.5
1982	12.5–13.5	12.0	8–12	10.8
1983	9	10.2	7–11	9.9

Source: Kate Barker et al., National Institute Economic Review, (Nov. 1984) p.75.

Using comparative data on the growth of government consumption and national income in sixteen, mainly European, advanced industrial societies from 1951 to 1980, Alt and Chrystal argue that generally and even in those countries, such as the United Kingdom, that were committed to government macro-economic manipulation of public expenditure, long-term inertia predominates over short-term change. Government consumption generally grew faster by just over 1 per cent per year because governments planned that this should happen and these plans were difficult to change to suit short-term fluctuations in political or economic circumstances. Whereas the participation of socialist parties in government tends to be associated with slightly faster increases in public expenditure, the fit is by no means perfect. Furthermore, from 1951 to 1974, in the case of France the growth of government consumption did not exceed that of national income, and over the period 1951–80 it only surpassed it by 0.1 per cent annually.[17] Such results and other investigations of the political business cycle are certainly not consistent with the ambitious model that leads Frey and Schneider to claim that public expenditure increases are correlated with periods of 'popularity deficit'.[18] The Mauroy Government was responsible for a modest expansion of public expenditure in 1981–2 at a time when it was enjoying the maximum popularity of the *état de grâce* and cut back on public expenditure in 1983–4 when its 'popularity deficit' reached record size! Given the propensity of French Governments to go easy on tax controls before general elections and to increase their severity afterwards, there might be more mileage in a political *fiscal enforcement* cycle rather than in a political *business* cycle.

Planning: Prometheus Bound

The heroic, Promethean conception of planning favoured by the Socialists came into collision with the fact that, in practice, planning 'has more the character of getting into step with the world than of changing it'.[19] The Left had long been commited to an ambitious conception of planning, based on the belief that the scope for social and economic change and the margin of political choice was much greater than anything even de Gaulle had attempted. Pierre Mendès France had sketched in 1962 the democratic and decentralized, yet rigorous national and regional planning institutions that were intended to become the centrepiece of political life, focusing political debate upon the alternative policy choices and simultaneously planning from above and from below.[20] Similar ideas had been developed by the CFDT in the 1959 report on democratic planning,[21] so that both on the political and industrial wings of the non-Communist labour movement, the ground had been prepared for a drastic change in the direction of French planning, both in its methods and in its objectives.

The immediate effect of the Mitterrand victory was to render the Eighth Plan, intended to cover the period 1981–5, stillborn. In fact, 1981 was the first year since 1947 when no national plan was in operation in France. The minister responsible for planning, Michel Rocard, who was very much in sympathy with the ideas formulated by Mendès France and the CFDT, concentrated initially upon preparing a two-year Interim Plan (1982–3) which had a dual purpose. It was intended to allow a reversal of policies that it was hoped would enable the French economy to resume its expansion, as well as to reform the planning process so that the Ninth Plan would coincide with the last five years (1984–8) of President Mitterrand's term of office. Such a synchronization of the planning and political timetable had been an important element in the Mendès France proposals and it would now be possible to see if the hazards of political and economic circumstance could be confined within the sedate limits of a quinquennial calendar.

Indicative of the desire to link planning with parliamentary democracy rather than the previous emphasis upon techno-bureaucracy with a corporatist camouflage, parliament playing a formal, negligible role,[22] the committee established in January 1982 to re-examine the techniques and methods of planning was placed under the chairmanship of the National Assembly's finance committee chairman Christian Goux. Its March 1982 report formed the basis of the 1982 Act on the reform of planning. Starting from an analysis of the decline in planning that had occurred from its early 1960s' Gaullist apotheosis as an 'ardent obligation', planning's fourfold functions conceived as forecasting, concerting interests with a view to making their demands more realistic, offering an attractive vision of the kind of society being developed or achieving administrative coordination, had all regressed.[23] Even the Priority Action Programmes experiment—aimed in part at overcoming administrative inertia—had succumbed to the Budget Division's hostility, so that the programmes scheduled for the Eighth Plan were shorn of all medium-term financial commitment. Returning to Monnet's view that planning should be based upon national consensus and not merely the will of the government—which had itself failed in recent years—the Goux committee stressed the need to create the conditions for a 'dynamic social compromise' based upon 'a widely shared diagnosis of the crisis'. The plan's implementation depended above all on establishing firm links between the five-year plan and the annual budgets, themselves based upon programme budgets in each ministry. To ensure that the plan's priorities were honoured in practice, programme laws would be necessary to give them legislative force and officials of the Planning Commissariat would need to take part in the annual spending ministry–Budget Division meetings. Ensuring the government's financial commitment to the plan was not sufficient. Contracts would have to be signed with public and private enterprises to ensure that the plan's objectives would be implemented by firms. Similar planning contracts were also to be signed with regional councils and local authorities.[24]

We have, in chapter 8, discussed the Priority Implementation Programmes (PIPs) of the Ninth Plan. As far as wider participation and decentralized planning are concerned, it should be borne in mind that recourse to a multiplicity of contracts has sought to combine concerted action and consistency with reciprocal commitment as a way of safeguarding comprehensive national planning from being overwhelmed by local priorities and preferences. A very diversified and selective set of specific planning agreements seek to reconcile the logic of central policies and extra-national constraints with the aims of peripheral actors. Without wishing to detract from the importance of what has been done, the bilateral character of such agreements is very much in the French tradition of central–regional–local relations, aimed at least as much at recentralization with consent as decentralist autonomy. This is even clearer in the case of the planning contracts between the government and public enterprises, where the managerial autonomy of the latter is circumscribed by more or less specific but not always consistent guidelines. Furthermore, one may anticipate that each public enterprise will put its commercial viability before conforming to government priorities, one of the problems of seeking to reconcile state planning and the market. The trade unions have continued, as in the past, to be faced with *faits accomplis*, leading to protests notably in the case of the 1984 EDF planning contract.

Parliament has undoubtedly played a more active part in the preparation of the Ninth Plan than in its predecessors. Not merely did parliament take a more active part in amending the Ninth Plan, but it will be able to monitor the conformity of the PIPs' performance with the programmes as part of the annual autumn budgetary process. While the Economic and Social Council continues to provide the major peak interest groups with little influence on the planning process, the regional economic and social committees may have been brought more fully into the process than heretofore. The new National Planning Commission (whose functions partly duplicate those of the Economic and Social Council in planning matters) which includes the presidents of all the regional councils monitors the Plan's progress twice yearly, in the spring as well as in the autumn.

Whether French planning continues its decline of the 1970s and early 1980s or enjoys a rejuvenation is likely to depend less upon the procedures used, the will of the many public decision makers or the goodwill of the even more numerous private decision makers as such, than upon France's ability to change the economic direction in which it is tending. If the country's political, administrative, industrial and financial leaders are unable to reverse an apparently inexorable trend towards economic stagnation rather than growth, to increasing unemployment and indebtedness, to large balance of payments and budgetary deficits, planning will be discredited owing to an unmerited 'guilt by association' with failure. The fact that the planners have been concerned to explore alternative scenarios, based upon plausible hypotheses about the interaction between an uncertain international environment and the priorities of national economic policy, to assess their expected consequences and to enumerate the preconditions of achieving policy objectives, cannot guarantee success. Particularly when it is associated with ambitious political rhetoric repudiating the non-interventionist 'muddling through' policy style—the dead dog drifting downstream—planning may seem to be too pretentious a label when all that is possible is improvising interim remedies to intractable problems, which seems difficult enough.

Industrial Ownership: Nationalization or Privatization?

The ideologically charged and interest-permeated issue of the ownership of the means of production and credit would seem at first sight an even more promising candidate for demonstrating that a change of the political majority in power will lead to a change in public policy. The early 1980s seemed to show a clear contrast between a Right-wing government in the United Kingdom hell-bent upon the privatization of any marketable public property and a Left-wing government in France embarked upon a massive programme of nationalization. Yet in a longer perspective, the alternatives do not seem so stark or the change of direction so radical as would be suggested by an adversarial interpretation of the interchange between public and private ownership in the United Kingdom and in France. More deep-seated cultural commitments to the public enterprise operating like a commercial business (which is the dominant model in the United Kingdom) and like a techno-bureaucratic entrepreneur (the dominant model in France) ensure much greater continuity, punctuated more often by pragmatic improvization to meet particular circumstances than ideologically inspired irreversible change.

Although in the immediate post-Second World War years, the

United Kingdom and France undertook comparable programmes of nationalization by governments wholly or partially composed of Left-wing parties, rather different kinds of state capitalism were developed, shame-faced and divisive in the case of the United Kingdom, and self-assertive and consensual in the French case. For whereas the Labour Party's 1945 public ownership programme stressed its socialist aspects, in France nationalization was presented by de Gaulle as a patriotic act to strengthen national economic power and independence. Whereas in the United Kingdom the nationalization legislation was bitterly contested in parliament and in two cases (road haulage and steel) partially reversed on the return of the Conservatives to power, in France the legislation was virtually unopposed and the preamble to the 1946 constitution enshrined a commitment to nationalize any property or enterprise having a monopoly or public service character. Thereafter, not until the early 1980s—with the advent of a Thatcher Government in the United Kingdom in 1979 and of a Mitterrand presidency in 1981—did the issue of nationalization/privatization in practice assume major significance in either country, although important incremental changes were made without exciting intense controversy. There was some symbolic privatization during the presidencies of Pompidou and Giscard d'Estaing, but this was deliberately kept partial, so that by the end of the Giscard presidency the results were modest. For example, the shares of the three public deposit banks were still publicly owned as to 91 per cent in the cases of *Crédit Lyonnais* and BNP, 87 per cent for the *Société Générale*, while the shares of the three public insurance companies were public as to 80 per cent for AGF, 91 per cent for UAP and 92 per cent for GAN.

Much more significant was the surreptitious and piecemeal extension of public ownership to which Edouard Bonnefous, chairman of the Senate Finance Committee, drew attention in the 1970s. He pointed out that in the years of Right-wing government a massive, incremental increase in the secondary and tertiary holdings of public enterprises had taken place, without public notice or public control, by capitalist-style diversification and establishment of subsidiaries.[25] Furthermore, when the 1982 nationalization programme was enacted, it transpired that the state already indirectly owned a minority shareholding of about 8 per cent in the industrial concerns through its banks and insurance companies, especially the *Caisse des Dépôts*. The latter alone owned 5.5 per cent of the *Compagnie Générale d'Electricité*, six per cent of *Saint-Gobain-Pont à Mousson*, 5.6 per cent of *Pechiney Ugine Kuhlmann*, 7.2 per cent of

Thomson–Brandt, 5.2 per cent of *Rhône-Poulenc*, 28.2 per cent of USINOR, and 33.2 per cent of SACILOR, while it also owned shares in the two major investment banks destined to be nationalized: 4.1 per cent of *Paribas* and 5.7 per cent of *Suez*. The basic steel duopoly had already been effectively nationalized under Giscard in 1978, the state indirectly owning 85 per cent of USINOR and 77 per cent of SACILOR.[26] This situation, the French state as a tentacular holding company passively accepted well before the advent of President Mitterrand, makes sense when seen in the French context of an interlocking economic directorate based upon recruitment of the managers of large public and private firms from the same *grandes écoles* that staff the senior civil service and provide the source of many top politicians, with *pantouflage* as the mechanism by which the elite circulates. This factor partly explains why so little fundamentally changed despite the massive Nationalization Law of February 1982.

While the extension of public ownership thus appeared from the 1950s to 1970s to be an example of an inexorable trend divorced from the political preferences of govenment and parties, the 1972 Socialist–Communist Joint Government Programme marked the emergence of an alternative partisan attitude. As its detailed proposals closely anticipated the 1982 legislation, its influence must not be underrated, although the decade that elapsed between programme and enactment produced a major switch in the justification offered. Dropping the promise that workers in a firm could request its nationalization—which would have given the PCF controlled CGT immense scope for expanding piecemeal the scale of public ownership—was indicative that 'whereas in 1972 nationalization was advocated primarily to shift power from capitalists to workers, in the wake of the 1970s' economic recession, nationalization was presented as a major instrument for overcoming under-investment and unemployment. Whilst trade unions have strengthened their position within the nationalized firms, the state-appointed managers remain firmly in control. Less emphasis was placed upon ideological imperatives and more weight was given to practical concerns, though nationalization as protection against multinationalization conveniently combined both preoccupations. Mitterrand appealed openly to the patron saint of industrial patriotism: "We must achieve through nationalization what de Gaulle achieved in nuclear strategy, provide France with an economic strike force".[27] The emphasis upon selecting industries of strategic importance to the government's undustrial policy and controlling the banking system to provide the financial resources to carry out that policy was reiterated by the Prime Minister, Industry Minister and all official spokesmen.

However, although this approach corresponded to the views developed particularly by the Communist party (as an adjunct of its theory of state monopoly capitalism and the peaceful transition to socialism), it did not correspond to the reasons underlying public support for nationalization or the managerial realities of publicly owned enterprises, which had little to do with 'ruptures with capitalism'. A public opinion poll conducted a year before the 1981 presidential election showed that when asked which were the two main objectives that public enterprises should set themselves in France, the majority—especially on the Left—gave priority to providing jobs over better service to consumers and sustaining national economic growth. Consequently, although the Socialist activists and leaders especially stressed the link between nationalization and planning, industrial policy, regional development and the workplace rights of workers, their supporters had other priorities of which job security was foremost, a notion borrowed from civil service employment. As consumers, they also expressed the opinion, by 51 to 22 percent, that if public firms were privatized their products would be more expensive and although the majority was higher in the case of Left-wing voters (58 to 20 per cent) the response of Right-wing voters was similar (50 to 28 per cent).[28] Since 1983, public opinion has become more favourable to privatization, partly because nationalization no longer provides a guarantee of employment and partly owing to the fact that the state seems to have lost its traditional hegemony for the present.

Table 10.3   The two main objectives public enterprises should seek

Objective	All (%)	Left (%)	Right (%)
Provide a large number of stable jobs	64	68	55
Give the best possible service to consumers	56	57	56
Contribute to the country's economic growth	48	49	57
Develop new techniques	17	16	21

Source: Alain Lancelot, 'Le service public industriel et commercial devant l'opinion', based on March–April 1980 SOFRES poll, reported in Le Monde, Dossiers et Documents, supplement (Oct. 1980) p.23.

As far as the management of French public enterprises is concerned, there has—since the 1967 Nora report on public enterprises—been an emphasis upon the need for them to operate as much like private enterprises as possible, putting commercial requirements before public service. However, in practice, pre-1981 Right-wing governments used public enterprises—especially those in deficit and therefore requiring financial assistance—as agents of short-term national economic management, keeping inflation down by public price restraint or promoting counter-cyclical investment in the public sector to compensate for the unwillingness of the private firms to invest, which was such a feature of the 1970s. However, in the case of those enterprises that were under strong management, notably EDF, ELF and Renault, there was substantial *de facto* autonomy despite piecemeal political and administrative intervention. Thus the economic restructuring, which was one of the objectives of post-1981 nationalization, had already been practised in a regular way, albeit without any overall, carefully thought-out strategy, carried out with continuity of purpose.[29]

The firms that were nationalized in 1982 were already national champions and although a few president/managing directors were replaced, they 'have not been subjected to the Plan or their firms dismembered, their strategic and managerial autonomy has scarcely been challenged and their internal power structure seems untouched', so that there has been 'a surprising continuity under the Fifth Republic. In practice, the public authorities, despite their liberal or volontarist rhetoric, give free play to the dynamics of cooptation: the continuity of industrial policies (of the firms) is guaranteed.'[30] So, despite the attempt at an integrated industrial policy, thanks to medium-term planning contracts signed with each of the public enterprises, it is likely that French industrial policy will continue to resemble an improvised combination of mainly piecemeal interventions based upon the specific strategies of the individual enterprises. The fact that they generally operate with similar managers and in a similar fashion to large private firms means that the case both for nationalization and for privatization is weakened.

This has not prevented the Right-wing parties (and Jacques Chirac as early as December 1981) from promising privatization as quickly as possible, with the RPR proposing the establishment of a financial agency to organize the process, whereas the UDF has stressed privatization of the banks as the top priority. Part of the attraction may be that whereas nationalization increases public borrowing privatization reduces it—both at the change of ownership and subsequently; an important consideration when, as in the

United Kingdom, it proves difficult to reduce public expenditure. There is little to suggest that a mere change of *ownership* will result in increased industrial or competitive capacity. In any case, there has been a massive 'natural' contraction—especially in employment—of the nationalized sector, which reminds us that underlying the spectacular policies dictated by partisan preference, humdrum forces are at work which impose changes that are at least as important in their effects.

Industrial Policy or Industrialists Policy? The Sub-Contractor State

We saw in Chapter 1 that 'industrial policy' is usually a symbolic, unitary fiction to cover a multitude of piecemeal, improvisatory and portentous claims by governments to be pursuing a comprehensive and consistent medium- and long-term industrial strategy. Because 'industrial policy' amounts to a number of specific practices that serve the interests and strategies of the large firms that belong to the industrial policy community, it should not be surprising that it frequently amounts to an industrialists' policy, such as would have appealed to Saint-Simon. Why should large enterprises—whether public or private—seek protection and assistance from the impact of market forces? 'Embedded in economies caught between external pressures and internal pressures and rigidities; confronted with an economic environment characterized by low growth, high unemployment, inflationary risks, a crisis of the welfare state, and structural adjustment; having to face important technical changes; engaged in fierce international competition; experiencing similar problems but having difficulties cooperating, European industrial firms . . . are in a very delicate situation. Hence it is not surprising if voices ask for industrial policies with intensities differing from one country to another.'[31] Such voices have been especially vociferous in France. Since the Second World War, more than any 'capitalist' country other than Japan, French governments have been concerned to regulate, recommend, subsidize, nationalize in the promotion of national industrial development through a variety of policies of which specifically industrial policy is not the most important. Quite apart from the impact of macro-economic policies upon industry, the significance of exchange rate, energy, employment, industrial training and research policies (to name but a few of the most directly relevant) is blindingly obvious. This also directs our attention to a major problem of conducting even a specifically industrial policy:

the involvement of many interdependent but autonomous actors, each with their own priorities and without a policy maker in command capable of pursuing a consistent policy free from indecision and confusion.

Where if anywhere is industrial policy coordinated in France? Is it in the wishfully renamed Ministry of Industrial Redeployment and External Trade? We have already discussed past failures at making the Industry Ministry the focus of industrial policy and since 1981 the rapid switch of ministers with diametrically opposed views has not helped increase its credibility. After the former head of Renault—Pierre Dreyfus—who favoured relying upon the autonomy of nationalized managers and reducing industrial policy to the policies of national champion firms, came the hyper-interventionist advocate of *volontarisme*. Jean-Pierre Chevènement was determined to boss the nationalized firms personally and to launch a series of ultra-ambitious industrial plans to rescue the dying machine tools industry, catch up on electronics, etc. with the help of massive inputs of public money. He was in turn succeeded by the future Prime Minister Laurent Fabius, who reverted to a classic policy of modernization in the service of competitiveness and completed the process of concluding planning contracts while abandoning the *dirigiste* proclivities of his predecessor in favour of a speedy return to profitability and coping with crises as they arose. He was helped by his close personal links with President Mitterrand and his adviser on industrial matters Alain Boublil, at which level official industrial decisions were often taken. The Industry Ministry was bolstered in 1984 by being given control of an Industrial Modernization Fund but many other influential actors continue to be involved in industrial policy, notably the Treasury and Budget Divisions of the Finance Ministry, as well as the Prime Minister and his advisers. The Planning Commissariat and DATAR also sought to influence the decisions on a case-by-case basis, but the endeavour to secure an overall formulation and coordination of industrial policy through the planning process has proved illusory. In 1984, another attempt was made through the establishment of a tripartite National Industry Commission to review annually the progress of French industrial policy with the help of thirteen industrial strategy groups. Like the planning contracts between nationalized enterprises and the government, this was an attempt to secure harmony between the industrial strategies of the government and the large firms, but such institutional devices are not capable of fulfilling so ambitious a function successfully.

The disparity between the ambitious hopes placed upon industrial policy and the varied achievements, ranging from spectacular success, through modest benefits relative to cost, on to disastrous failure, is also due to the need to differentiate between three types of situation which condition the government's capacity to carry out its own strategy. The key factor is the presence or absence of powerful national champion firms. Where such firms already exist (for instance, the firms nationalized in 1982) their strategy usually prevails over that of the various state actors. This is because the government is compelled to 'sub-contract' the implementation of its policies to them, which they 'redefine in terms of their own plans' with 'state policies providing sources of financial assistance into which industrial groups can dip.'[32] In the case of nationalized enterprises, the President of the Republic may use his power of appointment of the top manager as a way of overcoming one of the factors making for the industrial power of firms (the continuity of their management) but this has proved less significant than the copious press coverage would suggest. Either the existing management is confirmed in office, or the new head adopts the policy of his predecessor or he formulates a new policy which he will defend against the government as vigorously as his predecessors have done. In every case, the autonomy of the management—which is proclaimed in general and violated in practice by all governments—remains largely intact on the fundamental issue of pursuing its own strategy, helped by collusion between members of the same *corps* in the civil service and in the public enterprise. The replacement of the heads of *Rhône Poulenc*, ELF and USINOR by Mitterrand led to no change in their strategy.

In the case of industries whose firms were virtually bankrupt, ambitious schemes, sometimes using the advice of the Boston Consulting Group, were devised to concentrate production. They broke down because there were no industrialists capable of reorganizing the industry. This was notably true of machine tools and chemicals, while we have already seen that the decline of steel has not been arrested nor the retreat conducted with much semblance of good order. A third type of situation—characteristic of the oil, electro-nuclear, aircraft, space, armaments and telecommunications industries—arises where the inertia of the private sector leads the state to step in directly, using public purchasing and soft loans, forgoing short-term profitability and relying upon a 'homogeneous elite to convert the state's plan into that of a *corps*.'[33] However, if it succeeds, the government quickly finds itself facing a self-assertive national champion, whose power and resources may have been created by the state but are now used in the pursuit of its own strategy. The industrial policy community in practice disintegrates into its component elements and with it any hope of a comprehensive, continuous and consistent policy.

It was precisely to palliate the consequences of this tendency for the financial and industrial strategy of the major firms to diverge from that of the government (fixed generally through the planning process or piecemeal by specific decisions) that prompted the revival of the idea of planning contracts. Previous experiments in 1970–1 and in 1977 had been failures, largely because the government usually did not want to be financially committed for years to the strategy of a public enterprise and because both sides preferred to bargain in less formal ways. The Mitterrand presidency has witnessed a more determined attempt to generalize three- to five-year planning contracts to all major public enterprises. However, secrecy—insisted upon by the firms—makes it difficult to be specific about their significance, other than to stress their symbolic expression of the reciprocal commitment of government and firms to common objectives.[34] They include too many priorities to make any of them effective, with the really significant matters having to be read between the lines. Even the commitment to managerial freedom tends to break down in practice for some public utilities because, in the case of the railways, it can only decide tariff reductions not increases and wages (amounting to three-quarters of its costs) are often fixed by the Prime Minister. As far as the newly nationalized industrial firms are concerned, as well as powerful public utilities like EDF, their negotiations with the government are fundamentally aimed at securing state financial, regulatory and purchasing support from their strategies, with the national plan being modified to suit their 'contracts' rather than the reverse. Although 'planning contracts' were originally envisaged with private as well as public firms, none have been signed, which suggest that private ownership remains a real constraint upon government attempts to secure the *formal* cooperation of firms. Whether this amounts in practice to much more than a symbolic difference is dubious if the policies that emerge are those of the industrialists, with the state reduced to the role of sub-contractor.

Crisis Mismanagement

Rather than a Keynesian redistributive reflation in the service of go-it-alone 'socialism in one country' the early mistakes of the Mauroy Government were based upon the miscalculation—shared by the OECD and EEC—that there would be a revival in the world economy in the second half of 1981.[35] Furthermore, there had been a pre-electoral expansion of domestic demand by the Barre Government and as soon as the advent of a Left-wing president seemed a possibility, there was a classic run on the franc recalling that faced by the Popular Front Government of Léon Blum in 1936. The same mistake was made. In the spirit of the Mitterrand slogan of the *force tranquille*, there was a symbolic refusal to inaugurate his presidency with a devaluation.

Mauroy recounts how in the three months preceding the election of Mitterrand 5 billion dollars left the country, followed by a further 3 billion between 11 and 15 May 1981. Thereafter, the speculative outflow increased from half a billion to a billion dollars daily and was expected to increase further. The director of the Treasury Division had, at the beginning of May, advised that exchange control should be reinforced but the Barre Government refused to act. Despite Rocard's advice that the franc should be allowed to float, that is to accept an immediate devaluation, the future Prime Minister and Finance Minister (Delors) advocated a 'defence' of the franc within the European Monetary System (EMS). In the car travelling down the Champs-Elysées on 21 May 1981 after the transfer of presidential power, Mauroy secured Mitterrand's decision to support the franc.[36] Despite the Governor of the Bank of France's scepticism on their ability to maintain the franc's parity, Mauroy, Delors, Bérégovoy (Delors' successor as Finance Minister in 1984), the Governor and the head of the Treasury decided on the exchange control measures that staunched the immediate outflow but stored up the pressures that were to lead to three devaluations against the deutschmark on 4 October 1981, 12 June 1982 and 21 March 1983. Combined with the climb of the US dollar against all currencies, the franc lost more than half of its dollar value between 1980–4, exerting irresistible pressure to reverse 'socialist' policies.

At its very first cabinet meeting, the Mauroy Government launched a series of ambitious measures to deal with the problem of unemployment. The most important were steps to reduce the age of retirement and subsequently to encourage early retirement (notably through 'solidarity contracts') which made the largest contribution to the slowdown of unemployment in France of all the job-related policies adopted. The public sector directly employed over 200,000 more people, either in government service or in the nationalized industries. The most controversial issue of all, but ironically the one that saved fewest jobs, was the reduction in the workweek, over and above a fifth week's annual paid holiday which was promised as Proposal 23 in Mitterrand's presidential election programme. Although it was hoped to reduce the workweek by an hour a year from forty to thirty-five, it proved impossible to proceed beyond the fall to thirty-nine hours, partly because Mitterrand yielded to the refusal of the trade unions (apart from the CFDT) to countenance even a partial compensatory reduction in the wage rate. Having in 1983 managed to hold unemployment at about 2 million, the demotion of employment as the top policy priority led to an increase in the jobless to 2.5 million by the end of 1984.

However, the main reason for this reversal of initial policy priorities as well as of so many others was the need to restore the profitability and capacity to invest of firms, which we saw in Chapter 9 was the official reason given for prudence in workweek reduction during the preparation of the Giscardian Eighth Plan. The fight against unemployment becomes a secondary concern once one concedes that secure jobs will not be created without investment in internationally competitive industries that will earn the profits to finance them. (In 1983, of the hundred French firms with the largest turnover, fifty-two were not making profits but losses.) The decline of self-financed investment which preceded the advent of Mitterrand but accelerated thereafter meant that, as in the case of the exchange rate, all that he was able to do was delay the day of reckoning. This simply underlines the fact that one can abolish capital punishment by a sovereign political decision, but not similarly decide one's exchange rate or employment level. 'Whichever party is in office, the state of the economy is primarily determined by secular trends stronger than the intentions or skills of the party governing. This is true whether one examines economic inputs that governments can control or . . . the economic outcomes that reflect the interaction of government policy and international economic conditions.'[37] When the French Socialists came to power they said that they would refuse to manage the crisis of capitalism. Unfortunately, it transpired that the alternative was to mismanage it. The consequent involuntary change in economic policy may help the liberalized Socialists reconcile the role of the state and the market through a more judicious assessment of their limited capacity to assert political will over stubborn market realities. Recourse to revolution is another form of anti-fatalism but those who in despair of reform place their hopes in revolution should recall Ambrose Bierce's characterization of it as 'an abrupt change in the form of misgovernment'. Fatalism is more likely to follow in the wake of disillusionment with inordinate ambition than from a circumspect modesty of objective pursued with perseverence.

NOTES

Preliminaries

1. Nannerl O. Keohane, *Philosophy and the State in France. The Renaissance to the Enlightenment*, Princeton University Press, Princeton, N.J., 1980, p.160; cf. pp.159–66, 378–80, 389.
2. Léon Duguit, *Traité de Droit Constitutionnel*, Fontemoing, Paris, 1st ed. 1911, 3rd ed. 1927, Vol. II, pp.756–7.
3. SOFRES public opinion poll, *Le Monde*, 5 November 1984, p.6.

Chapter 1

1. James E. Alt and K. Alec Chrystal, *Political Economics* (Wheatsheaf, Brighton, 1983) p.35.
2. *ibid.*, pp.36–7.
3. James M. Buchanan *et al.*, *The Economics of Politics* (Institute of Economic Affairs, London, 1978) p.10.
4. Alt and Chrystal, p.131, referring to Jan Tinbergen, *On the Theory of Economic Policy* (North-Holland, Amsterdam, 1952) Ch. 6, and H. Theil, *Optimal Decision Rules for Government and Industry* (North-Holland, Amsterdam, 1968) Ch. 6.
5. Alt and Chrystal, pp.131–2.
6. *ibid.*, p.145.
7. Brian Hogwood, 'Analysing industrial policy: a multi-perspective approach', *Public Administration Bulletin*, no. 29 (April 1979) p.36; cf. pp.35–7.
8. Kenneth Dyson, in Kenneth Dyson and Stephen Wilks (eds.) *Industrial Crisis. A Comparative Study of the State and Industry* (Martin Robertson, Oxford, 1983) p.35; cf. p.45.
9. *ibid.*, p.46; cf. p.65.
10. Chalmers Johnson, *MITI and the Japanese Miracle. The Growth of Industrial Policy* (Stanford University Press, Stanford, 1982) p.11; cf. pp.21, 65–73.
11. *ibid.*, p.24, and Dyson, p.40.
12. Max Weber, *General Economic History* (Collier Books, New York, 1961) p.255; cf. pp.253-7.
13. *ibid.*, pp.257–8.
14. C.B. Macpherson, *The Political Theory of Possessive Individualism* (Oxford University Press, Oxford, 1962) p.58; cf. p.62.
15. John K. Galbraith, *Economics and the Public Purpose* (Penguin, Harmondsworth, 1975) p.37; cf. J.K. Galbraith, *American Capitalism. The Concept of Countervailing Power* (Penguin, Harmondsworth, 1963) p.35.
16. Friederich A. Hayek, *The Counter-Revolution of Science. Studies in the Abuse of Reason* (Free Press of Glencoe, New York, 1964) pp.133–5. *See also* Frederick Engels, in Marx–Engels, *Selected Works* vol. II, (Foreign Languages Publishing House, Moscow, 1962) p.151; cf. pp.122–3, from 'Socialism: utopian and scientific'.
17. Hayek, p.147; cf. part 2, ch. 4 *passim*.

18. Andrew Shonfield, *Modern Capitalism. The Changing Balance of Public and Private Power* (Oxford University Press, London, 1965) p.385; cf. pp.63, 66–7.
19. *ibid.*, pp.71–2.
20. *ibid.*, pp.73, 85.
21. Charles Lindblom, 'The sociology of planning: thought and social interaction' in Morris Bornstein (ed.) *Economic Planning, East and West* (Ballinger, Cambridge, Mass., 1975) p.54; cf. pp.53–7.
22. Charles Lindblom, *Politics and Markets* (Basic Books, New York, 1977) pp.326–7.
23. *ibid.*, pp.291–2.
24. *ibid.*, p.307; cf. pp.305–8.
25. *ibid.*, p.175.
26. *ibid.*
27. Charles Lindblom, 'Still muddling, not yet through', *Public Administration Review* (Nov.–Dec. 1979) p.520.
28. Galbraith, *American Capitalism. The Concept of Countervailing Power*, p.21.
29. Lindblom, *Politics and Markets*, p.356.
30. *ibid.*, p.116.
31. C. Wright Mills, *The Power Elite* (Oxford University Press, New York, 1959) p.244; cf. pp.245–7.
32. Karl Polanyi, *The Great Transformation* (Beacon Press, Boston, 1957) p.57.
33. Hugh Heclo and Aaron Wildavsky, *The Private Government of Public Money. Community and Policy inside British Politics* (Macmillan, London, 1974) p.xv.
34. *ibid.*
35. *ibid.*, p.xvi.

Chapter 2

1. Jack Hayward, 'Mobilising private interests in the service of public ambitions: the salient element in the dual French policy style?', in Jeremy J. Richardson (ed.) *Policy Styles in Western Europe*, (George Allen & Unwin, London, 1982) p.111.
2. *ibid.*, p.116.
3. John Zysman, *Political Strategies for Industrial Order. State, Market and Industry in France* (University of California Press, Berkeley, 1977) p.194, ch. 7 *passim*; Harvey Feigenbaum, *The Politics of Public Enterprise. Oil and the French State* (Princeton University Press, Princeton, 1985) p.173.
4. Feigenbaum, p.94.
5. Andrew Shonfield, *Modern Capitalism. The Changing Balance of Public and Private Power* (Oxford University Press, London, 1965) pp.386–7.
6. Zysman, p.51.
7. Paul Huvelin quoted in Lionel Stoléru, *L'Impératif Industriel* (Editions du Seuil, Paris, 1969) pp.151–2.
8. Zysman, p.140.
9. John Zysman, *Governments, Markets and Growth. Financial Systems and the Politics of Industrial Change* (Martin Robertson, Oxford, 1983) p.75; cf. p.91.
10. *ibid.*, p.115; cf. pp.114 ff.
11. *ibid.*, p.114. For a less Treasury-centred view of French economic policy-making processes, *see* Jack Hayward, *Governing France: the One and Indivisible Republic* (Weidenfeld and Nicolson, London, 1983) ch. 6; Guy Lord, *The French Budgetary Process* (University of California Press, Berkeley, 1972).
12. Feigenbaum, p.135. *See* Christian Stoffaës and J. Victorri, *Nationalisations*

(Flammarion, Paris, 1977) p.110; Philippe Simmonet, *Le Pouvoir Monétaire* (Seghers, Paris, 1975) pp.166–7. *See also* the testimony of a former assistant director of the Treasury Division and director general of the *Crédit Lyonnais*, Jean Saint-Geours, *Pouvoir et Finance* (Fayard, Paris, 1979) especially ch. 6.

13. Erhard Friedberg, 'Administration et entreprises', in Michel Crozier *et al.*, *Où va l'Administration Française* (Les Editions d'Organisation, Paris, 1976) pp.105–8.
14. *ibid.*, p.116; cf. pp.115–22.
15. Ezra N. Suleiman, *Politics, Power and Bureaucracy in France* (Princeton University Press, Princeton, 1974) pp.324–8; cf. pp.337–59.
16. Jean Monnet, *Memoirs*, 1976 (Collins, London, 1978) p.231. On the origins of the term 'concerted economy', *see ibid.*, p.258. For Hirsch's testimony, *see* François Fourquet, *Les Comptes de la Puissance. Histoire de la Comptabilité Nationale et du Plan* (Encres/Recherches, Paris, 1980) p.56.
17. Monnet, p.259.
18. François Bloch-Laîné, *Profession: Fonctionnaire* (Editions du Seuil, Paris, 1976) ch. 4 and 5.
19. François Bloch-Laîné, *A la Recherche d'une 'Economie Concertée'* (Les Editions de l'Epargne, Paris, 1964) p.18.
20. *ibid.*, pp.5–6.
21. *ibid.*, pp.7–10.
22. *ibid.*, p.14.
23. *ibid.*, p.17.
24. Bloch-Laîné, *Profession: Fonctionnaire*, p.164; cf. p.165.
25. *See also* René Bonéty *et al.*, *La CFDT* (Editions du Seuil, Paris, 1971), pp.64–96; Jean-Pierre Oppenheim, *La CFDT et la Planification* (Tema-Editions, Paris, 1973); Stephen S. Cohen, *Modern Capitalist Planning: the French Model* (Weidenfeld and Nicolson, London, 1969) part 6.
26. Claude Alphandéry *et al.*, *Pour Nationaliser l'Etat* (Editions du Seuil, Paris, 1968).
27. M.R. Fischesser and M.P. Lafitte, 'La formation des ingénieurs du corps des Mines', *La Jaune et la Rouge*, no. 238 (June 1969) p.3, quoted in Ezra N. Suleiman, *Elites in French Society* (Princeton University Press, Princeton, 1978) p.209; cf. pp.203 ff.
28. Suleiman, *Elites in French Society*, pp.241, 247, 250; cf. pp.219, 242–4, 248–50.
29. Michel Bauer and Elie Cohen, *Qui Gouverne les Groupes Industriels?* (Editions du Seuil, Paris, 1981) p.208; *see also* ch. 6 and 7.
30. Pierre Birnbaum, *et al.*, *La Classe Dirigeante Française* (Presses Universitaires de France, Paris, 1978) pp.69–70, 77, 123–4.
31. Chalmers Johnson, *MITI and the Japanese Miracle. The Growth of Industrial Policy, 1925–75* (Stanford University Press, Stanford, 1982) pp.24, viii; cf. p.12.
32. *ibid.*, pp.311, 21, 318–19.
33. *ibid.*, p.26, quoting R. Ozaki, 'Japanese views on industrial organisation', *Asian Survey*, X (October 1970), p.879. For a recent example of advocacy of the Japanese model, *see* Keith Smith, *The British Economic Crisis* (Penguin Books, Harmondsworth, 1984) ch. 12.
34. Chalmers Johnson, pp.272, 320; cf. pp.29, 195, 274.
35. On the role of trade associations and other business representative bodies, *see* Jack Hayward, 'Employer associations and the state in France and Britain', in Steven J. Warnecke and Ezra N. Suleiman (eds.) *Industrial Policies in Western Europe* (Praeger, New York, 1975) ch. 5.
36. Erhard Friedberg, *Le Ministère de l'Industrie et son Environnement* (CSO,

Microfiches de l'AUDIR, Hachette, Paris, 1973). *See also* Erhard Friedberg and D. Desjeux, *Le Système d'Intervention de l'Etat en Matière Industrielle et ses Relations avec les Milieux Industriels* (CSO, Hachette, Paris, 1973).

37. *See also* Erhard Friedberg, in Michel Crozier *et al.*, 1976, pp.122–40; Liliane Sardais, *L'Etat et l'Internationalisation du Capital; un Essai sur la Politique Industrielle en France*, doctoral thesis (Université de Paris X, 1977), pp.42–8, 215–27, 255–76, 288–94, 342, 400; Christian Stoffaës, *La Grande Menace Industrielle*, 2nd edn. (Calmann-Lévy, Paris, 1979), part 3, ch. 2; Diana Green, *Managing Industrial Change. French Policies to Promote Industrial Adjustment* (HMSO, London, 1981).
38. Yves Morvan, 'La politique industrielle française depuis la Libération: quarante années d'interventions et d'ambiguités', in *Revue d'Economie Industrielle*, no. 23, on 'Les Politiques industrielles' (1er trimestre 1983) p.33; cf. pp.28 ff.
39. Bauer and Cohen, pp.96–7, 107–13, 121, 157–64.
40. N.J.D. Lucas, *Energy in France. Planning, Politics and Policy* (Europa, London, 1979) p.139; cf. pp.9, 140–50.
41. *ibid.*, pp.23–7, 32–3, 56–8, 141, 144–7, 153, 186–7.
42. Quoted by Charles Debbasch, *L'Elysée Dévoilé* (Albin Michel, Paris, 1982) p.96; cf. p.57.
43. Lucas, p.163; cf. pp.20, 28, 257–8.
44. Feigenbaum, pp.88-9.
45. Lucas, p.19.
46. *ibid.*, p.29, quoting André Giraud, in *Revue Française de L'Energie*, (Jan. 1966).
47. *See* Simon Nora *Rapport sur les Entreprises Publiques* (La Documentation Française, Paris, 1967).
48. *See* Schvartz report, *Sur les Sociétés Pétrolières Opérant en France*, rapport de la commission d'enquête parlementaire (Collection 10/18, Paris, 1974) pp.230–1.
49. Harvey Feigenbaum, 'France's oil policy: the limits of mercantilism', in Steven Cohen and Peter A. Gourevitch (eds.) *France in the Troubled World Economy* (Butterworths, London, 1982) p.125, ch. 6 *passim*.

Chapter 3

1. Jean Meynaud, *Les Groupes de Pression en France* (Presses Universitaires de France, Paris 1960); *Nouvelles Etudes sur les Groupes de Pression* (Colin, Paris, 1962).
2. Jean Meynaud, *Technocracy* (Faber, London, 1965).
3. Henry W. Ehrmann, *Organized Business in France* (Princeton University Press, Princeton, 1957).
4. Henry W. Ehrmann, 'French bureaucracy and organized interests', *Administrative Sciences Quarterly* (March 1961) pp.534–55.
5. Andrew Shonfield, *Modern Capitalism. The Changing Balance of Public and Private Power* (Oxford University Press, London, 1965) ch. 8.
6. Ehrmann, *Organized Business in France*, p.487; cf. pp.91–4, 262–3, 274–5, 303. Note Ehrmann's remark that 'generally, pluralist doctrines and practices have travelled on the continent in corporatist clothes' (p.478).
7. *See* Ezra N. Suleiman, *Politics, Power and Bureaucracy in France* (Princeton University Press, Princeton, 1974) ch. 6.
8. Ehrmann is using the word in the French sense of the narrow pursuit of sectional interest.

9. Ehrmann, 'French bureaucracy and organized interests', pp.540, 554–5.
10. François Bloch-Laîné, *A la Recherche d'une 'Economie Concertée'* (Editions de l'Epargne, Paris, 1964). Monnet attributed parenthood of the concept to his collaborator and successor as planning commissioner, Etienne Hirsch. See Jean Monnet, *Mémoires* (Fayard, Paris, 1976) p.306.
11. Ehrmann, 'French bureaucracy and organized interests', p.555 (emphasis added).
12. Shonfield, *Modern Capitalism. The Changing Balance of Public and Private Power*, pp.71–2, 86, 99, 160, 164. See also Jack Hayward's 'Introduction', in Jack Hayward and Michael Watson (eds.) *Planning, Politics and Public Policy* (Cambridge University Press, London, 1975) pp.9, 16.
13. Ezra N. Suleiman, *Politics, Power and Bureaucracy in France* (Princeton University Press, Princeton, 1974) pp.337–59.
14. Samuel E. Finer, 'The political power of organized labour', *Government and Opposition*, Vol. VIII, no. 4 (Autumn 1973) p.393. In an earlier article on 'The political power of private capital', *The Sociological Review*, Vol. III, no. 2 (1956), Finer discussed the capacity to thwart government policy as constituting 'surrogateship'.
15. Grant McConnell, 'The public values of the private association', in J.R. Pennock and J.W. Chapman (eds.) *Voluntary Associations*, in *Nomos* XI (1969) p.157.
16. Finer, 'The political power of organized labour', p.394.
17. Andrew Cox and Jack Hayward, 'The inapplicability of the corporatist model in Britain and France. The case of labor', *International Political Science Review*, vol. IV, no. 2 (April 1983), pp.217–40.
18. Vincent Wright, *The Government and Politics of France*, 1st edn. (Hutchinson, London, 1978) pp.174–85.
19. Jack Hayward, 'Mobilising private interests in the service of public ambitions: the salient element in the dual French policy style', in Jeremy J. Richardson (ed.) *Policy Styles in Western Europe* (George Allen & Unwin, London, 1982) pp.119–20.
20. Frank L. Wilson, 'Alternative models of interest intermediation: the case of France', *British Journal of Political Science*, vol. XII, 2 (April 1982) pp.173–200; and 'Les groupes d'intérêt sous la Cinquième République: test de trois modèles théoriques de l'interaction entre groupes et gouvernement', *Revue Française de Science Politique*, vol. XXXIII, 2 (April 1983) pp.220–54.
21. Wilson, 'Les groupes d'intérêt sous la Cinquième République, p.253; cf. pp.252–4.
22. On the epithet 'toothless tripartism' see Jack Hayward, in Jack Hayward and Michael Watson (eds.) *Planning, Politics and Public Policy* (Cambridge University Press, London, 1975) p.12. More generally, see Wyn Grant and David Marsh, 'Tripartism: reality or myth', *Government and Opposition*, vol. XII, 2 (1977) pp.194–211; Jeremy J. Richardson and A.G. Jordan, *Governing Under Pressure* (Martin Robertson, Oxford, 1979) pp.48–53.
23. Jack Hayward, *Governing France. The One and Indivisible Republic*, 2nd edn. (Weidenfeld and Nicolson, London, 1983) ch. 5 *passim*.
24. *ibid.*, pp.226–8; cf. pp.222–40. See also N.J.D. Lucas, *Energy in France. Planning, Politics and Policy* (Europa Publications, London, 1979).
25. Jack Hayward, 'Mobilising private interests', in Jeremy J. Richardson (ed.) *Policy Styles in Western Europe* (George Allen & Unwin, London, 1982) p.136; cf. pp.128–37.
26. J.T.S. Keeler, 'The corporatist dynamic of agricultural modernization in the

Fifth Republic', in William G. Andrews and Stanley Hoffmann (eds.) *The Fifth Republic at Twenty* (State University of New York Press, Albany, 1981) ch. 16. *See also*, 'Alternative models of interest mediation', p.199, and the data reported in tables 4, 5 and 6 in Frank L. Wilson, 'Les groupes d'intérêt sous la Cinquième République', as well as Jack Hayward, 'Dissentient France: the counter political culture', in Vincent Wright (ed.) *Conflict and Consensus in France* (Cass, London, 1979) pp.56–7.

27. Jack Hayward, 'Interest groups and the demand for state action', in Jack Hayward and R.N. Berki (eds.) *State and Society in Contemporary Europe* (Martin Robertson, Oxford, 1979) pp.26–7. *See also* Hayward, *Governing France. The One and Indivisible Republic*, pp.68–9.
28. *See* Cox and Hayward, 'The inapplicability of the corporatist model in Britain and France', pp.217–40. More generally, *see* Klaus von Beyme, *Challenge to Power. Trade Unions and Industrial Relations in Capitalist Countries* (Sage, London, 1980).
29. It is not only political parties who receive time for broadcasts but six trade unions, the CNPF, two farm organizations (FNSEA and MODEF), one craftsmen's organization and the Chambers of Commerce, of Agriculture and of Craftsmen.

Chapter 4

1. Duncan Gallie, *In Search of the New Working Class* (Cambridge University Press, Cambridge, 1978) pp.301–2.
2. *ibid.*, p.305.
3. *ibid.*, p.314; cf. pp.280, 289–92. *See also* Duncan Gallie, *Social Inequality and Class Radicalism in France and Britain* (Cambridge University Press, Cambridge, 1983) especially part 2.
4. *See* Jean Dubois, 'Syndicalisme et politique: les associés rivaux', *Projet*, no. 149 (Nov. 1980) p.1068; George Ross, 'French labor and economic change', in Stephen S. Cohen and Peter A. Gourevitch (eds.) *France in the Troubled World Economy* (Butterworths, London, 1982) pp.158, 167–8. *See*, more generally, René Mouriaux, *La CGT* (Editions du Seuil, Paris, 1982) and Gérard Adam, *Le Pouvoir Syndical* (Dunod, Paris, 1983).
5. Ross, *ibid.*, pp.170–1. *See also* Jean-Daniel Reynaud, 'Trade unions and political parties in France: some recent trends', *Industrial and Labor Relations Review* (Jan. 1975) pp.211–2; W. Rand Smith, 'Paradoxes of plural unionism: CGT–CFDT relations in France', *West European Politics*, vol. IV, I (Jan. 1981); Hervé Hamon and Patrick Rotman, *La Deuxième Gauche. Histoire Intellectuelle et Politique de la CFDT* (Editions Ramsay, Paris, 1982).
6. *See* Jack Hayward, *Private Interests and Public Policy. The Experience of the French Economic and Social Council* (Longmans, London, 1966) especially ch. 5; 'Presidential suicide by plebiscite. de Gaulle's exit, April 1969' *Parliamentary Affairs*, vol. XXII, 4 (Autumn 1969) pp.305–7; cf. pp.291 ff.
7. Janice McCormick, 'Gaullism and collective bargaining: the effect of the Fifth Republic on French industrial relations', in William G. Andrews and Stanley Hoffmann (eds.) *The Fifth Republic at Twenty* (State University of New York Press, Albany, 1981) pp.353–5; cf. pp.348 ff.
8. Martin Schain, 'Corporatism and industrial relations in France', in Philip Cerny and Martin Schain (eds.) *French Politics and Public Policy* (Francis Pinter, London, 1980) pp.201–2, 212–3. *See also* Jeff Bridgford, 'The integration of

trade union confederations into the social and political system', in Philip G. Cerny (ed.) *Social Movements and Protest in France* (Frances Pinter, London, 1982) ch. 3.
9. Compare ch. 8 and 9 by Jack Hayward, 'Planning and the French labour market' and by John Corina, 'Planning and the British labour market', in Jack Hayward and Michael Watson (eds.) *Planning, Politics and Public Policy* (Cambridge University Press, Cambridge, 1975).
10. Quoted in Jack Hayward, 'Interest groups and incomes policy in France', *British Journal of Industrial Relations*, vol. VI (July 1966) p.165.
11. Michel Crozier, 'White-collar unions—the case of France', in Adolph Sturmthal (ed.) *White-Collar Trade Unions* (University of Illinois Press, Urbana, 1966) p.126.
12. Hayward, 'Interest groups and incomes policy in France', *op. cit.* pp.179–80.
13. *ibid.*, p.200, quoting a Fifth Plan working party report, *Réflexions pour 1985* (La Documentation Française, Paris, 1964) p.60. For a more sanguine view of the pre-1981 state involvement in industrial relations, *see* Douglas Ashford, *Policy and Politics in France* (Temple University Press, Philadelphia, 1982) ch 5.
14. *See* Jack Hayward, 'State intervention in France: the changing style of government–industry relations', *Political Studies*, vol. XX, 3 (Sept. 1972) pp.289 ff; cf. Jacques Delors, *Changer* (Stock, Paris, 1975) pp.82 ff, 102 ff, ch. 6–7 *passim*.
15. See Jack Hayward, *Governing France: The One and Indivisible Republic* (Weidenfeld and Nicolson, London, 1983) pp.233–4, 239, cf. pp.223 ff. *See also* Andre Delion and Michel Durupty, *Les Nationalisations 1982* (Economica, Paris, 1982).
16. George Ross, 'Gaullism and organized labor. Two decades of failure?', in Andrews and Hoffmann, *op.cit.* p.330, ch. 19 *passim*.
17. See the report to the President and Prime Minister by Minister of Labour Jean Auroux, *Les droits des travailleurs* (La Documentation Française, Paris, 1982) especially pp.30–8. See also Duncan Gallie, '*Les lois Auroux*: the reform of French industrial relations?' in Howard Machin and Vincent Wright (eds.) *Economic Policy and Policy Making under the Mitterrand Presidency 1981–1984* (Frances Pinter, London, 1985) ch.9.
18. Mikkal E. Herberg, 'Politics, planning and capitalism: National economic planning in France and Britain', *Political Studies*, vol. 29, 4 (Dec. 1981) p.513.

Chapter 5

1. This exchange was reported in *Le Nouveau Journal*, 1 Oct. 1969 and quoted in Jean G. Padioleau, *Quand la France's s'Enferre. La Politique Sidérurgique de la France depuis 1945* (Presses Universitaires de France, Paris, 1981) p.39; cf. pp.36–8.
2. Alain Boublil, *Le Socialisme Industriel* (Presses Universitaires de France, Paris, 1977) p.261; cf. pp.243–9, 268–77.
3. Henry W. Ehrmann, *Organized Business in France* (Princeton University Press, Princeton, 1957) pp.407–14; cf. pp.369 ff. and 'The French trade associations and the ratification of the Schuman Plan', *World Politics*, vol. VI (1954) p.453 ff.
4. Roger Priouret, *Origines du Patronat Français* (Grasset, Paris, 1963) p.19; cf. pp.13–18.
5. L. Lister, *Europe's Coal and Steel Community* (Twentieth Century Fund, New York, 1960) p.232; cf. pp.200–01, 404–08.

6. John Zysman, *Political Strategies for Industrial Order. State Market and Industry in France* (University of California Press, Berkeley, 1977) p.208.
7. *ibid.*, p.200; cf. pp.194 ff.
8. Michel Freyssenet, *La Sidérurgie Française, 1945–79. L'Histoire d'une Faillite. Les solutions qui s'affrontent* (Savelli, Paris, 1979) p.7.
9. Philippe Saint-Marc, *La France dans le CECA*, 1961, pp.248–9; cf. p.252. More generally, see Jack Hayward, 'Steel', in Raymond Vernon, *Big Business and the State. Changing Relations in Western Europe* (Harvard University Press, Cambridge, Mass., 1974) pp.265–9.
10. Saint-Marc, p.263; cf. 251–2, 266, 269.
11. Roger Biard, *La Sidérurgie Française* (Editions Sociales, Paris, 1958) p.77; cf. Jean-François Besson, *Les Groupes Industrielles et l'Europe* (Presses Universitaires de France, Paris, 1962) pp.503–4 and part 2, ch. 4 *passim*.
12. Besson, pp.315, 347–8. For a detailed description of the domestic and foreign links of the French steel companies and their ties with iron ore companies c1960, see *ibid.*, chart on p.89, list on pp.100–6 and pp.245–7, 257–60, 315 ff., 427.
13. Saint-Marc *op. cit.* p.36.
14. *Le Monde*, 7 Oc.t. 1959.
15. E. Arrighi de Casanova, 'Les quasi-contrats du Plan', *Droit Social* (June 1965) p.348.
16. See the very interesting interview with Jacques Ferry by Jean Boissonnat in *Expansion* (Feb. 1977) pp.113 ff. See also Jean Baumier, *Les Grandes Affaires Françaises. Des 200 Familles aux 200 Managers* (Julliard, Paris, 1967) pp.67–8 and J. Ferry interview reported in *Agence Economique et Financier*, 2 Aug. 1966, p.4.
17. See John H. McArthur and Bruce Scott, *Industrial Planning in France* (Harvard University Press, Harvard, 1969) pp.198–201. See also Rémy Prud'homme, *La Sidérurgie Française et le 3e Plan*, thèse complémentaire (Faculté de Droit de Paris, 1964) p.57; cf. Besson, p.507.
18. Michel Drancourt, *Les Clés du Pouvoir* (Fayard, Paris, 1964) pp.83–7; cf. Robert Catherine, *L'Industrie*, (Presses Universitaires de France, Paris, 1965), pp.116, 156–7.
19. On Fos, see Padioleau, *op. cit.* pp.105–17; Sidney Tarrow, 'Regional policy, ideology and peripheral defence: the case of Fos-sur-Mer', in Sidney Tarrow *et al.* (eds.) *Territorial Politics in Industrial Nations* (Praeger, New York, 1978) ch. 4 *passim*.
20. Prud'homme, *op. cit.*, p.25; cf. p.20, 71.
21. Henri Bustarret, in *Les Cahiers de l'Hexagone* (April 1964) pp.61, 63. On business domination of the Steel Commission and working party chairmanships and rapporteur positions see Jack Hayward, 'Le fonctionement des Commissions et la préparation du Ve Plan', *Revue Française de Sociologie*, Vol. VIII (1967) pp.464–5.
22. Jacques Ferry, 'Entreprise privée et secteur public', *Patronat Français*, no. 226 (Feb. 1963), p.24; cf. pp.18 ff.
23. *ibid.*, p. 25.
24. *Ve Plan*, I, pp.72–3.
25. Interview of J. Ferry in *La Vie Française*, 5 Aug. 1966.
26. *Rapport sur les Principales Options du Ve Plan*, part 2, ch. 2 (iiia); cf. J. Fabre, 'Le Ve Plan contre la nation', *Economie et Politique* (Dec. 1964) pp.9–30; J. Baumier, *op. cit.*, p.190.
27. *Ve Plan*, I, pp.68–9.
28. Jacques Ferry, 'Coordonner les investissements ou planifier les échanges', *Le*

Monde, 11 Oct. 1967; cf. 4 Oct. 1967, and Hayward in Vernon (ed.) *op. cit.*, pp.270–1.
29. *Le Monde*, 9 Oct. 1967, p.20. For similar criticisms of a purely market approach in matters of investment, *see* Ferry's speech as President of the ECSC Consultative Committee, reported *ibid.* 27 Jan. 1968.
30. *IISI First Annual Conference Report of Proceedings*, 1967, p.18.
31. *L'impératif industriel* (Editions du Seuil, Paris, 1969) pp.114–5; cf. pp.112–3, 148, 230.
32. Quoted in Padioleau, *op. cit.* p.51; cf. pp.52–3.
33. *ibid.* p.186; cf. pp.183–8. The three senior officials concerned were de la Rosière (Director of the Treasury Division, Ministry of Finance), de l'Estoile (Industry) and Oheix (Director of Employment, Ministry of Labour).
34. Jack Hayward, 'Employer associations and the state in France and Britain', in Steven J. Warnecke and Ezra N. Suleiman (eds.) *Industrial Policies in Western Europe* (Praeger, New York, 1975) pp.130–1.
35. Hugh Heclo and Aaron Wildavsky, *The Private Government of Public Money, Community and Policy inside British Politics* (University of California Press, Berkeley, 1974) pp.xv–vi, 366, whose conception of 'policy community' has been applied to industrial policy by Brian Hogwood, 'Analysing industrial policy: a multi-perspective approach', *Public Administration Bulletin* (April 1979) p.37. *See also* Wyn Grant, *The Political Economy of Industrial Policy* (London, Butterworth, 1982) ch. 2. We have simply applied the concept to a specific industrial policy community.
36. Freyssenet, *op. cit.* p. 181.
37. Commissariat Général du Plan and Ministère de l'Industrie et de la Recherche, *Rapport du Groupe Sectoriel d'Analyse et de Prévision. Mines de Fer, Sidérurgie, Première Transformation de l'Acier* (La Documentation Française, Paris, 1976), p.42; cf. pp.7, 26. Many of the key members of the steel policy community belonged to this 'sectoral group', the chairman and seven of its forty members belonging to the CSSF. (*See ibid.*, App. 3).
38. *ibid.*, p.21; cf. p.42.
39. *ibid.*, p.22; cf. p.23.
40. Quoted by Freyssenet, pp.188–9; cf. pp.185 ff.
41. Diana Green, *Managing Industrial Change? French Policies to Promote Industrial Adjustment* (HMSO, London, 1981) note 26, p.68–9.
42. *ibid.*, p.28; Freyssenet, pp.205 ff.
43. This paragraph draws on Catherine Omnès, *De l'Atelier au Groupe Industriel. Vallourec 1882–1978* (Editions de la Maison des Sciences de l'Homme, Paris, 1980) pp.271 ff., 337 ff., 377–91, 416–7.
44. Padioleau *op. cit.* pp.144–44, 153–4, 201–3. *See also* Anicet Le Pors, *Les Béquilles du Capital. Transferts Etat–Industrie: Critère de Nationalisation* (Editions du Seuil, Paris, 1977) pp.59–66, 78–84.
45. *Rapport du groupe sectoriel d'analyse et de prévision*, 1976, *op. cit.*, p.10; cf. p.11.
46. quoted in Freyssenet, *op. cit.*, pp.182–3.
47. George Ross, 'French labor and economic change', in Stephen S. Cohen and Peter A. Gourevitch (eds.) *France in the Trouble World Economy* (Butterworth, London, 1982) pp.165–7. For details, *see* two CGT publications: *Le Guide du Militant de la Metallurgie* (no. 136, Nov. 1978), and Centre confédéral d'études économiques, *Crise et Solution pour la Sidérurgie*, 1979. *See also Avenir de la Sidérurgie* (1979) published by the CFDT's Metalworkers Union.
48. On the steel riots of 1979, *see* R.W. Johnson, *The Long March of the French Left* (Macmillan, London, 1981), pp.10–21.

49. Jacques Malézieux, 'Crise et restructuration de la sidérurgie française. Le groupe USINOR', *L'Espace Géographique*, no. 3 (1980), pp.190–4.
50. On this merger, *see ibid.*, pp.189–90.
51. Christian Stoffaës and Pierre Gadonneix, 'Steel and the State in France', in the special issue on 'Steel and the State in Europe', *Annals of Public and Cooperative Economy*, no. 4 (1980), pp.417, 416; cf. pp.406–22. Stoffaës is head of the Ministry of Industry's *Centre d'Etudes et de Prévision* and Gadonneix is head of its Metallurgical Industries Division (DIMME) and on the board of directors, since 1982, of USINOR.
52. The other three reports were by the Audibert committee, representing the views of USINOR and SACILOR; the Delacotte committee (with representatives from the Ministries of Industry and Labour, as well as from DATAR), concerned with the regional impact of steel restructuring and will be dealt with in the next chapter; and the comparison of intermediate goods industries in France and Federal Germany (with a detailed analysis of the steel and chemicals industries) by Bernard Billaudot *et al.* based like Judet in the Grenoble University of Social Sciences. Sparse and vague references to steel are to be found in the *Plan intérimaire: Stratégie pour Deux Ans, 1982–83* (La Documentation Française, Paris, Nov. 1981), pp.151, 156, 174.
53. See the excellent article by François Renard, 'Une sidérurgie française oui, mais pas à n'importe quel prix', *Le Monde*, 13 July 1982, pp.17–8.
54. Reported in *Le Monde*, 11 June 1982, p.17.
55. François Renard, 'La sidérurgie et sa facture', *Le Monde*, 30 Sept. 1982, p.40; cf. Renard, 'Une sidérurgie francaise oui, mais pas à n'importe quel prix', *Le Monde*, 13 July 1982, p.18.
56. On the opposition of French trades unions to corporatism, *see* Andrew Cox and Jack Hayward, 'The inapplicability of the corporatist model in Britain and France: the case of labor', *International Political Science Review*, vol. IV, no. 2 (April 1983) pp.217–40.
57. For the text of President Mitterrand's press conference, *see Le Monde*, 6 April 1984.
58. The Prime Minister is chairman of the cabinet committee. In his absence the Minister of Industry acts as chairman. The other ministers represented are Finance, Social Affairs, Interior, Transport, Agriculture, Education, Housing, Trade, Industrial Training, Employment and Planning. The industry minister can directly call on the regional commissioners of the republic to assist him. *See Le Monde*, 8 April 1984, p.15.

Chapter 6

1. Most of the research for this chapter was undertaken in 1980–1 before the advent of the Mitterrand presidency. It was conducted as part of a project organized by Jerry Webman of the University of Princeton's Urban and Regional Research Center and was done in collaboration with Yves Mény, although his particular responsibility was for parts of the work only peripherally discussed in this chapter. I wish to thank especially Mr. Rubio (formerly of the Lille Chamber of Commerce) and Mr. Finzi (Valenciennes Chamber of Commerce) for their general advice and help in selecting the sample of twelve firms investigated as part of this study.
2. Alain Berger, 'Lille: le compromis historique', *Implantations*, no. 57 (Nov. 1980) pp.26–8.

3. Bernard Delebecque, *La Nouvelle Bataille de Tourcoing*, 1977. Delebecque was in 1981 excluded from the Socialist group on the Tourcoing council.
4. On this very important bank, see Gérard Dusart, *La Caisse des Dépôts et Consignations*, no. 4577–8 *(La Documentation Française, Notes et Etudes Documentaires) (Paris, June 1980)*. The Roubaix study, *La Ville Industrielle. Le Cas de Roubaix*, was published by the Ministry of the Environment (Paris, 1979).
5. For an industrial portrait of Roubaix in the early 1960s, see Pierre Belleville, *Une Nouvelle Classe Ouvrière* (Paris, Julliard, 1963) ch. 4.
6. Quoted in Bernard Frimat, *Conversion Industrielle et Système Economique: le Valenciennois*, doctoral thesis (University of Lille, Sept. 1979) p.243 note.
7. This discussion of the urban community and the new town draws heavily upon Georges Delbar, *La Ville Nouvelle de Lille Est, son Insertion et son Rôle dans les schémas d'Aménagement de la Région Nord*, doctorat de troisième cycle (Institute of Geography, University of Lille, 1977) especially p.52 ff; and Pascal Percq and Jean-Michel Stievenard, *Villeneuve d'Ascq, une Ville est née* (Editions Cana, Paris, 1980). On the establishment of urban communities, see Jean-Luc Bodiguel, 'Les communautés urbaines', in *Aménagement du Territoire et Développement Régional*, Vol. II, (University of Grenoble, 1968–9) pp.347–79. More generally see François d'Arcy and Bruno Jobert, 'Urban planning in France', in Jack Hayward and Michael Watson (eds.) *Planning, Politics and Public Policy. The British, French and Italian Experience* (Cambridge University Press, London, 1975) ch. 15.
8. Percq and Stievenard *op. cit.* p.14; cf. pp.12–38, ch. 10 and 11 *passim*.
9. Delbar *op. cit.* pp.178–9.
10. See, for example, the 'Letters to the mayors' sent from 1974–77, collected and updated in André Chadeau, *Etudes sur le Nord Pas-de-Calais*, S.A.I.E.N., Lille, 1977.
11. Rémy Prud'homme, 'Regional economic policy in France, 1962–72', in N. Hansen (ed.) *Public Policy and Regional Economic Development. The Experience of Nine Western Countries* (Ballinger, Cambridge, Mass., 1974) pp.41, 59.
12. *Conversion, Bulletin de l'APEX*, no. 27 (March 1980) p.2.
13. *ibid.*, p.7; cf. p.3. On the early history of the redevelopment commissioners, see Marie-Françoise Souchon, 'Les bureaux de reconversion industrielle', in *Aménagement du Territoire et Développement Régional*, vol. II (1968–9) pp.381–430.
14. Bruno Magliulo, *Les Chambres de Commerce et d'Industrie* (Presses Universitaires de France, Paris, 1980) p.101; cf. 75, 84–99, 121–2; *Actualité Services*, no. 340 (Nov. 1979).
15. See Jean-Marie Duprez, *Les Moyennes et Petites Industries dans la Société Locale: l'Opération de Promotion de la M.P.I. dans le Nord Pas-de-Calais*, sociology doctoral thesis (Institut d'Etudes Politiques, Paris, 1978) especially pp.102, 466–73.
16. Frimat *op. cit.* pp.266–73; cf. 225–7 and interview of the president of the regional chamber of commerce in *La Voix du Nord*, 26 Sept. 1980, p.2.
17. Delbar *op. cit.* p.138.
18. Frimat *op. cit.* pp.284–90, 296, 302–3, 309.
19. Diana Green, *Managing Industrial Change? French Policies to Promote Industrial Adjustment* (HMSO, London, 1981) p.34, quoting the Berthelot Report of 1978. On the organization of the French textile industry and its relations with the French state, notably through the CIRIT, see Erhard Friedberg, *Le Système d'Intervention de l'Etat en Matière Industrielle* (Hachette, Paris, 1973). See also Christian Stoffaës, *La Grande Menace Industrielle*, 2nd edn. (Calmann–Lévy, Paris, 1979) pp.81–91.
20. Diana Green, *op. cit.* p.38, ch. 5 *passim*.

21. *Le Monde*, 18 Jan. 1981, p.4; cf. 11 Oct. 1980. *See also Nord Eclair*, 6 Nov. 1980; 22 Nov. 1980.
22. *See* Prouvost S.A., *Informations Intérieures*, no. 28 (Feb. 1981, special issue on amalgamation) pp.4–7, 17. *See also* the BETURE–Nord report for Tourcoing, Lille, *Aménagement et Utilisation des Terraines Industriels* (1980) pp.24–9, 91.
23. 'Une entreprise type: la société Bidermann', in *Richesses du Valenciennois* (1979) p.106.
24. Frimat *op. cit.* pp.292–6; cf. pp.166–6, 214–5. *See also* Catherine Omnès, *De l'Atelier au Groupe Industriel. Vallourec 1882–1978* (Editions de la Maison des Sciences de l'Homme, Paris, 1980) pp.271 ff., 337–50, 377–91, 416–7.
25. *See* R.W. Johnson, *The Long March of the French Left* (Macmillan, London, 1981) pp.10–21.
26. On Alma-Gare, *see* AGIR, APU, 'Pour une économie du quartier', *Esprit* (March 1981) pp.65–79.
27. *See* Jack Hayward, 'Charles Gide and the social philosophy of cooperation', *Archives Internationales de Sociologie de la Coopération* VI, I (Jan.–June 1961) pp.19–48; 'Charles Gide as cooperative propagandist', *Archives Internationales de Sociologie de la Coopération*, XXII, 2 (July–Dec. 1967) pp.3–27.
28. Jean-François Jacquier, 'Le coût d'un emploi', *L'Express*, 10 Jan. 1981, pp.33–4.
29. This paragraph draws heavily on Douglas Yuill and Kevin Allen (eds.) *European Regional Incentives 1982* (Centre for the Study of Public Policy, University of Strathclyde, Glasgow, 1982) especially pp.195–6, 206-7, 217, 220–1.
30. *Conversion*, no. 27 (March 1980) p.4.
31. Jacquier, *op. cit.* p.34. On the PDR regulations, *see* pp.127–38 of *Aides au Développement Economique Régional* (OREAM Nord, Lille, Docamenor 1980) pp.185–8. This is a 507-page compendious description of all the incentives then available in the Nord Pas-de-Calais. For a succinct general description, *see* DATAR's *Aides au Développement Régional*. For a legalistic general review, *see* Yves Madiot, 'Les aides au développement régional', *Actualité Juridique. Droit Administratif* (May 1977) pp.227–47.
32. This paragraph draws heavily upon A. Cames, 'Une aide de l'Etat en faveur du développement industriel: la Prime de Développment Régional', *Profils de l'Economie Nord Pas-de-Calais* (July 1978).
33. Chris Hull, 'Regional incentives in France', in Douglas Yuill *et al.* (eds.) *Regional Policy in the European Community* (Croom Helm, London, 1980) p.71; cf. pp.80, 245.
34. *ibid.*, p.241; cf. *Conversion*, ch. 4, no. 25 (Sept. 1979) pp.7–8, special issue on incentives, and *Aides du Développement Régional, op. cit.*, pp.139–48.
35. *See* reports of National Assembly debates in *Le Monde*, 30 July–3 Aug. 1981.
36. *Note sur le Bilan de la Prime Régionale à la Création d'Entreprises Industrielles*, Mimeo, Prefecture of the Nord Pas-de-Calais Region, Mission Régionale, Lille (Jan. 1980). *See also Aides du Développement Régional, op. cit.*, pp.195–6.
37. Chambre de Commerce et d'Industrie de Lille–Roubaix–Tourcoing, 'Memorandum sur la taxe professionnelle', *Les Cahiers d'Etudes*, no. 1, (1978) app. 2A and B, pp.113–7. *See also* comments in Yuill *et al., op. cit.*, pp.71–8, 230.
38. Yuill *et al., op. cit.* p.233.
39. *See Aides au Développement Régional, op. cit.*, pp.210–1.
40. On aids to employment, *see Aides au Développement Régional, op cit.*, ch. 1.
41. It is the customary practice for incoming French firms to 'play the game' with local industry on wage rates (e.g. SMAN/Peugeot consulted Vallourec about

rates of pay prior to setting up, to avoid competitive bidding upwards).
42. Quoted by Bernard Frimat, *op. cit.*, p.166. More generally, *see ibid.*, pp.214–5, 292–6, 306–9.
43. Marianne Andrault, 'Une evaluation de l'impact des Primes de Développement Régional, 1976–81', *Politiques et Management Public*, vol. I, no. 4 (Autumn 1983) p.28.
44. Quoted, *ibid.*, p.31–2.
45. *ibid.*, pp.39–41, quoting reports by the Inspectors of Finance.

Chapter 7

1. Eugen Weber, *Peasants into Frenchmen. The Modernization of Rural France, 1870–1914* (Chatto and Windus, London, 1977) pp.98, 485. *See*, more generally, ch. 7 and 29. For an application of the 'internal colonialism' model to the French context, *see* Jack Hayward, 'Institutionalized inequality within an indivisible republic: Brittany and France', *Journal of the Conflict Research Society*, vol. I, no. 1 (Aug. 1977) pp.1–15.
2. Ezra, N. Suleiman, *Elites in French Society. The Politics of Survival* (Princeton University Press, Princeton, 1978) p.280; cf. p.278. *See also* p.156. In the French edition, *Les Elites en France. Grands Corps and Grandes Ecoles* (Editions du Seuil, Paris, 1978) p.281, in the sentence quoted, by a Freudian slip the hostility to decentralization is translated as a hostility to centralization!
3. Pierre Grémion, *Le Pouvoir Périphérique. Bureaucrates et Notables dans le Système Politique Français* (Editions du Seuil, Paris, 1976) pp.285–6; cf. pp.248 ff., 304 ff.
4. Quoted by Georges Dupuis in his preface to the excellent thesis of Yves Mény, *Centralisation et Décentralisation dans le Débat Politique Français (1945–1969)* (LGDJ, Paris, 1974) p.1.
5. Thiébaut Flory, *Le Mouvement Régionaliste Français. Sources et Développements* (Presses Universitaires de France, Paris, 1966) p.21 ff. Sidney Tarrow makes a helpful threefold distinction between regionalism as a 'policy or set of policies'; as an 'ideology of government intervention'; as a 'framework for peripheral defence'. (Sidney Tarrow *et al.*, *Territorial Politics in Industrial Nations* (Praeger, New York, 1978) p.98. The dual distinction used in this chapter, however, separates the first, instrumental sense—regional policy—from the last two, which are described respectively as 'regionalization' and 'regionalism'. It is hoped, thereby, to attain great terminological clarity.
6. *Tableau Politique de la France de l'Ouest sous la Troisième République*, 2nd edn. (A. Colin, Paris, 1913, 1964) p.222. One should not forget the contribution to the early twentieth-century emergence of regionalism in France of another geographer, Vidal de la Blache.
7. *See* Jean Hennessy, *Réorganisation Administrative de la France* (Berger-Levrault, Paris, 1923) and Henri Hauser, *Les Régions Economiques* (Grasset, Paris, 1918).
8. Jean-François Gravier, *Régions et Nation* (Presses Universitaires de France, Paris, 1942) p.63; cf. pp.62–4. The concept of 'functional regionalism' was popularized in the 1960s notably by Jean-Louis Quermonne, 'Vers un régionalisme "fonctionnel"', *Revue Française de Science Politique*, vol. XIII (Dec. 1963) pp.854 ff. and in his contribution to *Administration Traditionnelle et Planification Régionale* (A. Colin, Paris, 1964) pp.89 ff.
9. Jack Hayward, 'From functional regionalism to functional representation in France: the Battle of Brittany', *Political Studies*, vol. XVII, no. 1 (March 1969)

p.52; cf. pp.48–75, and *La Vie Bretonne*, 1952–4 *passim*. *See also* Michel Phlipponneau, *Le Problème Breton et le Programme d'Action Régionale* (A. Colin, Paris, 1957); *La Gauche et les Régions* (Calmann-Lévy, Paris, 1967) ch. 2, and *Debout Bretagne* (Presses Universitaires de Bretagne, Saint-Brieuc, 1970) ch. 2. For an alternative view, *see* Joseph Martray, *La Région. Pour un Etat Moderne* (Editions France-Empire, Paris, 1970) especially pp.54 ff. For a Marxist analysis, seeing regionalism in general and Brittany in particular as secondary to class conflict, *see* Renaud Dulong, *La Question Bretonne* (Presses de la Fondation Nationale des Sciences Politiques, Paris, 1975) and *Les Régions, L'Etat et la Société Locale* (Presses Universitaires de France, Paris, 1978).

10. Jean-Francois Gravier, *Paris et le Désert Français en 1972* (Flammarion, Paris, 1972), pp.94–7.
11. Catherine Grémion, *Profession: Décideurs. Pouvoir des Hauts Fonctionnaires et Réforme de l'Etat* (Gauthier-Villars, Paris, 1979) pp.143–8. *See also* Bernard Pouyet, *La Délégation à l'Aménagement du Territoire et à l'Action Régionale* (Editions Cujas, Paris, 1968) pp.50 ff.
12. Grémion, *op. cit.* p.169; cf. pp.166 ff.
13. Jean-Louis Quermonne, 'Planification régionale et réforme administrative' in a book based on the Grenoble Institut d'Etudes Politiques study of *Administration Traditionnelle et Planification Régionale*, *op. cit.*, p.110 anticipating Michel Rocard's title *Décoloniser la Province* in his *Rapport Général* to the 1966 *Rencontre Socialiste de Grenoble*. More generally, *see* Pierre Grémion, 'Réforme régionale et démocratie locale', *Projet* (Avril 1970) pp.412 ff; Howard Machin, 'Local government change in France—the case of the 1964 reforms', *Policy and Politics*, vol. 2, no. 3 (March 1974) pp.249–65; Machin, *The Prefect in French Public Administration* (Croom Helm, London, 1977) section 2, ch. 1.
14. Peter A. Gourevitch, 'Reforming the Napoleonic state: the creation of regional government (sic) in France and Italy', in Sidney Tarrow *et al.*., *op. cit.*, p.42; cf. pp.39 ff.
15. Hayward, *op. cit.*, p.50.
16. Jean-Luc Bodiguel (ed.) *La Réforme Régionale et le Référendum du 17 Avril, 1969* (Cujas, Paris, 1970). *See also* Jack Hayward, 'Presidential suicide by plebiscite: de Gaulle's exit, April 1969', *Parliamentary Affairs*, vol. XXII, no. 4 (Autumn 1969) pp.289–319. As the title of this article has been misunderstood (notably by Peter A. Gourevitch, *Paris and the Provinces. The Politics of Local Government Reform in France* (George Allen & Unwin, London, 1980) pp.123–4, who also misquotes the title of the article) it should be made clear that the term suicide was not intended to suggest a deliberate intention by de Gaulle to leave power, but an attempt that *miscarried* to force the voters to give him support, in the way that people sometimes *threaten* suicide to modify the conduct of others. As in de Gaulle's case, the threat sometimes has unintended, fatal results.
17. R.E.M. Irving, 'Regionalism in France', in James Cornford (ed.) *The Failure of the State* (Croom Helm, London, 1975) p.38; cf. pp.14 ff. For equally pessimistic assessments, *see* Vincent Wright and Howard Machin, 'The French regional reforms of July 1972: a case of disguised centralisation?', *Policy and Politics*, vol. III, no. 3 (March 1975) pp.3–28, and Vincent Wright, 'Regionalization under the French Fifth Republic: the triumph of the functional approach' in L.J. Sharpe (ed.) *Decentralist Trends in Western Democracies* (Sage, London, 1979) pp.193–234.
18. *Vivre Ensemble* vol. I (La Documentation Française, Paris, Sept. 1976) pp.91–2. The report devotes a mere five lukewarm pages to the regions (pp.157–61).
19. *ibid.*, p.96.

20. Pierre Grémion, *Le Pouvoir Périphérique, op. cit.* p.458.
21. *ibid.*, pp.460, 455.
22. Pierre Grémion, 'Crispation et déclin du jacobinisme', in Henri Mendras (ed.) *La Sagesse et le Désordre. France 1980.* (Gallimard, Paris, 1980) pp.334, 336.
23. Charles Vigouroux, *Quelques Eléments pour un Bilan des Etablissements Publics Régionaux* (Commissariat Général du Plan, Service Régional et Urbain, ronéoté Nov. 1979) app. 2 for detailed table; cf. p.39.
24. Michael Watson, 'A critique of development from above. The lessons of French and Dutch experience of nationally-defined regional policy', *Public Administration* (Winter 1978) p.478; cf. pp.457 ff.
25. Pierre Grémion, 'Crispation et déclin', *op. cit.*, pp.348–9.
26. Pierre Mendès France, *La République Moderne* (Gallimard, Paris, 1962) especially ch. 5 and 9.
27. Yves Mény, 'Decentralisation in Socialist France: the politics of pragmatism', *West European Politics*, vol. VII, I (Jan. 1984) pp.65–79; Douglas Ashford, 'The Socialist reorganization of French local government—another Jacobin reform?', *Government and Policy*, vol. I (1983) pp.29–44. *See also* Yves Mény, 'France: towards contractual regionalism', in Michael Hebbert and Howard Machin (eds.) *Regionalisation in France, Italy and Spain* (ICERD, London School of Economics, London, 1984) ch. 3.
28. Douglas E. Ashford, *British Dogmatism and French Pragmatism* (George Allen & Unwin, London, 1982) pp.337–8.
29. Dominique Flecher-Bourjol, 'Essai de typologie fonctionnelle des contrats passés entre l'Etat et les collectivités locales et établissements publics territoriaux', *Bulletin de l'Institut International d'Administration Publique*, no. 38 (April–June 1976) pp.60–1. *See also* J. Chevallier, 'Les formes actuelles de l'économie concertée', no. 1 (Publications de la Faculté de droit et d'économie d'Amiens, 1971–2) especially pp.68–72. On the background to these developments, *see* François Bloch-Laîné, *A la Recherche d'une Economie Concertée* (Editions de l'Epargne, Paris, 1959) and the Simon Nora *Rapport sur les Entreprises Publiques* (La Documentation Française, Paris, 1968).
30. Ashford, *op. cit.* p.325. On 'globalization' and 'contractualization' in the 1970s, *see* Yves Mény, 'Financial transfers and local government in France', in Douglas Ashford (ed.) *Financing Urban Government in the Welfare State* (Croom Helm, London, 1980) pp.153–5.
31. Ashford, p.328.
32. *ibid.*, p.329; cf. pp.312–3.
33. Flecher-Bourjol, *op. cit.*, p.89.
34. Quoted in J. Chobaux and J. Grammont, *Réflexions sur les conditions d'une Programmation Locales* (Ministère de l'Equipement SAEI, August 1934) p.19.
35. Commissariat Général du Plan, *IXᵉ Plan de Développement Economique, Social et Culturel, 1984–88*, vol. II (La Documentation Française, Paris, 1983) p.23.
36. *Rapport annexé à la Deuxième Loi de Développement Economique, Social et Culturel, 1984–88* (Journal Official, Paris, 30 Dec. 1983) p.155; cf. pp.156–7. Emphasis added.
37. François Bloch-Laîné, *Profession: Fonctionnaire* (Editions du Seuil, Paris, 1976), p.129; cf. pp.128–43. *See also* Pierre Beaudeux, 'Monsieur 200 milliards', *Expansion* (Nov. 1973) pp.139–43.
38. Ashford, p.314; cf. pp.313–6.
39. *Le Monde*, 17 Dec. 1982, p.40.
40. Gérard Dusart, *La Caisse des Dépôts et Consignations* (La Documentation Française, Paris, 1980), *Notes et Etudes Documentaires*, nos. 4577–8, pp.64–5.

This provides a good description of the *Caisse*'s activities just prior to 1981.
41. Interview of Pierre Richard in *Le Monde*, 27 Oct. 1983, p.38.
42. Pierre-Joseph Proudhon, *Idée Générale de la Révolution au XIXe Siècle*, 1851, quoted in George Woodcock, *Pierre-Joseph Proudhon. A Biography* (Routledge & Kegan Paul, London, 1956) p.171.

Chapter 8

1. Unpublished lecture by Michael Albert on 'La Planification Française' delivered at the Institut d'Etudes Politiques de Paris, on 8 Nov. 1979.
2. *ibid*.
3. *See* the extended extract from the May 1975 speech by the Minister of Industry, Michel d'Ornano, opening the colloquium on "Le Redéploiement Industriel", in *Les Cahiers Français*, special issue on the Seventh Plan, supplement no. 182 (July–Sept. 1977), p.19; cf. *Etudies de Politique Industrielle*, no. 6 (La Documentation Française, Paris, 1975).
4. Lionel Stoléru, *L'Impératif Industriel* (Editions de Seuil, Paris, 1969). the key document is the Montjoie report on *Le Développement Industriel* (La Documentation Française, Paris, Avril 1968). More generally, *see* Liliane Sardais 'Le planification industrielle' in *Les Cahiers Français*, *op. cit.*, supplement no. 4–5, and especially by the same author *L'Etat et l'Internationalisation du Capital. Un Essai sur la Politique Industrielle en France*, doctoral thesis (Université de Paris X (Nanterre, 1977). *See also* the discussion of French industrial policy by Jean-Jacques Bonnaud, in Jack Hayward and Michel Watson (eds.) *Planning, Politics and Public Policy* (Cambridge University Press, Cambridge, 1975) ch. 4. The quotation from Hamon is in 'Le Plan et sa signification politique', Jean-Daniel Reynaud (ed.) *Tendances et Volontés de la Société Française* (Futuribles, Paris, 1965) pp.210, 212.
5. Jacques Bravo, in Philippe Huet and Jacques Bravo, *L'Expérience Française de Rationalisation des Choix Budgétaires* (Presses Universitaires de France, Paris, 1973) p.151. On RCB and the Seventh Plan, *see* Jean Carassus, 'The budget and the Plan in France', in Jack Hayward and Olga Narkiewicz (eds.) *Planning in Europe* (Croom Helm, London, 1978) ch. 2.
6. Philippe Huet, in Huet and Bravo, *op. cit.*, p.16; cf. pp.12–4.
7. *ibid.*, p.10.
8. *ibid.*, p.22.
9. Diana Green, 'The Budget and the Plan', in Philip G. Cerny and Martin A. Schain (eds.) *French Politics and Public Policy* (Frances Pinter, London, 1980) p.110; cf. pp.105 ff. On the successful application of programme budgeting to achieve improved planning and coordinating within the Ministry of Education, *see* Michel Praderie, in Huet and Bravo *op. cit.*, ch. II; Jack Hayward, *The One and Indivisible French Republic* (Weidenfeld and Nicolson, London, 1973) p.201–3.
10. Gabriel Mignot, lectures at the Institut d'Etudes Politiques de Paris on *La Planification Française*, 1976–7, mimeo, p.180.
11. *ibid.*, p.182.
12. On this whole complex issue, *see Un dossier: La Liaison Rhin–Rhône*, no. 4547–8 (Notes et Etudes Documentaires, Paris, 28 Dec. 1979). *See also* Jack Hayward, 'Mobilizing private interests . . .' in Jeremy J. Richardson (ed.) *Policy Styles in Western Europe*, *op. cit.*, pp.128–37.
13. On this rather technical subject, *see* the very clear exposition by Jacques Bravo

and Bernard Walliser, 'Les systèmes d'indicateurs de programmes', *Statistiques et Etudes Financières*, no. 19, 1975, especially pp.12–7.
14. *Rapport d'Exécution du VIIe Plan*, annexe au Projet de Loi de Finances pour 1980 (Imprimerie Nationale, Paris, 1979) pp.33–5. For a statistical comparison of the PAPs' targets and implementation, *see* Green, *op. cit.*, pp.116–7.
15. Sir Andrew Shonfield, 'The VIIIth Plan: assumptions and constraints', *Revue Economique*, vol. XXXI, no. 5 (Sept. 1980) p.830. On the DMS model and its use for exploring alternatives, *see* two other articles in this special issue on the Eighth Plan, pp.894 ff.
16. Pierre Massé, 'Repenser le Plan', *Revue Economique* (Sept. 1980) p.818; cf. Jean Monnet, *Mémoires* (Fayard, Paris, 1976) p.270.
17. Jacques Delors, 'The decline of French planning', in Stuart Holland (ed.) *Beyond Capitalist Planning* (Basil Blackwell, Oxford, 1978) p.10. *See also* Jean Boissonnat, 'Le Budget contre le Plan', in *L'Expansion*, 5 Sept. 1980, pp.60–6.
18. Delors, *op. cit.*, p.26.
19. This letter was leaked to *Le Canard Enchaîné* and partially published in its issue of 10 Sept. 1980, p.3; cf. *ibid.*, 17 Sept. 1980, p.2.
20. *8e Plan de Développement Economique et Social, 1981–1985* (La Documentation Française, Paris, 1980) part III, pp.217–49.
21. Peter Holmes, 'Le Neuvième Plan: une perspective d'outre-manche', *Economie et Humanisme*, no. 274 (Nov.–Dec. 1983) pp.23–4.
22. Bernard Cazes, 'Les traits nouveaux de la planification française', *Economie et Humanisme*, no. 274 (Nov.–Dec. 1983) p.18.

Chapter 9

1. *Rapport sur l'Adaptation du 7e Plan* (La Documentation Française, Paris, 1978) p.13.
2. *ibid.*, pp.8, 15, 18–20, 34; cf. J. Pelletier and H. Guillaume, *Rapport de la Commission du Développement. Options du 8e Plan* (Commissariat Général du Plan, Paris, 1979) para. 212 and 521.
3. *Rapport sur l'adaptation, op. cit.*, p.9; cf. p.79.
4. Introduction to *Rapport de la Commission de l'Emploi et des Relations du Travail, 8e Plan* (Commissariat Général du Plan, Paris, July 1980) p.15; cf. pp.14, 234.
5. *ibid.*, pp.24–8; cf. *Rapport sur l'Adaptation du 7e Plan, op. cit.*, pp.81–3.
6. *Commission de l'Emploi, 8e Plan, op. cit.*, pp.31–3, 37–8, 41–2.
7. *ibid.*, pp.46–50. On motor cars, *see* Christian Stoffaës, *La Grande Menace Industriel*, 2nd edn. (Calmann-Lévy, Paris, 1978) pp.135 ff.
8. *Commission de l'Emploi*, pp.47, 52–7.
9. *Rapport sur les Principales Options du Huitième Plan* (La Documentation Française, Paris, April 1979) pp.26–30; cf. Pelletier and Guillaume, *op. cit.*, p.36. For an analysis of the structural causes of French unemployment in the 1970s, *see* an INSEE study in *Economie et Statistique*, no. 123 (July 1980).
10. *Commission de l'Emploi, 8e Plan, op. cit.*, pp.68–74, 83; *Révision du VIIe Plan. Synthèse des Travaux des Commissions et Comités Consultés pour la révision* (Commissariat Général du Plan, Paris, 1978) pp.16–17.
11. *Commission de l'Emploi, 8e Plan*, pp.74–82; *Révision du VIIe Plan, op. cit.*, pp.17–8, 72–3.
12. *Rapport sur les Principales Options du Huitième Plan, op. cit.*, p.33; cf. *Rapport sur l'Adaptation du 7e Plan, op. cit.*, pp.39–40.
13. *Rapport sur les Principales Options du Huitième Plan*, p.40.

14. *Révision du VIIe Plan, op. cit.*, pp.42–3. See also *8e Plan de Développement Economique et Social, 1981–85* (Journal Officiel, Paris, 1980) pp.85–5.
15. *Rapport sur les Principales Options du Huitième Plan, op. cit.*, pp.34–5.
16. *Commission de l'Emploi, 8e Plan*, pp.64–5; *Révision du VIIe Plan*, pp.55–7.
17. *Rapport sur les Principales Options du Huitième Plan*, p.8; cf. p.9.
18. *Révision du VIIe Plan*, pp.62–4.
19. SOFRES poll in *Le Nouvel Observateur*, no. 773 (3 Sept. 1979) p.23; cf. pp.21–4.
20. Jean-Luc Parodi, 'L'échec des gauches', *Revue Politique et Parlementaire*, no. 873 (1978) pp.5–6; Jean-Luc Parodi, 'Profil de l'année, Septembre 1978–Août 1979', *Pouvoirs*, no. 11 (1979) pp.174–5.
21. Parodi, in *Revue Politique et Parlementaire, op. cit.*, pp.5–6; Parodi, *Pouvoirs, op. cit.*, pp.174–6. See also Jean-Dominique Lafay, 'Les conséquences électorales de la conjoncture économique: essai de précision chiffrée pour mars 1978', *Vie et Sciences Economiques* (Oct. 1977).
22. *Rapport de la Commission Industrie, 7e Plan*, C.G.P. (La Documentation Française, Paris, 1976) pp.9–10, 49–51.
23. *Rapport sur l'Adaptation du 7e Plan, op. cit.*, pp.64–5. The Barre quotation is from an interview in *Le Progrès de Lyon*, 15 April 1980.
24. *Rapport sur les principales options du 8e Plan, op. cit.*, p.33.
25. *Le Progrès de Lyon*, 15 April 1980; *Le Monde*, 16 April 1980.
26. Liliane Sardais, *L'Etat et l'Internationalisation du Capital. Un Essai sur la Politique Industrielle en France*, doctoral thesis (University of Paris X, Nanterre, 1977) pp.387–91; cf. pp.380 ff.
27. *ibid.*, pp.444–9; cf. pp.350, 359–72. See also 'Les implantations étrangers en France au 1 Janvier, 1971', *Développement Industriel et Scientifique*, no. 17 (Dec. 1973); 'Les participations étrangères dans l'industrie française en 1971', *Economie et Statistique*, no. 52 (Jan. 1974).
28. *Rapport sur les Principales Options du 8e Plan*, p.73. On the impact of the recession on CFDT membership, see Françoise Lozier, 'La CFDT en chiffres', in the special issue of *Esprit* on 'La CFDT et la crise du Syndicalisme' (April 1980) pp.16–17. See also J. Bunel, 'L'action syndicale, crise et recentrage', *Economie et Humanisme*, no. 245 (Jan.–Feb. 1979).
29. *Commission de l'Emploi, 8e Plan*, p.176; cf. pp.175–81, 207–12, 227. See also *Révision du VIIe Plan, op. cit.*, pp.28–30; *Rapport sur l'Adaptation du 7e Plan, op. cit.*, pp.84–5; *Rapport sur les Principales Options du 8e Plan, op. cit.*, pp.70–2. On the issue in the mid-1960s, see Jack Hayward 'The reduction of working hours and France's Fifth Plan', *British Journal of Industrial Relations*, vol. VII, I (March 1969) pp.84–112. See also the book by Jacques Delors' Echange et Projets club: *La Révolution du Temps Choisi* (Edition A. Michel, Paris, 1980). *Le Monde, Dossiers et Documents* devoted a special issue to 'La durée du travail', no. 70 (April 1980).
30. See the declaration by the CGT and CFDT representatives appended to the Economic and Social Council's *Avis* on the *Adaptations du VII Plan* (Oct. 1978) pp.44–6 and on the *Principales Options du VIII Plan* (May 1979) pp.39–41. See also their views appended to *Commission de l'Emploi, 8e Plan*, pp.231–7 and the extended summary in *Le Monde*, 14 June 1980, p.41, of the twenty-seven scenarios for the Eighth Plan. For the earlier background, see Jean-Pierre Oppenheim, *La CFDT et la Planification* (Tema-Editions, Paris, 1973).
31. Ministère de l'Economie, *Rapport sur les Aides Publiques à l'Industrie*, 1979, summarized in *Le Monde*, 25 Dec. 1979, p.22.

Chapter 10

1. Pierre Mauroy, *C'est ici le Chemin* (Flammarion, Paris, 1982) pp.220–45. There is an appalling English translation of the '110 propositions for France', in Denis MacShane, *François Mitterrand. A Political Odyssey* (Quartet Books, London, 1982) pp.259–72.
2. '110 Propositions', quoted in Mauroy, p.225 and Parti Socialiste, *Projet Socialiste pour la France des Années 80* (Club Socialiste du Livre, Paris, 1980) p.180; cf. p.190.
3. *Projet Socialiste pour la France des Années 80*, p.10; cf. pp.14, 189.
4. *ibid.*, p.172.
5. *ibid.*, pp.182–3; cf. p.184.
6. *ibid.*, p.188. Early in 1985, unsold stocks of the *Projet Socialiste* were cleared out of Socialist Party Headquarters as wastepaper.
7. Jürgen Habermas, *Legitimation Crisis* (Heinemann, London, 1973, English ed. 1976) p.4; cf. pp.1–7, 24–341, 51–60. On the concepts of 'Promethean and Sisyphean planning' *see* Jack Hayward's 'Introduction: inertia and improvisation. The planning predicament', in Jack Hayward and Olga Narkiewicz (eds.), *Planning in Europe* (Croom Helm, London, 1978) p.19.
8. Michel Rocard, 'The challenges of the 80s', inaugural address to the French National Planning Commission, 8 Sept. 1982, mimeo (Commissariat du Plan, Paris) pp.2–3.
9. *ibid.*, pp.47–8.
10. *ibid.*, p.50.
11. Richard Rose, *Do Parties Make a Difference?*, 2nd edn. (Macmillan, London, 1984) p.157.
12. Kate Barker *et al.* 'Macroeconomic Policy in France and Britain', *National Institute Economic Review* (Nov. 1984) p.68.
13. Raymond Barre, 'Le budget de l'Etat est entré dans une crise grave et durable', *Le Monde*, 16 Oct. 1984, p.9; cf. p.1.
14. Barker *et al.*, *op. cit.*, p.74.
15. *Le Monde*, 18 Oct. 1984, p.9, report of the National Assembly debate.
16. Barker *et al.*, pp.73–4. On the rather late and restricted impact of Keynesian ideas in France, *see* François Fourquet, *Les Comptes de la Puissance. Histoire de la Comptabilité Nationale et du Plan* (Recherches, Paris, 1980) pp.21–8, 39–47, 71.
17. James Alt and K. Alec Chrystal, *Political Economics* (Wheatsheaf, Brighton, 1983) pp.212–7.
18. *ibid.*, pp.228–31; cf. B.S. Frey and F. Schneider, 'A politico-economic model of the United Kingdom', *Economic Journal*, vol. 88, 1978, pp.243–53 and Frey and Schneider, 'An econometric model with an endogenous government sector', *Public Choice*, vol. 34 (1979) pp.29–43. See also Kristen Monroe, 'A French political business cycle?', in Philip G. Cerny and Martin Schain (eds.) *French Politics and Public Policy* (Frances Pinter, London, 1980) ch. 7, especially pp.151–3.
19. Hermann R. van Gunsteren, *The Quest for Control. A Critique of the Rational-Central Approach in Public Affairs* (J. Wiley & Sons, London, 1976) p.2; cf. p.9. See also numerous publications by Aaron Wildavsky, notably 'If planning is everything, maybe it's nothing', *Policy Sciences*, vol. IV (1973) pp.127–53.
20. Pierre Mendès France, *A Modern French Republic* (Weidenfeld & Nicolson, London, 1962) especially ch. 5–9.
21. *See* the 1959 Declercq report 'Pour une planification démocratique', republished in *La CFDT* (1971) pp.64–96. *See also* Jean-Pierre Oppenheim, *La*

CFDT et la Planification (Tema, Paris, 1973).
22. On the role of the ESC in plan preparation, *see* Jack Hayward, *Private Interests and Public Policy*, 1966, pp.65 ff. On the role of parliament, *see* P. Corbel, *Le Parlement Français et la Planification* (Editions Cujas, Paris, 1969) pp.163–78, 278–81.
23. For a thorough critique of pre-1982 planning, *see* the report of the Bloch-Laîné Commission du Bilan, *La France en Mai 1981* (La Documentation Française, Paris, 1981) ch.6.
24. Report of the Commission de Réforme de la Planification, March 1982. *See also Plan Intérimaire: Stratégie pour Deux Ans 1982–1983* (La Documentation Française, Paris, 1981) pp.46–7; and *Projet Socialiste, op. cit.*, p.187. For the most comprehensive and up-to-date review of French planning, see the special issue of *Documents pour l'Enseignement Economique et Social*, no. 57, Oct. 1984, on 'La Planification Française et le 9e Plan: analyses et débats'.
25. André G. Delion and Michel Durupty, *Les Nationalisations 1982* (Economica, Paris, 1982) pp.32–3; cf. pp.27–8; Jack Hayward, *Governing France. The One and Indivisible Republic* (Weidenfeld & Nicolson, London, 1983) pp.224–5.
26. Delion and Durupty, *op. cit.*, pp.42, 45, 48–9, 52–9, 70, 72, 119.
27. Jack Hayward, *Governing France, op. cit.*, p.236; cf. Delion and Durupty, pp.6–10, 79–81, 118–22, and especially p.206. For pre-1981 PCF views on nationalization, *see* Henri Sègre *et al.*, *Les Entreprises Publiques en France* (Editions Sociales, Paris, 1975) and by a future minister from 1981–4, Anicet Le Pors, *Les Béquilles du Capital. Transferts Etat–Industrie: Critère de Nationalisation* (Seuil, Paris, 1977). For socialist views, *see* the book by the future presidential adviser on industry, Alain Boublil, *Le Socialisme Industriel* (Presses Universitaires de France, Paris, 1977) and two 1980 party publications *L'Agression. L'Etat Giscard contre le Secteur Public* and *Socialisme et Industrie* (Club Socialiste du Livre, Paris). *See also* PS, PCF and MRG, *Programme Commun de Gouvernment*, 1973 ed. (Flammarion, Paris) pp.49–51. On the continuity between the pre- and post-1981 role of multinationalization, *see* Julien Savary, *French Multinationals* (Frances Pinter, London, 1984).
28. Alain Lancelot in *Le Monde, Dossiers et Documents* (quoted at the bottom of Table 9.2 in the text), p.25.
29. Delion and Durupty, pp.199–201.
30. Michel Bauer and Elie Cohen, 'Les managers du secteur public en France', Colloque du CERI *'Entreprise Publique et Société Politique'*, Paris (Jan. 1983) mimeo, pp.9, 18.
31. Jacques Lesourne, 'The changing context of industrial policy: external and internal developments', in Alexis Jacquemin (ed.), *European Industry: Public Policy and Corporate Strategy* (Clarendon Press, Oxford, 1984) p.28.
32. Elie Cohen, 'Le politique, l'administratif et le pouvoir industriel', Association Française de Science Politique conference on *Alternance et Changements de Politique*, Paris (Jan. 1985) mimeo, pp.10–11. For a review of post-war French industrial policy which also emphasizes the key role of large firms, *see* Yves Morvan, 'La politique industrielle française', *op. cit.*, *Revue d'Economie Industrielle*, no. 23 (1983) especially pp.28, 30.
33. Cohen, *op. cit.*, p.16; cf. pp.9–17, on which this paragraph leans heavily.
34. *See* Jean-Pierre Anastassopoulos, 'Les entreprises publiques entre l'autonomie et la dépendance: une analyse des divers instruments de régulation des entreprises publiques par l'Etat', *Politiques et Management Public*, no. 9 (May 1985). *See also* Dominique Strauss-Kahn, 'Plan et autonomie de gestion', Fifth Spanish–French Planning Conference (May 1983) mimeo, Commissariat du

Plan.
35. A. Fonteneau, 'Les erreurs de prévision économique pour 1982', *Observations et Diagnostics Economiques*, no. 4 (June 1983). For the oft-repeated 'Keynesian' explanation, see the well-argued version by Peter A. Hall, 'Socialism in one country: Mitterrand and the struggle to define a new economic policy for France', in Philip G. Cerny and Martin A. Schain (eds.) *Socialism, the State and Public Policy in France* Frances Pinter, London, 1985) pp.83–5, 87.
36. Pierre Mauroy, *C'est ici le chemin*, *op. cit.* (1982) pp.18–25.
37. Richard Rose, *op. cit.*, p.136. For a contrasting view, backed by data on the 'output' of British local government but dealing with the wide-ranging issues suggested by the title, *see* Kenneth Newton and L.J. Sharpe, *Does Politics Matter?* (Clarendon Press, Oxford, 1984) especially ch. 10.

INDEX

Aerospace industry, 64, 118, 137, 139, 143-4, 146, 211, 232
   Dassault, 211
AGREF, *Association des Grandes Entreprises Faisant Appel à l'Epargne*, 80
agriculture, farming, 13, 46, 49, 52, 153, 194-5, 218
   Ministry of Agriculture, 52
   Mouvement de Défense de l'Exploitation Familiale (MODEF), 52
Air France, 38
Albert, Michel, 171-2, 185
Alt, James, 3, 221
Anglo-American approach, xii, 10, 39, 46, 125, 220
APEX, *Association pour l'Expansion Industrielle de la Région Nord Pas-de-Calais*, 117, 119, 121-3, 135-6, 143, 147
Argenson, Marquis d', xii
Aron, Raymond, 60
Ashford, Douglas, 162-3, 167
Auchan, Mulliez group, 130-2
Auroux Laws, 62, 66
Austria, 42
Automobile industry, 68, 99, 122-3, 137-8, 145, 194, 207
   Citroën, 135
   Peugeot, 128, 135-7, 142, 145-6
   Renault, 24, 52, 229, 231
   Talbot, 127-8, 135

banks, bankers, 11-12, 17, 23, 28-9, 31, 35, 38, 51-2, 64, 72, 77, 91-2, 97, 108, 124-5, 143, 149, 166-7, 173, 200, 226, 228-9
   Bank of France, 22-4, 51, 123, 234
   central, 3, 6
   CAECL, *Caisse d'Aide à l'Equipement des Collectivités Locales*, 167-8
   Caisse des Dépôts et Consignations, 23-4, 27, 91-2, 110-11, 163, 166-8, 226
   Caisse Nationale des Marchés de l'Etat, 125
   Crédit d'Equipement des Petites et Moyennes Entreprises, 125
   Crédit Hotelier, 124-5
   Crédit National, 23-4, 33, 74, 92, 124-5, 136, 144
   Paribas, 227
   Suez, 227
bankruptcy, 80, 97, 102, 104, 111, 117-18, 120, 133, 205, 232
Barre, Raymond, 34, 90-1, 95, 97, 177, 190, 200, 203-6, 208, 210, 218, 220
Barre Government, 90-1, 100, 173, 184, 200-1, 204, 210, 220, 234
Bauer, Michel, 30-1, 34
Belgium, 96, 127
Benda, Julien, 150
Bérégovoy, Pierre, 234
Bergeron, André, 58
Bloch-Lainé, François, 26-9, 166
Blum, Léon, 234
Bodin, Jean, 9
Boiteux, Marcel, 35
Bonnefous, Edouard, 226
Boston Consulting Group, 232
Boublil, Alain, 68, 104, 231
Brittany, 117, 121, 152-4, 160, 196
   Breton Plan, 153-4
Buchanan, James M., 2
budget, 174-85, 187, 195, 197, 204, 220, 223-5
   Finance Act, 184, 187
   see also Finance, Budget Division; public expenditure, RCB
building industry, 95, 99, 115, 118, 194-5, 199
bureaucracy, *see* civil servants

Canada, 120
capitalism, capitalist, capital, 6, 8-9, 11, 16, 19, 32, 40, 53, 63, 65-6, 72-4, 76, 79, 96, 109, 113-14, 150, 161, 200, 208, 214-15, 226-8, 230, 235
Carous, Pierre, 112-13
Catholicism, Social, 56, 59
CELIB, *Comité d'Etudes et de Liaison des Intérêts Bretons*, 117, 153
centralization, 20-1, 151-6, 161, 167, 224
CERES, *Centre d'Etudes et de Recherches Socialistes*, 213, 215
Ceyrac, François, 208
Chaban-Delmas, Jacques, 63, 157, 163
Chadeau, André, 119
Chalandon, Albin, 37-8

258

Index

chambers of commerce, 4, 119-21, 125-8, 143, 153, 159
  Dunkirk, 128
  Lille—Roubaix – Tourcoing, 111-12, 126-8, 131
  Nord regional chamber, 126-7
  Paris, 147
  Valenciennes, 111-12, 120, 126-8, 130-1, 135-6, 139, 144-5, 147
Channel Tunnel, 114
Chemical industry, 79, 88, 133, 191, 207, 232
  Rhône-Poulenc, 227, 232
Chevènement, Jean-Pierre, 94, 213, 215, 231
Chirac, Jacques, 93, 178, 184, 186, 203-6, 208, 229
Chrystal, Alec, 3, 221
CIASI, Interministerial Committee for the Adaptation of Industrial Structures, 123, 129, 206-7
CIDISE, Interministerial Committee for the Development and Support of Employment, 123, 129
CIRI, Interministerial Committee for Industrial Restructuring, 123, 207
civil servants (senior), bureaucrats, 4, 7, 11-12, 17-18, 20, 22, 27-8, 30-4, 41-2, 48-51, 64, 73, 86, 97, 109, 120, 123-4, 151-60, 164, 168, 174, 206, 217, 227, 232
  see also pantouflage, technocrats
CNPF, *Conseil national de Patronat Français*, 21, 24, 39, 51, 59, 69, 79-80, 88, 121, 128, 209-10
coal industry, 60-1, 66, 69, 71, 74, 103, 107, 109, 121, 124, 127, 138-9, 191, 211
  Northern Coal Corporation, 112, 121, 124
CODEFI, *Comités départementaux de financement des enterprises*, 123
CODER, Regional Economic Development Councils, 155
CODIS, Strategic Industries Development Committee, 129-30
Cohen, Elie, 30-1, 34
COMECON, Council for Mutual Economic Assistance, 14
Comité des Forges, 69, 73
Common Government Programme, PS-PCF (1972), 96, 205-6, 214, 227

communist, communism, 13-14, 32, 63, 72, 77, 107
  French Communist Party, 54, 56, 58, 65-6, 68-9, 86, 95-6, 102, 109, 113, 132, 142, 145, 184-5, 203, 206, 208, 214, 227-8
competition, competitiveness, 12, 21, 25-6, 30-2, 38, 69-70, 78-9, 83, 85-7, 89-90, 93, 96, 100, 103, 129, 134, 136, 147, 173, 191-2, 194-7, 201, 206, 212, 215, 218, 230-1, 235
computer industry, 64, 101, 118, 211
Comte, Auguste, 10
concerted economy, concerted action, 27-9, 32, 40-1, 64, 66, 77, 155, 162, 166, 172, 177, 210, 223-4
  concerted politics, xiv, 44-5, 48, 50-1, 53
constraints, 1-3, 36, 38, 54, 68, 162, 168, 172, 184, 186, 213, 215, 218, 224
consumers, consumption, 2, 13-14, 18, 64, 70, 99, 199-200, 221, 228
contracts (medium-term), 36, 53, 64, 79-82, 104, 129-30, 152, 157, 160, 162-9, 180, 223-4, 229, 231, 233-4
cooperative (producer), 118, 132-3
  Marketube, 132-3
corporatist, neo-corporatist, xiv, 15, 40-2, 46-7, 52-3, 59, 61-5, 81, 86-8, 90, 101, 153, 155, 158, 216, 223
Corps des Mines, 29-30, 33-4, 38
credit, 3, 22-3, 25, 33, 71, 124-5, 220
Creusot-Loire, 96, 104, 211
crisis, 44-5, 50-1, 213-16, 231
  capitalist crisis, 235
  economic crisis, 68, 73, 87, 149, 173, 202, 214, 223
  oil crisis, 170, 190-1, 197, 201-2, 204, 207, 214-15, 218
  steel crisis, 100, 102
cumul des mandats, 108, 162

DATAR, Regional and Spatial Planning Delegacy, 22, 24, 34, 75, 91, 110, 117, 119-22, 127, 130, 134-6, 139, 144, 155, 159, 165, 208, 231
Debré, Michel, 81, 86, 150, 171, 174, 184
decentralization, 54, 65, 109, 141, 151, 154-6, 158-9, 161-2, 164, 168, 175,

222, 224
democracy, 12, 16, 18, 21, 44, 54, 57, 108, 113-14, 149, 157-8, 161-2, 223
democratic planning, 28, 54, 59, 64, 161, 164, 172, 214, 222
Defferre, Gaston, 162
Delebarre, Michel, 117
Delmon, Pierre, 121
Delors, Jacques, 28-9, 63, 65, 185, 213, 234
Delouvrier, Paul, 35
dirigisme, 21, 27-8, 37, 62, 71, 80, 110, 173, 204, 231
DNEL, Denain-Nord-Est-Longwy holding company, 87, 91-3, 131
Dollé, Claude, 96
Dreyfus, Pierre, 94, 96, 231
Duguit, Léon, xiii
Dunkirk, 74, 92, 105, 128, 144
Durkheim, Emile, xiii
Dyson, Kenneth, 7

EC, European Community, 5, 21, 70, 83, 94-5, 99-102, 114, 124-5, 129, 136, 140, 191, 196, 234
 Coal and Steel Community (ECSC), 69-71
 Commission, 5-6, 99-101
Ecole Nationale d'Administration, 31
Ecole Polytechnique, polytechnicien, 10, 31, 95-6
Economic and Social Council, 24, 59, 63, 172, 208, 210, 224
Economic and Social Development Fund, 23, 125, 139
economic policy, xv, 1-2, 4, 7-9, 13, 15-39, 48, 57, 60, 65-6, 105-6, 162, 169-73, 192, 202, 208, 212, 217, 220, 225, 235
 macro-economic policy, 10, 18, 172, 216-22, 230
economists, xi-xii, 2-3, 9-10, 12, 39, 90, 110, 148, 203, 205, 215
education policy, 179, 187-8
Ehrmann, Henry, 39-41
elections, 87, 97, 102, 202, 212, 222
 1965 local elections, 155
 1977 local elections, 90, 93, 116, 202
 1973 National Assembly elections, 77
 1978 National Assembly elections, 65, 93, 202-6
 1981 National Assembly elections,

212, 235
 1974 Presidential elections, 202
 1981 Presidential elections, 65, 185-6, 228
 trade union, 58
electrical industry, 207
 CGE, *Compagnie Générale d'Electricité*, 211, 226
electronics industry, 79, 101, 142, 195, 207, 211, 231
 Thomson-Brandt, 211, 227
employment, unemployment, job creation, 9-10, 18, 23, 62, 65-6, 75-6, 78, 83, 93-5, 97, 99-100, 102-4, 109, 113, 120, 122-3, 135-49, 173, 183-8, 192-6, 201-2, 204-5, 209-11, 216, 218-19, 225, 227-8, 230, 234-5
 ANPE, *Agence Nationale pour l'Emploi*, 183, 195
 Délégation à l'Emploi, 134
 Departmental Committee for the Encouragement of Employment, 139
 full employment, 10, 54, 107, 172, 186, 192, 214
 pactes pour l'emploi, 146, 183
 redeployment, 95, 115, 123, 128, 131-2, 144
  see also CIDISE, retirement
energy policy, 18, 23, 29-30, 33, 35-8, 64, 119, 188, 200-2, 204, 211
 CEA, Atomic Energy Commissariat, 35-6
 EDF, *Electricité de France*, 24, 35-6, 52, 101, 180, 200, 224, 229, 233
 and electro-nuclear policy, 35-6, 101, 180, 186, 200, 207, 232
 ELF, *Essences et Lubrifiants de France*, 24, 35-8, 52, 96, 229, 232
Engels, Friedrich, 10
engineering industries, 68, 71, 88, 99, 207, 211
environment policy, 179
Etchegaray, Claude, 95

Fabius, Laurent, 94, 97, 231
Faure, Edgar, 154
Feigenbaum, Harvey, 20
Ferry, Jacques, 72-3, 76-7, 79-83, 85, 87, 90-1, 95
FIAT, *Fonds Interministériel d'Aménage-*

ment du Territoire, Regional Intervention Fund, 122, 166
FIM, Industrial Modernization Fund, 123, 129, 231
Finance:
   Minister of Finance, 10, 22, 24, 63, 73-5, 81-2, 86, 103, 174, 180, 185, 198, 204, 213, 220, 234
   Ministry of Finance, 22-3, 26, 33, 35-7, 40-1, 51, 72-4, 76, 86, 88, 91, 93, 97, 102-3, 120, 123, 139, 163, 166-8, 175-8, 207, 210-11, 223
   Budget Division, 22-5, 35, 41, 51, 134, 142, 175, 177-82, 187, 231
   Budget Minister, 96-7
   Competition Division, 123, 134
   Foreign Relations Division, 207
   Inspectors, 29-31, 37
   Price Control Division, 123
   Taxation Division, 88, 123, 134
   TPG, Treasurer and Paymaster-General, 123, 163-4
   Treasury Division, 22-5, 27, 33, 35, 41, 51, 73-5, 81, 93, 100, 123-4, 129, 134, 136, 166, 207-8, 231, 234
Finer, Samuel E., 42-3
firm, business, corporation (private), 4, 7, 12-14, 16-18, 21, 25, 27-43, 47-9, 51-3, 55, 58-64, 68-104, 107, 109-13, 117-18, 120-49, 172-3, 187-8, 192, 194, 199, 205-11, 217, 223, 226-7, 229-35
   multinational corporation, 6, 17, 30, 38, 140, 149, 227
   see also self-financing
forecasts, 12, 28, 62, 77-8, 103, 157, 223
Fos, 75-7, 92, 103
franc exchange rate, 23, 99, 186, 191-2, 205, 213, 234-5
Frey, Bruno, 222
Friedberg, Erhard, 33
FSAI, Special Industrial Adaption Fund, 122, 129, 134-8

Galbraith, John Kenneth, 10-11, 13, 15-16
Gallie, Duncan, 57
Gaulle, Charles de, 12, 27, 36, 41, 53, 59, 61, 63, 81, 107, 156, 170-1, 184, 191, 198, 204, 222, 226

Gaullism, 56, 62, 155, 206, 223
Germany, Federal, 7, 11, 28, 42, 76, 93-4, 101, 120, 125, 144, 191, 193, 197-8, 204-5, 213, 220
Gide, Charles, 133
Giraud, André, 36-8
Giraudet, Pierre, 209
Giscard d'Estaing, Valéry, xv, 34, 36, 53, 86, 104, 125, 130, 158, 161-3, 170-1, 174, 184, 186, 190, 197-8, 202-4, 206, 226-7, 235
Goux, Christian, 223
Gravier, Jean-François, 153
Grémion, Pierre, 151, 158-9, 161
growth, economic, 41, 56, 66, 70, 88-9, 98-9, 138, 155, 170, 186, 191-4, 196-201, 204-5, 214-15, 218-19, 228, 230
Guesde, Jules, 107
Guichard, Olivier, 121, 155, 158, 165
Guillaumat, Pierre, 36

Habermas, Jürgen, 215
Hamon, Léo, 172
Hannoun Report, 210-11
Hauriou, Maruice, 152
Hayek, Friedrich von, 11
health policy, 179, 188
   Ministry of Health, 181
Heclo, Hugh, 16
Hennessy, Jean, 153
Hirsch, Etienne, 26
Hogwood, Brian, 7
housing policy, 109-11, 115-19, 147, 166-7
   HLM, *Habitations à Loyer Modéré*, 116-18, 167
   Société Centrale pour l'Equipement du Territoire, 166-7
   Société Centrale Immobilière, 167
Hull, Christopher, 140

IDI, Industrial Development Institute, 130
IMF, International Monetary Fund, 5-6, 221
incomes policy, 12, 18, 23, 29, 59-63, 201-2
   national income, 3, 11, 211
industrial policy, 4, 7-8, 13, 18, 23, 25, 29-35, 38, 63-4, 77, 80, 83, 86, 97, 105, 107, 145, 148-9, 173, 183,

202, 207, 215, 228-33
Industrialization Commissioners, 121
National Industry Commission, 231
Industry, Industrial Development, Industrial Redeployment and External Trade:
  Minister, 35, 37, 81-82, 86, 94, 96, 98, 104, 181, 211, 228
  Ministry, 33-4, 36-7, 73-5, 86, 97, 102-3, 123, 125, 134, 207-8, 215, 231
  Direction des Carburants (DICA), 33, 36-8
  Direction des Industries Mécaniques et Electriques (DIMEE), 33
  Direction des Industries Métallurgiques, 73-4
  Direction de la Sidérurgie, 75, 88
  Direction Général de l'Industrie, 207
inertia, 3, 112, 171, 180-1, 198, 213, 221, 223, 232
inflation, 3, 61-2, 155, 177, 193, 197, 203-6, 212, 219, 229-30
Interministerial Committee for Aid to the Localization of Activities, 134
Interministerial Economic Committee, 22, 25
investment, 12, 23, 27-28, 36, 51, 62, 70-2, 74, 76, 78-9, 81, 83, 85, 87-8, 90, 92-6, 98-104, 117, 120, 124, 129, 133, 135-6, 138-49, 155, 157, 159, 163-8, 173-83, 185, 187, 194, 197, 199-200, 204-5, 207-8, 210, 214, 218, 229, 235
Ireland, 136
Italy, 76, 93, 125, 129, 137, 197-8

Japan, 7-8, 13, 22, 30-3, 85, 89, 104, 120, 220
  MITI, Ministry of International Trade and Industry, 32-3
Johnson, Chalmers, 32-3
Judet Report, 98
judiciary, 48-9, 51, 88
  Ministry of Justice, 182

Keynes, John Maynard, 10
Keynesian, 220, 234
Krasucki, Henri, 58, 66

Labour:
  Minister, 117

Ministry, 60, 86, 95, 123, 183
labour force, workers, employees, 9-10, 13, 53-4, 57-67, 71, 78, 83, 87, 90, 93-5, 100, 104, 128, 131-2, 146-7, 150, 193-6, 200-1, 206, 208-10, 218, 227-8
  see also trade unions
Lagrange Report, 167-8
laissez-faire, xii-xiii, 9, 29
land use policy, 109-18, 126-7, 131, 136, 143-5
  FNAFU, National Land and Urban Planning Fund, 127
  POS, Land Use Plan, 114, 145
  SDAU, Urban Development Master Plan, 114, 145
Laurent, Augustin, 108, 115
Le Chapelier Law (1791), 56
Le Garrec, Jean, 96
Lévy, Raymond, 96, 104
liberal, liberalism, xii, 7-10, 27-8, 37, 39, 42, 64, 70, 90, 97, 217, 229, 235
Lille, 105, 107-16, 118, 120-1, 124, 126, 130, 132, 135, 138, 140-3, 149
  metro, 111, 114-15, 118
  University, 114-15
  Urban Community, 111, 113-16, 130, 132
Lindblom, Charles, 13-16
local authorities, 18, 76, 107-20, 127, 130-2, 141-5, 148-9, 153, 157-60, 162-8, 180, 223-4
  CAECL, *Caisse d'Aide à l'Equipement des Collectivités Territoriales*, 167-8
  communes, mayors, 108-17, 141-3, 145, 158-9, 164, 167
  départements, departmental council, 108, 117, 141-3, 157-60, 162, 167
  urban community, 108, 111, 113-17, 130, 132, 143, 160, 163
Lorraine, 66, 68, 73, 75-7, 91, 94-5, 102-5, 132, 135, 196

machine tools industry, 207, 231-2
Macpherson, C.B., 9
Maire, Edmond, 58
managers, businessmen, employers, 14-15, 32, 34, 49, 56-64, 73-4, 95-6, 107-12, 121-4, 131, 135, 138, 148, 192, 195, 200, 208-11, 225, 227-9, 231-3
Marshall, Alfred, xi

Martray, Joseph, 153
Marx, Karl, xi
  Marxist, 19, 46
mass media, 4, 48-9, 54-5
  press, 18, 55, 210, 213
  radio & TV, 55
Massé, Pierre, 60, 63, 184
Mauroy, Pierre, 95, 108-9, 112-13, 115, 117-18, 165-6, 212, 234
  Mauroy Government, 60, 63-6, 94, 96, 99-100, 109, 116, 127, 185, 222, 234
May 1968 'events', 61, 63, 155, 170, 193
Mayoux, Jacques, 95
McConnell, Grant, 43
Mendès France, Pierre, 28, 154, 161, 186, 222-3
mercantilism, xii-xiii, 9, 69, 213
Meynaud, Jean, 39
Michelet, Jules, 150
military, 1, 36, 48-9, 51, 69, 173, 176
  Ministry of Defence, 208
Mills, C. Wright, 16
ministers, 20, 22, 24, 40, 48, 66, 96, 171, 231
Ministry of Equipment, 180-1
Ministry of the Interior, 143, 163, 168
Mitterand, François, xv, 36, 50, 53, 65, 74, 94-5, 97, 100, 103-4, 158, 171, 186, 206-7, 211-13, 216, 222-3, 226-7, 231-5
modernization, 26, 73, 75, 82, 87, 100, 126, 131, 148, 150, 157, 162, 170, 188, 200
  commissions, 172, 177-8, 208, 210
monetary policy, 23, 33, 191-2, 204, 218-21, 230
  European Monetary System, 205, 213, 234
  exchange rate, see franc
Monnet, Jean, 26-7, 184, 192, 223
Monod, Jérôme, 121
Monory, René, 211
Montchrétien, Antoine de, xii
Montjoie, René, 34, 174

national champions, 30, 34-8, 68, 83, 96, 103, 192, 208, 229, 231-33
nationalism, economic, 7-9, 69, 227
nationalization, public enterprises, 11, 17, 20, 23, 28-9, 34-6, 38-41, 51-5, 58, 62, 64, 70-1, 86-8, 95-8, 101, 127, 200, 208, 211, 215, 217, 224-35
  banks (1982), 52, 227-8
  steel, 70-1, 90-2, 94-7, 102
Netherlands, 197-8
Notebart, Arthur, 111, 114-16
Nora, Simon, 29, 164
  Nora Report, 34, 38, 228
Nord, 66, 68, 75, 91, 94-5, 105, 107, 109-49, 153, 160, 165-6, 196

O'Connor, James, 215
oil companies, 20, 35, 37-8, 96, 207, 232
  Antar, 127
  CFP, *Compagnie Française des Pétroles*, 37-8
  ELF *see* energy policy
Ortoli, François-Xavier, 116, 155

pantouflage, 7, 32, 73, 227
PAP, Priority Action Programmes, 118, 159, 164, 172, 174, 176-88, 200, 223
  PAPIR, Regional and Local Priority Action Programmes, 159-6, 164, 179
Paris, 7, 26, 109, 113, 120, 123, 127, 141, 143-4, 146-8, 150-4, 157, 163, 181, 191, 196
parliament, 3-5, 18, 48-9, 54, 65, 82, 88, 90, 96, 166, 186-7, 204, 210, 216, 223-4, 226
  National Assembly, 88, 96, 223
  deputy, 108, 110-11, 113, 117, 157, 204
  legislation, 18, 32, 56, 82, 88, 193
  Senate, 59, 63, 88, 156, 226
  senator, 112, 157
parties, political, 3-5, 14, 18, 44, 48-50, 54-5, 69, 77, 90, 161, 217, 235
PDR, *Prime de Développement Régional*, 134, 137-40, 142-3, 148
Pflimlin, Pierre, 154
Phlipponneau, Michel, 153
Pinay, Antoine, 75
Pisani, Edgard, 115
planning, 11-13, 15-16, 19, 27-9, 32-3, 37, 47, 64-5, 68, 72-104, 153-90, 192, 206, 208-10, 214-15, 222-5, 228, 231-3
  Central Planning Council, 171, 184-5
  land-use, town planning, 110-11,

132, 144-5, 163
Minister for Planning, 134, 186, 214, 222
National Planning Commission, 187, 214, 224
Planning Commissariat, 23-5, 28, 41, 73-5, 77-9, 81, 98, 120, 153, 157, 159-60, 171-2, 175, 177-80, 183, 185, 190, 210, 223, 231
Planning Commissioner, 22, 26, 47, 60, 81, 86, 134, 171, 178, 180, 185
regional planning, 117-24, 153-61
steel commission, 76-9, 89
First Plan, 27
Fourth Plan, 76, 79
Fifth Plan, 76, 79-83
Sixth Plan, 34, 76, 89, 93, 115, 119, 164, 174, 176-7
Seventh Plan, 89, 91, 118-19, 157, 159, 161, 164, 172, 174-6, 178-80, 182-3, 186, 190, 200, 204-5, 209-10
Eighth Plan, 184-7, 190, 192, 198, 205, 209-10, 222-3, 235
Interim Plan, 97, 186, 215, 222-3
Ninth Plan, 165, 187-8, 216, 223-4
democratic planning, *see* democracy
planning contracts, *see* contracts
see also PAP (Priority Action Programmes), PPE (Priority Implementation Programmes)
PLAR, Research Activities Localization Grant, 140-1
PLAT, Location of Service Activities Grant, 140-1
pluralist, pluralism, xiv, 6-9, 13-16, 18, 23, 27, 38-48, 52, 64
Polanyi, Karl, 16
police, 48-9, 51, 61, 95
policy community, xiv-xv, 4-8, 13, 15-38, 57, 65-6, 68, 83, 85-9, 97, 102, 105, 148-9, 162, 169-70, 172, 189, 217, 230, 233
political economy, xi-xiii, 15
Pompidou, Georges, 36, 53, 63, 81, 121, 155-8, 162, 170-1, 191, 204, 226
Popular Front (1936), 59, 209, 234
PPE, Priority Implementation Programmes, 164-6, 168, 187-9, 224
PRCEI, *Prime Régionale à la Création d'Entreprises Industrielles*, 141-2
prefect, commissioner of the republic, 120-1, 134, 154-5, 157, 159, 161, 164
economic sub-prefect, 119
regional prefect, 116, 118-21, 130, 134, 154-5, 157, 159-61, 165, 179
President of the Republic, 20, 22, 24-5, 35-8, 48, 50, 53-4, 65, 68, 86, 94, 100, 103-4, 121, 125, 130, 135, 156-8, 161, 163, 170-1, 174, 179-80, 184-7, 190, 202-4, 208, 211, 213, 216, 223, 226-7, 231-5
pressure groups, interest groups, 12, 25-6, 39-55, 62, 153, 155-7, 162, 217, 224
prices, price control policy, 12, 23, 25, 37-8, 62, 64, 70-1, 79, 93, 99, 123, 128, 173, 201-2, 204-5, 210, 229
Prime Minister, 20, 22, 24-5, 35, 48, 60, 63, 74, 78, 86, 90-1, 93, 95, 97, 102-3, 109, 116-17, 119-20, 135-6, 157, 165, 171, 173, 178, 180, 184-5, 189-90, 200, 202-4, 208, 212, 220, 228, 231, 233-4
privatization, 225-6, 229
production, GDP, 27-9, 33, 70, 72, 78, 83, 85, 89, 96, 98, 100, 102, 194, 197, 218-20
productivity, 93, 133, 146, 193-4, 197, 218
profit, xii, 9, 71, 80, 87, 93-6, 136, 143, 146, 148, 173, 192, 197, 200, 209, 211, 214, 231, 235
profit sharing, 62, 90, 132, 136-7
property, private, xii, 11, 80, 111, 225-7, 229-30
Proudhon, Pierre-Joseph, 11, 152, 168
Prouvost, Pierre, 110-11
public expenditure, 3, 99, 119, 157, 159, 164, 173-89, 197-9, 214, 217, 221-3, 230
public policy, 2, 16, 19, 35, 40, 52, 54, 61, 74, 154, 212-13, 216-17, 222, 225
public works and housing, 95, 116, 194
Minister of, 115
Ministry of, 113-14, 116, 123
PUK, Pechiney-Ugine-Kuhlmann, 76, 226

Rank-Xerox, 120-1, 132, 139-40, 144
RCB, *rationalisation des choix budgétaires*, 173-6, 179

Redoute, La, 110, 130-1
regional council, 106, 108-9, 134, 141, 155, 157, 159-60, 161, 223-4
  Nord Regional Council, 109, 116-18, 141-2
  President of Regional Council, 165
Regional Development Grant, *see* PDR
Regional Economic Expansion Committee, 154-5
  CELIB, 117, 153
  CERES, 115, 117, 153
Regional Economic and Social Committees, 121, 134, 224
Regional Employment Grant, 134
regional policy, 23, 62, 75-6, 105-66, 177, 194-6, 211, 228
regionalism, 152, 154, 156, 161
regionalization, functional, 152-62
Renan, Ernest, 150
Republic:
  Third, xiii, 10-11
  Fourth, 41, 82, 120, 216
  Fifth, 36, 41, 50, 53, 59, 196, 202-3, 208, 229
research, 12, 134, 210, 230
  PLAR, Research Activities Localization Grant, 140-1
retirement, age of, 95, 100, 131, 234-5
Rhine-Rhône waterway, 52, 180, 183
Richard, Pierre, 168
Ripert, Jean, 28, 174
Rocard, Michel, 65, 186, 206, 214-16, 222, 234
Rose, Richard, 217
Roubaix, 107-12, 114, 116, 126, 129-33, 135, 149
RPR, *Rassemblement pour la République*, 68, 112, 186, 205-6, 229
Rueff, Jacques, 220

SACILOR, 24, 84, 91-3, 95-7, 99-102, 104, 227
Saint-Simon, Henri de, 10, 39, 230
Sanguinetti, Alexandre, 150
Say, Jean-Baptiste, 10, 89
Say, Léon, 10
SDR, *Société de Développement Régional*, 124, 132
self-financing, 71, 79, 93, 173, 199-200, 235
self-management, 59, 63, 66
Servan-Schreiber, Jean-Jacques, 68

shipbuilding industry, 66, 95, 101, 103, 135, 191
Shonfield, Andrew, 11-13, 21, 217
Siegfried, André, 152
Sismondi, Jean Charles Leonard Simonde de, 10
Smith, Adam, xi, 9
Social Security, 180, 195, 197-201, 205
socialist, socialism, 9, 11, 57, 107, 132, 198, 217, 221, 226, 228
  French Socialist Party, 14, 36, 54, 56, 58, 60, 65-6, 68, 93, 96-7, 107-11, 114, 116-19, 142, 161, 184-5, 203, 206, 208, 211-15, 222, 235
SNCF, *Société Nationale des Chemins de Fer*, 118-19, 233
sovereignty, state, xiii, 2, 99, 152, 162
Soviet Union, 13-15
Spain, 76, 120
Spencer, Herbert, xi
steel industry, 64, 66, 68-105, 107, 109, 112, 121-2, 127-8, 131-2, 135, 147, 191, 194, 196, 226, 232
  CSSF, *Chambre Syndical de la Sidérurgie Française*, 68-9, 72-4, 77-82, 87-8, 90-1, 93-4, 97-9
  Eurofer, 5, 85; 95
  GIS, *Groupement de l'Industrie Sidérurgique*, 73-4, 88, 92
  IISI, International Iron and Steel Institute, 85
  international cartel, 70, 83, 85
  plan professionnel, 72, 80-3, 86, 88
  special steels, 76, 83, 85, 96, 101, 104
  see also DNEL, SACILOR, USINOR, Wendel
Stock Exchange, 24, 90
Stoléru, Lionel, 34, 85
strikes, 44, 54, 56, 60-2, 191
  general strike, 56, 191, 209
subsidies, 101, 133, 152, 163, 229-32
  national subsidies, 134-41, 207, 210-11
  regional and local subsidies, 134, 141-9, 154, 166-8
  steel industry subsidies, 87, 93, 97, 99-104
Suleiman, Ezra, 25, 29-30, 151
Sweden, 120, 197-8
Switzerland, 120

Taine, Hippolyte, 150
taxation, fiscal policy, xii, 3, 14, 25, 33, 71, 82, 88, 111, 122, 125-6, 128, 130, 162, 176, 179, 197-8, 210, 215, 220, 222
   taxe professionnelle, local business tax, 142-3
technocrats, techno-bureaucrats, technostructure, 6, 10, 13, 15, 21, 39, 50, 52, 64, 92, 113-14, 156, 162, 164, 167, 216-18, 223, 225
   see also civil servants
technology, advanced, 101, 114, 118-20, 123, 187-8
   robotics, 101
   telematics, 64
telecommunications industry, 183, 200, 232
textile and clothing industries, firms, 81, 107, 110-11, 116-17, 121, 128-33, 137, 139, 142, 194
   Bidermann, 130
   Boussac, 130
   Central Wool Committee, 128
   CIRITH, Textile and Clothing Industry Restructuring Committee, 128-9
   Prouvost, 129-30
   Willot brothers, 130
Thatcher, Margaret, 51
   Thatcher Government, 226
Tinbergen, Jan, 2
Tourcoing, 107-12, 114, 116, 126, 132-3, 135, 139
trade, international, xiii, 9, 23, 33, 69, 78, 85, 128-9, 197, 199, 201, 204-5, 207, 213, 218
   balance of payments, 186, 191-2, 205, 210, 212, 218-19, 225
   Ministry of Trade and Craft Industries, 181
   tariffs, 25, 71, 129
trade associations, 4, 25, 33, 42, 49, 54, 68-9, 72-4, 80-3, 88, 98, 121, 128
trade unions, xv, 4-5, 18, 27-8, 43-5, 47, 53-67, 77-8, 82, 87, 94, 100-3, 117, 128, 132, 155, 174, 192, 201, 208-10, 224, 235
   anarcho-syndicalism, 56-7, 64
   CFDT, *Confédération Française Démocratique du Travail*, 28, 53, 58-66, 94-5, 100, 104, 161, 172, 208, 210, 235
   CFTC, *Confédération Française des Travailleurs Chrétiens*, 59, 208
   CGC, *Confédération Générale des Cadres*, 59, 61, 208
   CGT, *Confédération Générale du Travail*, 53, 58-60, 64-6, 87, 94-5, 100, 104, 132, 153, 208, 210, 222, 227
   FEN, *Fédération de l'Education Nationale*, 53
   FO, CGT – *Force Ouvrière*, 53, 58-9, 62, 94, 132, 208
   see also, labour force
training, industrial, 12, 60, 82, 101, 122, 125, 146, 187-8, 230
transport, 79, 95, 99, 118, 127, 144-5, 147, 179
   Ministry of Transport, 180
Tullock, Gordon, 2

UDF, *Union pour la Démocratie Française*, 202, 229
United Kingdom, Britain, xi, 3, 7-9, 21, 39-48, 50-3, 57-8, 60, 63, 65, 85, 89, 93, 114-15, 140, 144, 173, 192-3, 197-8, 209, 216, 218-21, 225-6
United States of America, xi, xv, 3-4, 7-8, 11, 30, 36, 39, 42, 76-7, 85, 99, 120, 131-2, 137, 214, 220, 234
USINOR, 24, 68, 74-5, 77, 79, 84, 87, 91-3, 95-7, 99-102, 104-5, 107, 112, 128, 131, 135, 137, 144, 227, 232

Valenciennes, 94, 102, 105, 107-9, 112-13, 120, 124, 126, 130-1, 135-9, 141-7, 149
Vallourec, 92-3, 107, 112-13, 127, 131, 144, 146, 148
Villeneuve d'Ascq, 110-16, 118
volontarisme, 2-3, 21, 215-16, 229, 231, 235-6

wages, 29, 60-3, 65, 132, 146, 193-4, 197, 199-201, 206, 209, 218-19, 233, 235
   SMIC, *Salaire minimum interprofessionnelle de croissance*, 61, 200-1
Waldeck-Rousseau Law (1884), 56

Weber, Eugen, 150-1
Weber, Max, xi, 9
Wendel, de, 68-9, 76-7, 79, 84, 87, 91
Wildavsky, Aaron, 16
Wilson, Frank, 46-7
Wison, Harold, 212
working hours, 65-6, 95, 100, 185, 188, 193-4, 209-10, 235
Wright, Vincent, 44

Zysman, John, 20-3

LIBRARY OF DAVIDSON COLLEGE

two wee'